PARAS

The new low-level parachute (LLP) which is now in service with 5 Airborne Brigade, providing the capability to drop into action at 250 ft.

PARAS

AN ILLUSTRATED HISTORY OF BRITAIN'S AIRBORNE FORCES

DAVID REYNOLDS

FOREWORD BY HRH THE PRINCE OF WALES,
KG KT GCB AK QSO ADC
COLONEL-IN-CHIEF,
THE PARACHUTE REGIMENT

EPIGRAPH BY BRIGADIER ADRIAN FREER, OBE

SUTTON PUBLISHING

First published in 1998 by
Sutton Publishing Limited · Phoenix Mill
Thrupp · Stroud · Gloucestershire · GL5 2BU

British Library Cataloguing in Publication Data
A catalogue record for this book is available from the British Library.

ISBN 0-7509-1723-7 (hardback)
ISBN 0-7509-2059-9 (paperback)

Endpapers, front: men of 'B' Company 2 Para brace themselves against the down-draught of a Chinook helicopter as it lifts off behind them during multinational exercises in Egypt; *back*: the bridge at Arnhem which was renamed Frostbrug, Frost Bridge, in memory of Lieutenant Colonel John Frost, who commanded 2 Para in their epic battle there.

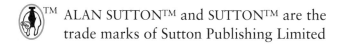 ™ ALAN SUTTON™ and SUTTON™ are the
trade marks of Sutton Publishing Limited

Typeset in 11/14 pt Sabon.
Typesetting and origination by
Sutton Publishing Limited.
Printed in Great Britain by
Butler & Tanner, Frome, Somerset.

CONTENTS

HRH The Prince of Wales, KG KT GCB AK QSO ADC, Colonel-in-Chief, The Parachute Regiment.

FOREWORD

HRH THE PRINCE OF WALES, KG KT GCB AK QSO ADC, COLONEL-IN-CHIEF, THE PARACHUTE REGIMENT

The Parachute Regiment has been at the heart of Britain's airborne forces throughout its short, but distinguished, history and I take great pride in having served as Colonel-in-Chief of the Parachute Regiment for the past 21 years. PARAS has been published to coincide with the presentation of new Colours to the three battalions of the Parachute Regiment in June 1998.

Many unique photographs have been brought together to illustrate the development of the airborne forces. They range from the early pioneers of military parachuting at Ringway during the dark days of the Second World War to today's paratroopers jumping with the remarkable low-level parachute from as low as 250 feet.

Our airborne forces have always been a truly joint capability and their unique characteristics are recognised by their position at the core of today's Joint Rapid Deployment Force. PARAS is a fitting tribute to the brave men and women who have served with Britain's airborne forces.

The current Commanding Officer of 5 Airborne Brigade, Brigadier Adrian Freer OBE.

EPIGRAPH

BRIGADIER ADRIAN FREER, OBE
Commander 5 AB Brigade

As the Commander of 5 Airborne Brigade and former Commanding Officer of 2 Para I am delighted that *PARAS* is being published to coincide with the presentation of Colours to the regular battalions of the Parachute Regiment. However, it would be remiss of me to introduce this prestigious volume without reference to our forefathers, principally those who served in the 1st and 6th Airborne Divisions, who set the standard that we strive to emulate today. Airborne warfare is a coherent, all-arms approach to warfare and without our affiliated combat support and combat service support units we would be emasculated.

In this modern world, we should not forget the impact of air power that provides so much more than just the 'lift' into battle. Air power is, increasingly, a vital component in the Brigade's ability to sustain itself in theatre. Looking through this book and at 5 Airborne Brigade today, I am reminded of Field Marshal The Viscount Montgomery of Alamein's words:

> What manner of men are these who wear the maroon beret? They are, firstly, all volunteers and are then toughened by physical training. As a result they have that infectious optimism and that offensive eagerness which comes from physical well-being. They have jumped from the air and by doing so have conquered fear. Their duty lies in the van of battle: they are proud of their honour and have never failed in any task. They have the highest standards in things, whether it be skill in battle or smartness in execution of all peacetime duties. They have shown themselves to be as tenacious and determined in defence as they are courageous in attack. They are in fact, men apart. 'Every man an emperor.'

Little has changed. As General 'Windy' Gale once said: 'Drive on.'

Rapid reaction. A paratrooper makes his exit from a C-130 Hercules. His equipment container can be seen in front of him and static line strops from paratroopers who have jumped seconds before him stretch out of the door.

INTRODUCTION

At the end of the Second World War Field Marshal Montgomery concluded that Britain's airborne forces had a secure future, stating that 'a nation without airborne forces will be severely handicapped and at a great disadvantage in future warfare'. His words could never be more relevant than in the late 1990s, when rapid intervention forces have taken a leading role following the end of the Cold War and the increasing global instability of the modern era.

The role of airborne forces is possibly the most misunderstood and underestimated capability in the modern British Army. Over the years many military observers, not privileged to be members of the airborne forces, have suggested that if the parachuting role is not being used it should be retired – perhaps they do not understand that this is only a means of insertion. It is the training to achieve very high standards that has made airborne forces so effective in battle. Parachute selection training is designed to be physically testing. It instils an inner confidence in both officers and soldiers that they can overcome any adversity, and this belief gives paratroopers the mental strength not to give up when the going gets tough. This unique spirit has well served the Parachute Regiment and airborne forces wherever they are, whether on active operations in Arnhem, North Africa or the Falklands, or humanitarian operations in Rwanda.

The high professional standards set by airborne forces have established a respected benchmark of quality within the British Army which has often resulted in units of the Parachute Regiment and the Airborne Brigade being mobilised at short notice for operations anywhere in the world. In the past decade the Parachute Regiment has also provided more candidates for special forces selection than any other unit in the British Army. A former Regimental Colonel, Hamish McGregor MC, described airborne forces as having the finest soldiers in the world, adding: 'their skills, flexibility and sheer professionalism make them a force very much in demand'.

During the Second World War the Airborne Brigade consisted of air-landed troops, who arrived by glider, and parachute forces. Both wore the red beret although only parachute-trained soldiers wore wings. After the war the glider role was made redundant and only the parachute capability was retained.

The modern brigade includes two parachute-trained battle groups but has also reintroduced the air-landed concept to enhance its manoeuvre readiness. Parachute-trained personnel wear parachute wings as they did during the war while air-landed personnel are entitled to wear the Pegasus emblem of the airborne brigade, and in

In the first few minutes after landing the men must quickly form up into their respective company groups and move off to the drop zone. Marker panels are used to identify forming-up points and each group meets at these points. During a night drop a coloured strobe is used.

some cases the maroon beret.

Two infantry battalions, currently drawn from the Gurkhas and the Princess of Wales's Royal Regiment (PWRR), form the basis of the brigade's air-land force. They regularly train in Tactical Air Land Operations (TALO), during which they go into battle aboard a C-130 Hercules aircraft. This means of delivery proved highly successful at Entebbe in 1977 and Kabul in 1979.

The flexible capability of the airborne brigade to deploy by parachute, TALO, a fleet of support helicopters or more conventional means of transport, its ability to react to a broad spectrum of operations with rugged determination, and its ability to sustain itself independently in difficult terrain, all resulted in its selection as a core component of the UK's Joint Rapid Deployment Force, formed in August 1996. And although the last battalion drop was at Suez, readers may be surprised to learn that there have been several planning orders in recent years to use parachute troops. In 1982 a drop by a small force from the 3rd Battalion the Parachute Regiment was planned to capture Great Island in the Falklands, but it had to be cancelled because of poor weather.

In October 1996 5 Airborne Brigade was ordered to plan a parachute insertion of its spearhead battalion into Zaire. This was part of a multinational humanitarian operation to save thousands of refugees who had been routed from their villages by armed tribesmen and had fled to remote jungle areas. The mission, codenamed

Operation 'Purposeful', was ordered by the UK Defence Secretary after the world's media had focused on these starving refugees in the central African state. A parachute insertion was therefore approved by senior officers at the Permanent Joint Headquarters in Northwood. At their Aldershot base paratroopers prepared for the jump. Security was tight and there were no leaks to the media. In the age of modern communications the Brigade Commander did not want to alert armed tribesmen or anyone else. At Arbroath too, 45 Commando Royal Marines were also preparing for the operation; they would join the force and come under command of 5 Airborne Brigade. The plan included more than twenty C-130 Hercules, twelve of which would carry the leading elements of the force into Zaire.

The big problem identified by planning staff at Northwood was the fact that the refugees had disappeared into the bush and could not initially be located by satellite.

The soldiers were due to fly from the UK and land in Cyprus at night, jumping into Africa at first light the following day. But just as soldiers prepared to say goodbye to their families news came that the refugees had been located and within twenty-four hours the international aid agencies announced that there was no longer a need for a military intervention force. The parachute assault operation was cancelled but it had proved that the airborne capability was still very much a vital asset to any modern fighting force, particularly in the area of humanitarian operations, where refugees can be isolated in remote areas that are difficult to access by conventional means.

Also, as recently as early 1997 one of the brigade's TALO battalions (The Princess of

The RAF is crucial to the airborne capability. The C-130 Hercules can airlift the Leading Parachute Battle Group or the Leading Tactical Air-Land Battle Group into action.

As a key part of the UK's Rapid Reaction Force, elements of the modern airborne force is ready to be sent anywhere in the world – by parachute, helicopter or other conventional means of insertion – and are expected to become Britain's primary theatre entry force in future operations.

Into action! The brigade regularly carries out exercises in which the readiness of the formation is tested.

Wales's Royal Regiment) was alerted for operations in the Balkans. This was cancelled but months later elements of the PWRR together with specialists from the brigade's logistics battalion and medics from 23 Parachute Field Ambulance, deployed to the Congo to prepare for an evacuation of British nationals. And in early 1998, specialist Tactical Air Control Parties from the brigade were deployed in Northern Iraq and Kuwait ready to co-ordinate Allied air strikes if they were needed.

But most important in modern eyes is the brigade's capability to airlift an entire parachute battle group aboard a stream of Hercules aircraft which fly at low level to avoid air defence systems, and in future operations can provide the capability to deploy the Paras at night, from a height of 250 ft, using a revolutionary new low-level canopy. This type of joint service operation offers major advantages as a strategic intervention force, and trials are currently under way to enhance the firepower capability of the Lead Parachute Battle Group to ensure that airborne forces are ready to play a leading role in the future British Army.

Britain is the leading exponent of the new Low-Level Parachute (LLP) concept and the use of airborne troops, either in isolation ready to deploy as a demonstration of political intent or used as a deliberate intervention force, has the potential to make a major psychological impact on an enemy. As such, Britain's airborne forces are well prepared for the twenty-first century both as a combat-ready force and as specialists in humanitarian emergencies.

A stick of trainee paratroopers from Manchester's Ringway parachute training school is pictured deploying from a Whitley. The paratroop exit hole is in the belly of the aircraft.

1. THE EARLY DAYS OF AIRBORNE FORCES

The story of Britain's airborne forces in the Second World War is one of measured professionalism and determination against a backdrop of inadequate equipment and a slow start in relation to that of the Germans. Nevertheless, when Britain's units were operational they had a significant effect on the war in Europe and in the Mediterranean where, on experiencing their ferocious fighting spirit, the Afrika Korps nicknamed them 'Red Devils'.

The advance by German forces across Europe in 1940 had been rapid: in just three months they had occupied Denmark, Norway, Holland, Luxembourg, Belgium, France and the Channel Islands. Following the fall of France in May 1940, Prime Minister Winston Churchill was eager to create fighting forces that could strike at enemy-occupied Europe. Among the troops he had in mind were parachute forces, which he was aware had been used to great effect by the enemy.

During their assault on Europe, Hitler's military commanders had mounted several successful operations with paratroops. By using a joint force of parachute and glider troops the Germans had perfected the art of dropping ahead of their own advancing ground forces to seize key objectives, therefore maximising the element of surprise. These *coup de main* operations, which the British War Office had previously dismissed, had attracted the attention of the newly appointed Prime Minister Winston Churchill, who called for more information about this new military development. He was soon to decide that Britain should raise its own airborne force.

The world's first parachutist, André Jacques Garnerin, made his historic jump in Paris on 22 October 1797,* but since then progress had been slow, the most significant development being the introduction of emergency parachutes for wartime pilots at the end of the First World War. After the war the Americans carried out small-scale experiments in dropping parachutists, but it was the Russians** who saw the potential for airborne forces and began to develop the skill. By the mid-1930s the Soviets had created an effective airborne force capable of dropping large contingents of men and equipment.

This new capability was demonstrated at the Red Army autumn manoeuvres near

---

* On 22 October 1997, B Company of 2nd Battalion the Parachute Regiment marked the 200th anniversary by dropping in to Egypt as part of a multinational airborne force.

** Although Russia helped pioneer military parachuting, their achievements during the war years were limited and when deployed were operationally ineffective.

The 'pull-off' method. This dare-devil system was pioneered by professional stuntmen who climbed on to the wing of an aircraft and while holding on to the strut of the fuselage pulled their own ripcord, deploying the canopy into the slipstream, which pulled the parachutist off. In the late 1930s these stuntmen staged spectacular shows around the country and their experience was invaluable to the training staff at Ringway.

Moscow in September 1936. A British delegation, headed by Major-General A.P. Wavell (later Field Marshal The Earl Wavell), was invited to Kiev to watch the exercise in which a force of about 1,500 Russian troops dropped by parachute from 2,500 ft to seize a river crossing with apparent success and few casualties. Wavell described it as a 'spectacular performance', but was doubtful of its tactical value.

In Britain, the reaction of the War Office appears to have been that there was little scope for the employment of parachute forces on a scale sufficient to exert any major influence on a campaign or battle, and so the concept was dismissed. However, the use of parachuting as a form of insertion into occupied territory for agents of the Special Operations Executive was to be adopted.

By the mid-1930s, the Germans had already started to build an airborne force. They had identified a future for such troops who could play a vital role in deliberate attack operations, their silent arrival at night or dawn on or near the objective ensuring that they maintained the key element of surprise. By the start of the war they had gained six years of experience in training their parachute and glider troops and in early 1940 they mounted several parachute assaults into Norway, one operation on to an airfield at Stavanger. The mission was a total success, the target being secured in just 35 minutes. Then, in May, German airborne troops launched a raid on the fortress of Eben Emael to destroy the gun fortifications that were the backbone of Belgium's main defence against Hitler's advancing army. The heavily defended guns had been regarded as impregnable, but the unexpected and unconventional nature of the airborne raid took the Belgians completely by surprise and within minutes of the assault the paratroopers had paralysed the base.

The German airborne troops were proving their capabilities in warfare and gave

Hitler's war machine a significant boost. Such 'shock troops' could be used to mount small raids, 'leapfrog' a force forward into battle by parachuting ahead of the main assault, or perhaps even to launch a major airborne drop into England. This invasion threat resulted in road signs being removed in Britain and Home Guard units being placed on the alert in case of an airborne assault on East Anglia or southern England.

Now, as Britain struggled to recover from the retreat at Dunkirk and the fall of France, Winston Churchill sought to create a new force to match the Germans. These troops would need to be flexible, highly motivated and well trained, and would be drawn as volunteers from regiments and corps across the British Army. Churchill, who had only taken office on 10 May 1940, had already told the House of Commons in his first speech that he had nothing to offer but 'blood, toil, tears and sweat'. Following the evacuation of Dunkirk he warned the country about the risk of invasion and now looked to his military commanders to give him direction at this darkest hour.

On 22 June 1940 he directed the War Office to investigate the possibility of forming a corps of at least 5,000 parachute-trained troops, which, he added, should include a proportion of Canadians, Australians and New Zealanders. But the shortage of resources meant it was difficult to train any volunteers fully. Priority was given to the RAF, which desperately needed pilots and other aircrew trades to fight the Battle of Britain and develop the bomber force, while the Army was still reorganising and re-arming at home and abroad. The Prime Minister told the Joint Chiefs of Staff: 'We ought to have a corps

A student at Ringway parachute school drops through the paratroop exit hole of the Whitley.

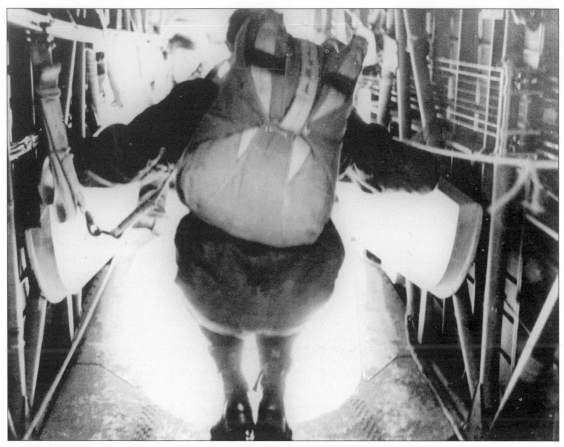

A student poised for an imminent drop from a Whitley.

of at least 5,000 parachute troops . . . advantage of the summer must be taken to train these troops, who can none the less play their part meanwhile as shock troops in home defence.' In fact a study had already commenced a month earlier when the RAF established a base at Ringway, near Manchester, with the aim of investigating procedures and the resources required to establish a full-scale parachute training programme. Ringway was commanded by Squadron Leader Louis Strange, a former RFC officer, who, assisted by Major John Rock of the Royal Engineers, was tasked with the 'military organisation of British airborne forces'. It was soon named the Central Landing School and was directed to train both parachute and glider troops. Initially 3,500 men volunteered for service, of whom 500 were further selected for parachute training. However their training was held up owing to the lack of suitable aircraft.

The American Douglas DC-3 Dakota was the preferred aircraft with its side exit door, but there were none available so it was decided that with minor modifications the British Armstrong Whitworth Whitley bomber could be adapted for parachuting, although these aircraft were also in limited supply. In addition there were only a few civilian gliders and these could not be converted for military operations owing to their light construction. The twin-engined Whitley was considered suitable for parachuting because at the time it was the slowest of the available RAF aircraft and it also had the capability to tow gliders. However, these aircraft were primarily built for bombing and the long thin fuselage did not leave much room for paratroopers; at first they carried only eight soldiers, this number later increasing to ten.

The first application of the parachute by the British military had taken place at the end of the First World War as an emergency escape for pilots about to crash. This had resulted in the establishment of the Parachute Test Centre at Henlow, Bedfordshire, which evolved to train all aircrew in parachute drills, should they be needed. Instructors from the Test Centre now formed the nucleus of staff at Ringway. The team of parachute jump instructors based at Henlow was headed by Flight Sergeant Bill Bereton and included several civilian 'show jumpers' called upon to assist in training.

First trials of the static line parachute at Ringway in 1941. The project was very sensitive, as the 'secret' stamp on the picture indicates.

During the First World War 'show jumping' was the only direct way in which parachuting was promoted. The jumpers themselves were brave men who had started their careers as balloonists and took to the parachute to improve their public appeal and boost their income. They performed at events all over the country, standing on the wings of an aircraft and deploying their parachute by means of the pull-off method. It was therefore a natural progression that a select group of these pioneers should be called on to give advice at Ringway, particularly in the area of landing drills.

The instructors had limited equipment and training facilities and initially used a supply of manually operated Irvin parachutes, which had a 28 ft canopy, and were designed as emergency parachutes for pilots and aircrew. Fitted with a rip-cord which had to be pulled manually, these parachutes were by no means ideal for training. This design feature resulted in the initial style of jumping known as the 'pull-off' method, in which students stood outside the aircraft and after they had activated the rip-cord the slipstream caught their parachute and deployed it, pulling the soldier – or pilot – away from the aircraft.

The first jumps from the Whitleys were carried out on 13 July 1940 by RAF Parachute Jump Instructors and men from No. 2 Commando who displayed outstanding courage. One at a time a parachutist and a dispatcher crawled on hands and knees to the rear of the aircraft, where the gun turret had been removed. There they knelt in the open tail of the Whitley ready to make their jump. Holding on to a small metal bar the jumper positioned himself carefully on a small platform, about one foot square, and then stood up. Standing outside the aircraft and exposed to the elements, the jumper went through the drill with the instructor; then, when he was given the signal, he pulled his rip-cord. Within seconds the slipstream caught hold of the parachute and opened it, jerking the jumper away from the aircraft. It was a crude and risky procedure, but the shortage of aircraft had forced the staff to improvise and adapt the Whitley in the best way they could, with the only parachute available to them.

Captain Martin Lindsay of the Royal Scots Fusiliers, who had been a polar explorer before the war, was one of the first army volunteers to jump from the Whitley gun turret. The terror he experienced on that first jump can only really be appreciated by those who jumped from the Whitley tail turret:

We climbed into the aircraft and sat on the floor of the fuselage. The engines roared and we took off. I noticed how moist the palms of my hands were. I wished I didn't always feel slightly sick in an aircraft.

It seemed an age, but it cannot have been more than ten minutes when the instructor beckoned me. I began to make my way down the fuselage towards him, crawling on my hands and knees into the rear-gunner's turret, the back of which had been removed. I tried not to overbalance and fall out, nor to look at the landscape speeding across below me as I turned to face forward again.

I now found myself on a small platform about a foot square, at the very back of the plane, hanging on like grim death to the bar under which I had had such difficulty in crawling. The two rudders were a few feet away on either side of me; behind me was nothing whatsoever.

As soon as I raised myself to full height, I found that I was to all purposes outside the plane, the slipstream of air in my face almost blowing me off. I quickly huddled up, my head bent down and pressed into the capacious bosom of the flight sergeant. I was about to make a 'pull-off', opening my parachute which would not pull me off until fully developed – a procedure calculated to fill me with such confidence that I should be only too ready to leap smartly out of the aircraft on all subsequent occasions.

The little light at the side changed from yellow to red. I was undeniably frightened, though at the same time filled with a fearful joy. The light changed to green and the instructor's hand fell down indicating for me to jump. I put my right hand across to the D-ring in front of my left side and pulled sharply.

A pause of nearly a second and then a jerk on each shoulder. I was whisked off backwards and swung through nearly 180 degrees beneath the canopy and up the other side.

But I was quite oblivious to all this as I had something akin to a black-out. At any rate, the first thing I was conscious of after the jerk on my shoulders was to find myself, perhaps four seconds later, sitting up in my harness and floating down to earth.

These pioneers jumped into Tatton drop zone (DZ), which belonged to Lord Egerton. The base commander, Squadron Leader Louis Strange, said: 'We cut down his trees, we knocked down his gateposts, we landed all over his park, yet I cannot remember Lord Egerton ever complaining. It was to his co-operation that I attributed a great deal of the early success of our work.'

Paratroopers fit parachutes as they prepare for a demonstration jump at Ringway to show Prime Minister Churchill their skills.

Qualified paratroopers of No. 2 Commando, later to be re-badged as the 1st Battalion the Parachute Regiment, pictured inside the fuselage of a Whitley bomber.

In the initial days of training the first two descents were by the 'pull-off' method. Shortly after training commenced the instructors decided to tie a secure line to the rip-cord which was then fastened in the aircraft with the aim of achieving automatic opening. This system worked well at first, but it was very dangerous and a number of parachutists lost their lives. The system meant that now parachuting would be from an exit *inside* the aircraft, not from side doors like American paratroopers in their Dakotas, but from a hole in the floor of the Whitley bomber. This exit needed maximum courage, although it was perhaps an improvement on standing in the open air at the back of the rear turret.

On the order 'Action Stations', the first two jumpers sat opposite each other with their feet dangling out through the hole. On the order 'Go' the number one launched himself through the hole while trying to maintain the position of attention. This was not 'bull' but an attempt to get the exit just right. Too hard a push-off could result in the jumper smashing his face against the opposite side of the hole, while too feeble an effort caused the parachute pack on the man's back to catch on the edge of the hole and tip him forward, with the same outcome.

With training and practice it was possible to drop ten paratroopers from the Whitley. A well-trained stick of men could exit an aircraft within nine to ten seconds. With the aircraft flying at 100mph this resulted in the ten jumpers being dispersed over 500 yards. From a Dakota, the time and dispersal could be halved.

In early 1940 the only aircraft the RAF had which offered a door exit was the Bristol Bombay. It was an underpowered monoplane that lacked range, but it was slow and had a side door which made it suitable for parachuting. The problem was that these aircraft were simply not available in the early days of parachuting training.

The first jump by a pupil at Ringway took place from a Whitley on 21 July 1940. Just four days later, on 25 July 1940, Private Evans, a driver with the Royal Army Service Corps who had volunteered for special service, was killed when his parachute rigging lines twisted around his canopy, preventing it from deploying. His jump was only the 136th since Ringway had opened and training was suspended for several weeks while trials with dummies were carried out.

It was at this point that Raymond Quilter of the GQ parachute company demonstrated a new parachute system which he had designed with his colleague James Gregory. The system used the same 28 ft canopy, packed in a bag carried on the soldier's back. A static line was fitted to the apex, the top of the parachute, and secured inside the aircraft. This enabled the rigging lines to be pulled out and fully extended before the canopy deployed. It also had the advantage of delaying opening until the parachute was well clear of the aircraft. The parachute itself broke away from the soldier's back and remained attached to the static line and the aircraft. As he continued to fall, his weight pulled first the lift webs, then the rigging lines, out of the bag. Finally, at the end of the taut and extended rigging lines, the canopy pulled out of the bag, a final tie broke, and the canopy developed. The opening shock was negligible and the danger of becoming entangled was also greatly reduced.

Within five days of the first fatality, a modified version of the GQ system was being developed in conjunction with Irvin Parachutes to produce the GQ X-Type statichute system. This very effective system remained in service for the remainder of the Second World War. It was produced by two rival companies, Irvin and GQ, which are still supplying parachutes to Britain's airborne forces today.

Jumping resumed two weeks after the death of Driver Evans using the new static line parachute. But despite the improved parachute the difficulty in making a good clean exit from the 'hole' in the Whitley often resulted in 'twists' and more accidents. These horrific incidents, in which twisted rigging lines prevented the parachutes from deploying, became known as 'Roman Candles' and were greatly feared by trainees. In the first few months of operations at Ringway more than 2,000 descents had been recorded but by the end of 1940 at least three men had died. The 'Roman Candle' was – and still is – the greatest fear of any paratrooper.

In September 1940 the school at Ringway was expanded to become the Central Landing Establishment and was divided into a Parachute Training School, a Technical

Winston Churchill during a visit to the parachute training school at Ringway to see for himself how training was developing.

Unit and a Glider Training Squadron. The role of the establishment was to train parachute troops, glider pilots and aircrew for airborne work, develop the tactical handling of airborne troops, carry out technical research and recommend operational requirements.

Squadron Leader Strange and Major Rock of the Royal Engineers, the two men who pioneered parachute training, had one thing in common – they knew nothing about training paratroopers. They had no standing operational procedures to follow and were equipped with just three obsolete Whitley bombers to train Britain's new airborne force. On the plus side, they did have three former circus fliers among their ranks, one of whom had made pull-off jumps from a biplane in the 1930s, and he would plan the initial parachute drills. At this time enthusiasm rather than experience was the keynote to future success. Major Rock and Squadron Leader Strange faced a daunting task in training 5,000 paratroopers for operations and although the organisation worked well, the dual RAF/Army control of training created difficulties in agreement over operational priority.

At the Air Ministry senior officers were not convinced that parachute operations had a tactical role in major operations and consequently did not give it priority; instead they favoured small-scale airborne operations with greater emphasis on glider operations. They even proposed a scheme in which gliders might be used to refuel heavy aircraft. The Prime Minister agreed that the scheme should be taken seriously, but he feared that the pursuit of the doubtful and experimental glider policy might cost the country an airborne force whose efficiency had already been proved by the Germans. He therefore asked for a full report of what had been done on the gliders.

In the same month, in a report to the Prime Minister, the Air Ministry proposed the following tasks for which airborne troops could be used: a parachute raid on a selected

A paratrooper makes a descent from the balloon. On average a jumper fell 200 ft before the canopy fully deployed – but the system was very safe. The balloon was retired in the early 1990s.

position followed by evacuation by air; a parachute raid followed by evacuation by sea; dropping parachutists secretly to act as saboteurs. The Ministry concluded that for any operation about 1,000 men would be needed of whom just 100 would parachute in, while 900 would be glider-borne. The report recommended that the total airborne force should comprise 500 parachute troops, 2,700 glider troops and 360 glider pilots to fly the glider-borne troops. The number of parachutists was considerably lower than initially planned.

At the end of 1940 the Air Ministry and War Office had agreed to produce four types of glider. The four were an 8-seater to be named the Hotspur, a 25-seater named the Horsa, a 15-seater to be produced in small numbers and called the Hengist, and a large glider called the Hamilcar which could carry either a tank or forty troops.

By early 1941 the first 500 parachutists had been trained for operations and in April that year the first service glider, a Hotspur, arrived at Ringway with a further fifteen being delivered in August. On 26 April 1941, a parachute and glider demonstration was given at Ringway for the Prime Minister, Mr Churchill. A formation of six Whitleys dropped just sixty men – considerably fewer than the Prime Minister had expected to see. In fact 800 had been trained by this time, but the lack of aircraft prevented a mass drop. On his return to London Churchill wrote to General Ismay asking for the minute which he had written in the summer of 1940 directing that 5,000 parachute troops were to be prepared. He also asked for all the staff papers relating to his agreement to reduce the number to just 500.

Before the Prime Minister could be convinced that the decision to reduce the number of parachutists from 5,000 to 500 was correct, Germany's 7th Airborne Division invaded Crete with parachute and glider-borne troops. Just two weeks before the air assault the Air Ministry had advised Churchill that Crete could never be taken by such a method. The German success in Crete convinced the Prime Minister that there was an important role for parachute and glider troops and he invited the Chiefs of Staffs to make proposals to try to improve training and ensure that the original target figure of 5,000 was met as soon as possible. The Chiefs of Staff told him that by May 1942 there would be 5,000 paratroopers available, supplying one brigade at home and another in the Middle East. There would also be sufficient gliders and tug aircraft to carry another force of 5,000 men and supporting arms.

The problems they faced in preparing this airborne force were lack of aircraft and resources, and too little experience to reflect upon for training standards and procedures. One senior RAF officer summed up the situation, saying: 'We are trying to do what we have never been able to do hitherto, namely to introduce a completely new arm into the Service at about five minutes' notice with totally inadequate resources and personnel. Little if any practical experience is possessed in England of any of these problems and it will be necessary to cover in six months what the Germans have covered in six years.'

In July 1941 Wing Commander Maurice Newnham, a fighter pilot from the First World War, took command of the Parachute Training School at Ringway. Newnham

A demonstration at Ringway of the tactical value of airborne troops.

An RAF parachute jump instructor checks the equipment of a present-day paratrooper. It was the RAF that took charge of parachuting at Ringway and more than 50 years on they are still responsible for training airborne forces.

The balloon. It was first introduced at Ringway in 1941 and remained a vital part of parachute training until the early 1990s when the system was replaced by a small transport aircraft.

was instrumental in establishing RAF control of parachute training and he guided the PTS successfully through the Second World War.

Newnham was responsible for training more than 60,000 British and Allied parachutists as well as several thousand special agents who were dropped behind enemy lines. He also introduced the balloon to speed up training jumps and meet the target to train 5,000 paratroopers as set by the Chiefs of Staff.

The first balloon was delivered to Ringway in April 1941 and it soon became a distinctive feature of the Tatton Park skyline. It provided a cheap and relatively safe introduction to parachuting, but a terrifying one, as recalled by one of Ringway's first students, Major John Frost, later Major General:

> Then came that morning when we found ourselves sitting side by side in the crazily swaying basket of a balloon which was slowly rising to a height of 600 ft above Tatton Park and we smiled at each other with the learner parachutist's smile – which has no humour in it. One merely uncovers one's teeth for a second or two then hides them again quickly lest they should start chattering.
>
> We fiddled anxiously, threw a quick agonised glance at the ground below, but in the main we started upwards, praying. . . . The first sensation of falling drew breath from my lungs, then a cracking sound from above and a sudden pull on my harness told me that my parachute was open, and the rest was heavenly.

The balloon was adopted for full-scale training and within six months more than 6,000 descents had been made. But the balloon was feared by many, even though it offered a better exit than from an aircraft and the students did not suffer air-sickness in the aircraft prior to the jump. The experience of jumping from a balloon is summed up by a Parachute Regiment sergeant:

> Everyone was very nervous, there was no noise and as the balloon was raised into the air you could hear a pin drop.
>
> Often the parachute jump instructor would crack a joke and everyone would either start laughing before he had finished or not laugh at all. Then when he was ready the PJI would call the first man forward and you would jump. I can only relate it to committing suicide. As you leave the balloon you simply drop straight down, there is no slipstream.
>
> After what seems hundreds of feet you are convinced that any minute you will die, then suddenly you are jerked back as your parachute opens and for a few seconds you feel like God. Then you suddenly hear the instructor shouting and realise that you are almost on the ground and he is yelling at you to put your feet together and lock your arms in. It was a hell of an experience.

In September 1941 the Central Landing Establishment was renamed the Airborne Forces Establishment, No. 1 Parachute Training School being part of the establishment. As further changes were made Squadron Leader John Callastius Kilkenny (known as JCK) arrived at Ringway and took charge of the development of the syllabus and ground training methods.

British troops were not the only forces to be trained at Ringway: French, Belgian, Czech, Norwegian and Polish troops also trained in England. Harry Ward, the former air-circus jumper, was very involved in training the Polish Brigade who arrived in Britain after the fall of France. Parachute jump instructors from Ringway also served overseas to support airborne operations in Middle and Far East campaigns. No. 2 Parachute Training School was formed at Kabrit in North Africa in 1942, to train and support airborne forces in the Middle East. No. 3 PTS was established in India at New Delhi in 1941, then later on at Chaklala. Gurkha troops were trained here to form the 50th Indian Parachute Brigade who took part in the assault on Rangoon in 1945.

The war effort had been a success. The Airborne Forces Establishment had trained three Air Landing Brigades of glider-borne troops in a training package which saw soldiers from a wide selection of the British Army being sent to Ringway. Among those trained were men from the 1st Battalion the Border Regiment, 12th Battalion the Devonshire Regiment, 2nd Battalion the Oxfordshire & Buckinghamshire Light Infantry, 7th Battalion the King's Own Scottish Borderers, 1st Battalion the Royal Ulster Rifles, 2nd Battalion the South Staffordshire Regiment, 2nd Battalion the Black Watch and 1st Battalion the Argyll and Sutherland Highlanders.

Trained paratroopers passed out of Ringway to serve in seventeen parachute battalions. The 1st Parachute Battalion was formed from No. 2 Commando and No. 11 SAS Battalion in September 1941, the 2nd, 3rd and 4th Battalions were drawn from all arms volunteers, while the 5th Battalion was drawn from the Cameron Highlanders. The 6th Battalion was made up from the 10th Battalion the Royal Welch Fusiliers, the 7th Battalion from the Somerset Light Infantry and the 8th Battalion from the Royal Warwickshire Regiment. The 10th Battalion Essex Regiment provided the initial manpower for the 9th Parachute Battalion, and the 10th Battalion was drawn from the Royal Sussex Regiment and units stationed in the Middle East. The 11th Battalion also recruited from units based there. The 12th Battalion was created from men serving with the Green Howards, in the 13th Battalion from the South Lancashire Regiment, the 14th Battalion from the Royal Hampshires, the 15th Battalion from the King's Regiment in India, the 16th Battalion from the South Staffordshires in India and the 17th Battalion from volunteers in the north of England.

At the end of the war General 'Windy' Gale, commanding the 1st British Airborne Division, said: 'To all who qualified and subsequently fought as parachutists, the happiest memories are associated with this great school. Here no less than sixty thousand British and Allied parachutists were trained. The spirit that has inspired so many of them to perform such grand and courageous tasks was largely laid at the Parachute Training School.' Ernie Chinery, a student on the very first parachute course at Ringway, was a guest at RAF Brize Norton in 1994 to congratulate fifty-seven trainees and hand them their wings when they completed the 1,000th basic parachute course. Since the first parachute courses began in 1940 more than 166,000 trainees have received their wings.

'C' Company of 2nd Battalion the Parachute Regiment – the Bruneval raiding force pictured during preparations for the raid. At this stage soldiers still wore the beret and cap badge of their parent unit.

2. THE FIRST OPERATIONS

TRAGINO, BRUNEVAL AND VERMORK

The first airborne operation took place in early 1941 when Britain's fledgling force was still developing. There were few airborne resources available at this time and Whitley bombers were still the only approved parachuting aircraft – even their modification was in its infancy. The only parachute-trained troops around were the 11th Special Air Service Battalion, formed from No. 2 Commando the previous November. However, it was desirable to do anything that would hamper the Italian war effort and the Tragino aqueduct in southern Italy was selected as the target for the first airborne raid.

Water from the Tragino aqueduct supplied Italian military units and the two million people who lived in the Apulia Province, and its destruction would cause chaos. But it was too far inland for a seaborne raid and difficult to bomb accurately. An airborne assault was the obvious answer and it gave the Chiefs of Staff the opportunity to test Churchill's new force.

In early January 1941, when the 11th SAS was asked for volunteers to take part in a raid on the Tragino aqueduct, every member of the battalion stepped forward. Major T.A.G. Pritchard of the Royal Welch Fusiliers was selected to command 'X' Troop which would conduct the raid – thirty-eight officers and men including a demolition team and three Italian interpreters. Following training against a mock-up of the aqueduct at Tatton Park, 'X' Troop took off from Mildenhall in Suffolk on 7 February and headed for Malta. The men had been given just three weeks to prepare for the operation, and during their training one man, Sergeant Dennis, was killed when he landed in a lake and drowned. The force arrived in Malta on 9 February and prepared their orders and equipment for the raid. Lieutenant Tony Deane-Drummond was already in Malta as part of the advance party, having flown ahead several weeks earlier in a Sunderland flying boat from Plymouth in Devon.

The next day, 10 February, six of the eight Whitleys that had flown them to the island were loaded with weapons, explosives, ammunition and rations, while the other two were bombed-up for a diversionary raid on the railway marshalling yard at Foggia.

The aircraft lifted off: Operation 'Colossus' was under way. The officers under Major Pritchard were Captain Lea, Lieutenant Deane-Drummond and 2nd Lieutenant Jowett leading the covering parties with Captain Daly and 2nd Lieutenant Patterson in charge of the Royal Engineers, who would be responsible for placing the explosives once the party reached the target. The drop itself was to be made to the north of the aqueduct. Once the operation had taken place, the men were to split into small groups and make their way to the west coast, where they would be picked up by the submarine HMS *Triumph*.

At around 2145 hours the men were dropped; however, the sixth Whitley dropped the party of Royal Engineers and the majority of the explosives in the wrong valley. First to land was Lieutenant Deane-Drummond; his job was to destroy a small bridge over the River Genestra to hinder the arrival of any Italian forces, and to round up local villagers and hold them in nearby cottages. The commanders of the other covering parties, Captain Lea and 2nd Lieutenant Jowett and their troops were positioned on either side of the Genestra bridge to keep an eye on movements up the valley. Casualties on the drop were light but Major Pritchard was short of sappers and the bulk of his explosives were with the Engineers. Luckily one of the sappers, Lieutenant Patterson, had dropped in a different aircraft and was with the party. He began laying his charges at the aqueduct, though Captain Daly's explosives were still missing. Nevertheless, when the explosives were detonated at half past midnight, the aqueduct was destroyed, as was the Genestra bridge.

'X' Troop had achieved maximum success, but then events took a turn for the worse. As the teams made for the coast (Captain Daly and his party of Royal Engineers who had missed the operation heard the explosions and immediately set off for the pick-up point), they were unaware that the *Triumph*'s sailing orders had been cancelled after one of the two Whitleys bombing Foggia had made a forced landing at the mouth of the River Sele. It was assumed that the area would be crawling with Italian units looking for the downed aircrew, and therefore that the submarine rendezvous would be compromised.

Major Pritchard and his men made their way to the Sele, but were then spotted and identified by a lone peasant, who was soon joined by armed police and more civilians, including women and children. The British Paras could have fought their way out, but Pritchard was reluctant to engage in a firefight against civilians and so ordered his men to lay down their weapons. The men of 'X' Troop were taken to Naples and then to the prisoner-of-war camp at Sulmona. Thus ended the attack on the Tragino aqueduct, although captured the troops of the first airborne campaign had achieved their aim.

The British had proved they could carry out an effective airborne operation, a fact acknowledged with relish by the new Director of Combined Operations, Lord Louis Mountbatten. Late in 1941 the 11th Special Air Service Battalion became the 1st Parachute Battalion and by September it was joined by the 2nd and 3rd Battalions in the 1st Parachute Brigade, which had been formed by Brigadier Gale. In October Brigadier Frederick 'Boy' Browning was appointed Commander of Airborne Forces and promoted to Major-General, and in November he was ordered to form an Airborne Division.

By late 1941 British scientists had alerted the War Office to the giant Würzburg radar system that the Germans were using. They were desperate to inspect the system, believing it sent out medium-length transmissions that identified aircraft and enabled

Map of the raid on Bruneval. The Bruneval raid took place in February 1942 and was codenamed Operation 'Biting'. The airborne troops were drawn from 'C' Company of 2nd Battalion the Parachute Regiment, commanded by Major Frost, who later led the battalion at Arnhem.

flak gunners to engage unseen Allied aircraft. One such radar was located 12 miles north of Le Havre, near the village of Bruneval. Major-General Browning proposed a raid on the site and by December plans were being prepared for an assault against the German radar station at Bruneval. In early 1942 the Director of Operations approved the mission, codenamed Operation 'Biting'.

The Bruneval raid was planned for late February 1942 and would be a combined operation involving paratroopers, a naval evacuation force and an infantry party landed from the sea to cover the beach evacuation. The parachute element was to be 'C' Company, 2nd Parachute Battalion, commanded by Major John Frost. ('C' Company was also known as 'Jock' Company because of the large number of men from Scottish regiments in the unit.) The naval element was led by Commander F.N.

Cook of the Royal Australian Navy, and consisted of a small fleet of assault landing craft, support landing craft, gunboats and two escort destroyers. The beach protection party was made up of thirty-two officers and men from the Royal Fusiliers and South Wales Borderers. In addition, the RAF were to carry out a diversionary raid at the time of the assault. The radar itself was located in front of a large villa, not far from a farmhouse called La Presbytère, which was used as the headquarters of a German garrison of 100 troops who manned fifteen defence posts along the cliffs. In addition, there was a German infantry regiment and a tank battalion based not far inland. The ground itself suited an air drop, being flat and open.

On 27 February the tides and weather conditions were favourable, and Operation 'Biting' got under way. That afternoon Frost and his paras of 'C' Company arrived at Thruxton airfield in Hampshire. The company was divided into three sections for the raid which were named Nelson, Drake and Rodney after famous naval commanders. 'Nelson', led by Lieutenant Ewen Charteris, comprised forty men whose task was to drop first, knock out the cliff machine-gun posts and then move into Bruneval village.

Paratroopers search German prisoners taken at the Bruneval raid, February 1941. The men are wearing 'step-in' smocks and the first design of para helmets which had a flared piece at the back to protect the head on exit from the aircraft.

Major Frost, right, who led the Bruneval raid, briefing a colleague.

The fifty-five men of 'Drake' were further divided into two sections, one under Lieutenant Young and Captain Vernon. Lieutenant Young and his team would seize the radar installation, while Captain Vernon's troop were to assist in the dismantling of the radar. The last party, 'Rodney', which comprised forty men under Lieutenant Timothy, had orders to prevent the German garrison from reaching the villa. They would also act as a reserve force.

A key member of the raid was RAF Flight Sergeant Charles Cox, an electrical expert, who had been 'volunteered' by Air Commodore Victor Tait, the RAF's Director of Radar, to oversee the dismantling of the radar installation. Cox joined 'C' Company and parachuted into occupied France with the rest of the paratroopers. His action and bravery won him high praise from Frost and he was later decorated for his work.

The twelve Whitley bombers from 51 Squadron took two hours to reach the French coast near Le Havre, the men inside playing cards, singing or trying to sleep to pass the time. The aircraft came under anti-aircraft fire and two of the pilots were forced to alter course. The drop zone (DZ) was situated 1,000 yards east of the villa, and apart from the sticks in the two Whitleys which had to divert, all of 'C' Company made an excellent landing. The Paras, less the two missing sections, quickly collected their equipment from the containers and moved off to the assembly area. Charteris and half of the 'Nelson' group in the two diverted Whitleys landed 3,500 yards south of the villa – close to the village but a long way from the cliff machine guns. 'Drake' and 'Rodney' proceeded towards the radar station and the wood surrounding the farmhouse. When Young and his men reached the radar they found it manned, though with a quick burst of gunfire they killed or captured the crew. Frost and 'Drake' established a cordon around the villa and then stormed the building and captured it; Frost then concentrated his men around the radar set. Soon word reached Frost that the radar had been dismantled and was ready to be carried away. It seemed all too easy.

Suddenly gunfire from La Presbytère opened up on the Paras, and the machine-gun positions on the cliffs which 'Nelson' had not reached were still in action. Lieutenant Charteris, commander of the 'Nelson' group who had been dropped in the wrong area, was desperately trying to catch up on his task to attack the cliff-top machine-gun posts. Demonstrating outstanding courage Lieutenant Charteris and his section attacked the German machine-gun post and silenced the enemy. Now all they had to do was wait for the Navy, but by 0215 hours the men on the beach were still waiting for the boats. Worryingly, radio contact could not be established with the senior service. By this time more machine-gun fire was being directed at Frost's men from the cliffs, and the situation became desperate. Finally, the naval vessels appeared out of the mist and approached the beach. As the Paras and their precious cargo were loaded on to the boats, the infantry in the torpedo boats leapt ashore and saturated the enemy cliff positions with gunfire. Operation 'Biting' was a resounding success and had yielded much important information regarding enemy radar equipment. In addition casualties had been light. This success, combined with the continuing expansion of

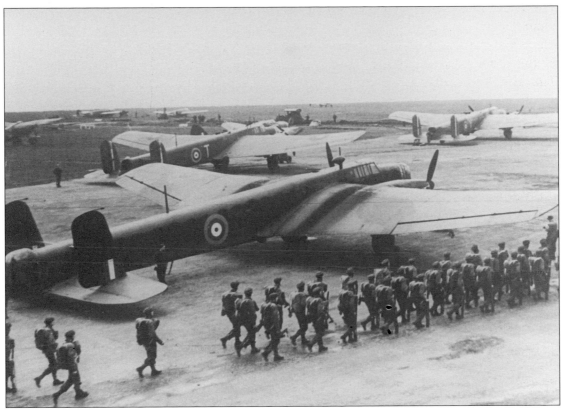

Paratroopers march towards their Whitley aircraft. The Whitley was used to drop the Tragino force at Bruneval and in the Norwegian operation at Vermork.

airborne forces, influenced the decision to give the new battalion its own identity and on 1 August 1942 the Parachute Regiment was officially formed, becoming part of the Army Air Corps and the Glider Pilot Regiment which had been formed on 21 December 1941. Under the guidance of Major-General Browning the Parachute Regiment gradually expanded until the end of the war when it comprised seventeen battalions, three of which were formed in India and two in Egypt. As the battalions grew so did the support organisation created by the Royal Air Force for training and dropping parachutists. These tasks were entrusted to squadrons of 38 and 46 Groups whose history is closely linked with the Parachute Regiment and airborne forces.

In mid-1942 Major-General Browning decided that his troops should have some form of distinctive headwear and after much debate the maroon beret was selected. Legend has it that the author Daphne du Maurier, the Major-General's wife, provided the inspiration for the colour of beret in one of her books. A character in *Frenchman's Creek* wore a maroon beret and stood out from the crowd, and it is said that this influenced the General's decision. This theory is dismissed by others who say there was a more formal selection process in which General Browning presented several coloured berets before the Chief of the Imperial General Staff, General Sir Alan Brooke. Unable to make up his mind he asked the opinion of the soldier who had been asked to pose wearing the different coloured berets. The soldier selected maroon and thus the choice was made. Whatever the real truth of the selection, the hallmark of Britain's airborne forces had been decided. Interestingly, the famous maroon berets were issued in 1942, but soldiers continued to wear the cap badges of their units until later in 1943 when their new regimental cap badge, incorporating the parachute canopy and wings, was minted.

American and German airborne forces also adopted the maroon beret for their parachute units and today almost every country in the world, except Russia, has adopted the same colour, generating an easily identified airborne brotherhood.

A PIAT (Projector Infantry Anti-Tank) weapon used by a member of the Parachute Brigade in North Africa.

Major-General Browning also wanted the 1st Airborne Division to have its own emblem and he commissioned Major Edward Seago, a well-known artist, to produce one. The result was the now famous badge showing the mythical warrior Bellerophon riding Pegasus. The first recorded instance of an airborne warrior, Bellerophon's exploits are recounted in Greek mythology, where he is chiefly famous for slaying the fire-breathing monster Chimera. Bellerophon, spear in hand, mounted Pegasus, rode into the air and swooped down on the monster to destroy it.

A far less successful airborne operation was Operation 'Freshman' on 17 November 1942. This was the attempt to destroy the Norwegian heavy water plant at Vermork – which was linked to German atomic bomb research – a few miles south-west of Rjukan. Vermork stands on one side of an inland fjord with steep sides, so the gliders used in the operation had to land a night's march from the target.

The volunteers for the raid were from the 9th Field Company (Airborne) RE and the 261st Field Park Company (Airborne) RE, the latter being specialists in demolition. Two separate parties, led by Lieutenants Alex Allen and David Methven, were transported in two Horsa gliders. The tug aircraft were two Halifax bombers from 138 and 161 Squadrons under the command of Group Captain Tom Cooper, 38 Wing.

But the mission ended in tragedy. The aircraft flew into a blizzard and one glider crash-landed in thick snow on a mountain, killing three troops on impact. The Halifax flew into a mountain and all on board died. The glider survivors were quickly rounded up by the Germans and were executed within hours. The second glider had problems with the intercommunications link with the tug and cast off prematurely, flying into high ground and killing eight of the seventeen men on board. Of the survivors four were injured and five unhurt – the injured were taken to Stavanger where they were poisoned by German doctors, while the others were shot two months later by the Gestapo. The Halifax carrying Group Captain Cooper returned safely to Scotland.

INTO NORTH AFRICA

The opportunity for Britain's airborne forces to prove their true value came in November 1942, when Major-General Browning learned that only one American airborne battalion was scheduled to take part in the forthcoming North Africa campaign. Browning believed there were tremendous opportunities for airborne forces in this vast desert terrain where the theatre of operations would be spread over great distances and vulnerable to the surprise of parachute raids.

Accordingly the 1st Parachute Brigade was placed under the command of General Eisenhower, the Supreme Allied Commander for the North African campaign, but it was short of men and equipment and resources had to be re-allocated from the 2nd Parachute Brigade and other units of 1st Airborne Division. Air support was to be provided by the United States Army Air Force (USAAF) and thus the brigade had to

A British airborne soldier pictured in North Africa. This was an opportunity for the newly formed force to cut its teeth where General Browning believed there were tremendous opportunities for parachute raids.

learn a new skill – jumping from a Dakota. Training took place at Netheravon in Wiltshire, although it was soon halted by problems with the length of the static line on the British parachute. The line was too short, causing several incidents in which four Paras were killed after their lines got hooked up under the fuselage or became entangled because their canopies had deployed too quickly. The problem was resolved by lengthening the static line. With the static lines refitted the 2nd Battalion, the Parachute Regiment became the first complete battalion to jump from the Dakotas – a significant improvement from jumping through a hole in the floor of a Whitley!

It was also discovered that 'trimming' the aircraft forward (and thus raising the tail) helped to eliminate the danger of parachutes snagging on the aircraft's tail wheel.

North Africa, as Major-General Browning had suggested, was to provide a more fruitful theatre for Britain's airborne forces, and on 9 November 1942 Lieutenant-Colonel Geoffrey Pine-Coffin's 3rd Parachute Battalion flew to Algiers from England via Gibraltar. The remainder of the 1st Parachute Brigade travelled by sea and arrived on 12 November, as the first airborne mission in North Africa was already under way. Earlier, on 8 November, the Allies had launched their assault on the North African coast, codenamed Operation 'Torch'. The immediate strategic objective was northern Tunis, and the intention was to cut off the Axis line of retreat from the advancing British 8th Army in the western desert.

On 11 November the 3rd Battalion took off from Gibraltar and flew into Maison Blanche airfield, near Algiers, early in the morning. Here, the Commanding Officer, Lieutenant-Colonel Pine-Coffin, was briefed by Lieutenant-General Sir Kenneth Anderson, Commander of the 1st British Army, aboard a ship in Algiers harbour. The 1st Parachute Brigade was now assigned to the 1st British Army who were eager to see what the Paras could do.

As Operation 'Torch' got under way the 3rd Battalion were ordered to seize the airfield at Bone on the morning of 12 November and hold it until No. 6 Commando, who would carry out a seaborne landing at Bone, could link up with the airborne force. A total of twenty-nine Dakotas dropped 360 men, just minutes before the Germans had intended to carry out a similar operation – which they then abandoned.

On 16 November the 1st Battalion, under the command of Lieutenant-Colonel James Hill, dropped near Souk el Arba airfield, situated 8 miles south-east of Bone, and advanced on Beja where they were tasked to capture a vital road junction and occupy the town, then held by 3,000 French troops. The Germans had already warned the French that there would be serious consequences if they allowed the British to enter Beja. Hill stopped on the outskirts of Beja and opened negotiations with the French commander. He told the French that Allied armoured divisions were nearby and indicated that the British Paras outnumbered the garrison in Beja – which, of course, they didn't. It was agreed that the British should enter the town and to continue his deception Lieutenant-Colonel Hill marched his men through the town twice, once wearing helmets and once wearing berets, to disguise the battalion's true strength.

Learning from the French that a German armoured patrol visited Sidi N'Sir each day to exchange cigarettes with the French and then drove back to Bizerta, a fortified base on the coast, Hill decided that this would be an ideal opportunity to hit the enemy and show the French what the Paras were capable of.

Major Peter Cleasby-Thompson's 'S' Company, together with a team of sappers, was dispatched to make contact with the French commander and set the ambush. The following day the armoured convoy drove past the Paras' position towards Sidi N'Sir, as it had done on a regular basis for some time. After it had passed them, 'S' Company's sappers (engineers) laid necklaces of anti-tank grenades across the road and withdrew, waiting for the patrol to return.

They waited until the first of the anti-tank grenades detonated then opened fire

Paratroopers pictured in a Douglas aircraft en route from Algiers to Tunisia in North Africa. Several of the paratroopers are wearing special kneepads designed for airborne forces. Like 'step-in' smocks these were initially used by German airborne forces and adopted by the British, albeit for a short period of time.

using 3-inch mortars to force the enemy into a main killing ground. Many Germans were killed while others were taken prisoner and their vehicles destroyed. The ambush was a total success. The wounded were loaded on to the two enemy armoured cars that were still working and the company withdrew to Sidi N'Sir before returning to Beja, where Lieutenant-Colonel Hill took advantage of this success and ordered that the armoured vehicles and prisoners be driven through the streets to demonstrate to the French garrison that the Germans were not invincible. Although two members of 'S' Company were injured in the ambush, it had been such a success that the British were able to convince the French that they had used a secret weapon against the German armour – another deception that played a significant part in persuading them to rally to the Allied cause.

Several days later, on the night of 23/24 November, the commanding officer was informed of an Italian force, numbering some 300 men, with some armour, located in a position north-east of Sidi N'Sir. Lieutenant-Colonel Hill took two companies, plus a contingent of Senegalese troops, and attacked the position at Gué Hill, 9 miles up the valley to Mateur.

The attack, conducted at bayonet point, was fierce. Hill captured two tanks by tapping on their turrets with his walking stick – when they opened the turret and found themselves facing his pistol the Italians quickly surrendered. But when the CO tried the same tactic on a third tank the crew emerged with guns blazing and Hill was hit three times in the chest. His adjutant Captain Miles Whitelock was also hit by shrapnel. Major Alistair Pearson took over command of the battalion and Hill and Whitelock were evacuated to Beja in a captured enemy motorbike and sidecar. The CO was seriously wounded but a field surgical team from 16th Parachute Field Ambulance operated on him, and an RAMC surgeon saved his life.

In an attempt to reach Tunis before the wet season, the 2nd Parachute Battalion was ordered to jump near Depienne airfield, south of Tunis, seize it and destroy any aircraft there as the 6th Armoured Division headed for Tunis. Under the command of Lieutenant-Colonel John Frost, the battalion dropped on the night of 29 November and the men reached the airfield to find it unoccupied. Frost then pushed on to Oudna airfield on the outskirts of Tunis. Again there were no aircraft, but skirmishes with German troops prompted the battalion to withdraw to Prise de l'eau.

Locals assured the Paras that the German forces were retreating, but the reverse was true. Enemy opposition had halted the advance of the British 1st Army leaving the 2nd Parachute Battalion isolated 50 miles behind enemy lines. As Frost was informed of the perilous situation, a German column advanced from Oudna. This was ambushed, but a second column mauled the Paras. Frost's command was now surrounded, and so he ordered a fighting withdrawal. On the afternoon of 1 December, 'B' and 'C' Companies, with 'A' Company in reserve, formed defensive positions based on two small hills. Enemy infantry, artillery and tanks proceeded to attack these positions, inflicting heavy casualties on the Paras ('C' Company was all but wiped out).

Frost's men had to conduct a desperate retreat over inhospitable terrain, in the

British airborne troops carry out training in North Africa before the invasion of Sicily.

process almost exhausting their ammunition. Fortunately the local French farmers were friendly and gave food and water to the by-now small groups of Paras. On 3 December they reached Allied lines. Only 180 men, less than 25 per cent of the battalion, had reached Medjez el Bab.

This was the last airborne operation in North Africa, but it was not the end of the fighting for the airborne troops. The 3rd Battalion was engaged in the fighting around Hunt's Gap and Green Hill, west of Mateur, while in February the 1st Parachute Brigade held the Bou Arada sector on the right of the Allied line. On the night of 2/3

February 1943, Major Pearson's 1st Battalion was ordered to capture the heights of the Jebel Mansour. 'R', 'S' and 'T' Companies captured the Jebel, with the help of the French Foreign Legion, but then had to endure three days of enemy shelling and a counter-attack. With little ammunition left and no sign of relief, Pearson ordered a withdrawal. The battalion had lost 200 men killed or wounded.

As the Allies resumed their offensive in North Africa, the parachute brigade continued to fight on the ground. On 17 March, for example, the battalions assisted in the drive to Bizerta. Following the Axis surrender in Tunis, Brigadier Lathbury's 1st Parachute Brigade assembled near Mascara, its reputation famous among friend and foe alike. The price in blood had been high, though: 1,700 killed, wounded or missing. The fighting spirit of the British airborne troops and their determination to win whatever the odds were feared by the enemy in North Africa. Stories about the 'Red Berets' launching surprise parachute raids spread across the desert and the Germans nicknamed them *Rote Teufel* – 'Red Devils'.

On 15 January 1945 General Alexander sent a signal to Major-General Browning directing him to inform 1st Parachute Brigade that the Germans had given them the nickname of 'Red Devils' and to congratulate them on this high distinction.

The surviving men of the 1st and 2nd Battalions witnessed a unique mark of respect as they travelled by train to Algiers. As they passed one of the huge prisoner-of-war camps outside the city German POWs spotted the men in red berets leaning out of the windows. More than a thousand POWs ran towards the train, cheering and throwing their own hats in the air. 'That', said Frost, 'was the tribute I liked best.'

In January 1943 President Roosevelt and Prime Minister Churchill held a conference in Casablanca. It was clear that the campaign in North Africa would be successful and their agenda now focused on the operations that would follow the German withdrawal from Tunis. An immediate invasion of north-west Europe was an obvious option, but at this time Allied resources did not permit such a course of action. So it was decided that the next step should be the capture of Sicily, followed by the invasion of Italy. At the same time Roosevelt and Churchill agreed that the concentration of all available forces in Britain should continue and that the planning of the invasion of north-west Europe should begin at once.

By April 1943 the 2nd Parachute Brigade under Brigadier Down and the 1st (Air-Landing) Brigade under Brigadier Hicks had arrived in North Africa. In addition, Brigadier 'Shan' Hackett's 4th Parachute Brigade arrived by sea from Libya. On 16 May 1943 the 1st Battalion the Border Regiment left the UK aboard the troop ship MV *Staffordshire* to join the 1st Airborne Division in North Africa. These men would provide the backbone of the force that would be airlifted by glider for the airborne assault on Sicily.

Eric 'Johnny' Peters joined the 70th Battalion the Border Regiment in February 1941 at the age of eighteen. He passed his basic army selection training at Barton Stacey camp and quickly volunteered for service with the airborne division. After undergoing

Sergeant Eric 'Johnny' Peters who served with the Border Regiment and volunteered for airborne training.

glider training at Ringway he was transferred to 1st Border Regiment in November 1942 where he was selected for training as a sniper. 'We were taught street fighting in and around Portsmouth, using the bombed areas of the city. We were used as live loads for trainee glider pilots and then we were off to North Africa. Here we were introduced to the American Hadrian, better known as the Waco, a larger version of the Hotspur', said Eric.

SICILY

The British 1st Airborne Division was a strong force on the eve of the Allied invasion of Sicily, and its commander, Major-General 'Happy' Hopkinson, persuaded General Montgomery that the force would be an asset in Sicily, and that glider-borne troops should lead the assault. The capture of Sicily was planned as a pincer movement, with the US 7th Army invading on the west coast between Licata and Scoglitti and the British 8th Army on the east coast south of Syracuse. Airborne troops were to capture the key points of the Ponte Grande, the bridge over the canal at the entrance to the port of Syracuse, and the Ponte di Primosole, the main coastal bridge on the approach to Catania. The British airborne contingent consisted of 2,200 men of the 1st (Air-Landing) Brigade loaded into 444 gliders, seven of which failed to leave the African mainland. The success of the glider attack depended on surprise, so the aircraft took a long route to the target via Malta and then north-east towards Sicily.

On 9 July 1943 the moon was bright and the sky clear, and the lights of Malta provided a valuable checkpoint. However, strong winds caused serious problems. The telephone communications between gliders and their tugs broke, the wing-tip lights on the gliders failed and it became very difficult for the tugs to maintain position within the formations. The Hadrians had no blind flying instruments and despite the bright moonlight the haze generated by the winds made it difficult for the glider pilots to identify the landing zones after being released from their tugs.

More than seventy gliders crashed into the sea and the mission was in dire straits. Major Ballinger of the 2nd Battalion South Staffordshires, who was to lead the Ponte Grande assault, was killed immediately after stepping out of his glider, but Lieutenant Withers of 15 Platoon and fourteen soldiers did manage to seize the objective before midnight and were later reinforced by more troops. By morning eighty-seven airborne troops held the bridge, but the Italians mounted a counter-attack and by 1530 hours the next day constant shelling had resulted in seventy-two casualties among the British force. The bridge was retaken by the enemy, albeit for a short time, as the 2nd Battalion the Royal Scots Fusiliers recaptured it.

Back in Tunisia the 2nd Parachute Brigade was stood down (it was to have dropped near Augusta), but the 1st Parachute Brigade was ordered to take the Primosole bridge on 13 July to secure the line of advance to Catania. The 1st, 2nd and 3rd Battalions loaded into more than 105 Dakotas and 11 Albemarles, with 8 Waco and 11 Horsa gliders carrying gunners, anti-tank guns, sappers and medics. The plan, codenamed 'Fustian', called for landings on four DZs and two LZs west of the main road from Syracuse to Catania. The 1st Battalion was to approach the bridge from both sides, while the 2nd and 3rd Battalions were to seize the high ground north of the River Simeto and south of the Gornalunga Canal. The Primosole bridge was the only bridge across the Simeto River on the Catania Plain, and the seaborne invasion forces had to pass it in their advance north. Loss of the bridge would have imposed a serious delay in the capture of the island.

En route to the target two of the Dakotas were shot down by mistake by the invasion ships, while a further nine were forced to turn back after also being hit by friendly fire. This was nothing compared to the Axis flak the air fleet then encountered, which resulted in ten aircraft turning back and thirty-seven crashing on to the beaches and into the sea. This meant that of the 1,900 men of the 1st Parachute Brigade who had taken off, only 250 from the 1st and 3rd Battalions reached the Primosole bridge. Once there Lathbury assigned its defence to Lieutenant-Colonel Alistair Pearson. The winner of four DSOs, Pearson was one of the greatest airborne warriors of the Second World War and among the chaos of the Sicily landings it was the quality of such officers that averted total disaster. Pearson ordered his men to dig in on the north side of the river, their positions supported by three anti-tank guns, two 3-inch mortars, light machine-guns and a Vickers machine-gun. German paratroopers of Heidrich's 1st Parachute Division had flown in from Rome, and these were now ordered to retake the bridge. It was Para versus Para, and the British acquitted themselves well.

However, enemy tanks and self-propelled guns from Catania forced the 'Red Devils' back. It seemed that defeat was inevitable, but John Frost's 2nd Battalion, with elements of the 4th Armoured Brigade, came up in support and a fierce battle developed. Both sides fought superbly (German Paras, like their British counterparts, never wanted for courage), but eventually, after two days of fighting, the Germans were forced back. Messina fell to the Allies on 17 August, by which time the 1st Parachute Brigade was back in Africa. The total casualties suffered by the 1st Airborne Division in Sicily amounted to 454 dead (including 57 glider pilots), 240 wounded and 102 missing. The conquest of Sicily was only part of the greater prize – the Italian mainland itself.

In late August 1943 the 1st Airborne Division was concentrated at Sousse, Tunisia, and on 3 September the Allies landed in Italy. Their objective was Taranto and six days later Hopkinson's 1st Airborne Division secured the port with no opposition. But the success was marred by tragedy: the troops arrived by ship in Taranto harbour, but HMS *Abdiel* hit a mine and sank within two minutes, killing 58 and injuring 154 men of the 6th (Royal Welch) Battalion.

The headquarters of 4th Parachute Brigade and 10th Battalion travelled in the cruiser HMS *Penelope*. Once ashore, the British Paras moved inland. Brigadier Down,

British paratroopers were back in the North African desert during 1997 as part of a multinational exercise in which they parachuted into the desert to mark the 200th anniversary of the first parachute jump.

commander of the 2nd Parachute Brigade, was determined to regain the initiative in the east, and the 10th and 156th Battalions were continually probing forward, the 10th Battalion taking Gioia Delle Colle airfield on 16 September which was urgently needed for the RAF to provide air support for the Salerno landings. During the advance at Castellaneta the divisional commander, Major-General Hopkinson, was killed as he watched an attack by the 10th Battalion. He was replaced by the promoted Major-General Eric Down.

The Air-Landing Brigade and 1st Parachute Brigade now landed and took over the advance, pushing on to Foggia 125 miles inland. In October the 1st Army was withdrawn to Taranto and in the following month returned to the UK, leaving the 2nd Parachute Brigade as General Alexander's airborne assault force. The brigade was to remain in Italy until the end of hostilities, fighting as an infantry unit, and in April 1944 it took part in action at Cassion.

Winter once again delayed operations and while the Allies prepared to assault the line between Pisa and Rimini, the 2nd Parachute Brigade was withdrawn for an airborne attack on Southern France to coincide with the Normandy invasion. The German armies in Italy finally capitulated on 2 May 1945. As the enemy withdrew they destroyed bridges behind them in an attempt to hamper the Allied advance. General Sir Oliver Leese, the commander of the 8th Army, decided to drop airborne troops along the route from Sara to the Avezzano road. A force of sixty men from the 6th Parachute Battalion, who had been left behind, dropped near Torricella from three Dakotas in daylight and with pinpoint precision.

Additional dummy drops were made to exaggerate the size of the raiding force, and in three groups the troops mounted attacks on the road for more than a week, keeping an entire German division pinned down and away from the front line at a time when its presence might have been invaluable This was the last action by 1st Airborne Division in the Italian campaign.

While the 1st Airborne Division cut its teeth in North Africa back in the UK preparations continued to train more airborne troops at Hardwick Hall, the Airborne Forces Depot, which was established in 1942 and was responsible for preparing all volunteers for parachute training. The training at Hardwick lasted two weeks and focused on physical fitness, the men being raced around assault courses, and on aerial confidence to make sure they were suitable for parachute training. There was even an 'airsickness test' in which students were swung around on a fairground-type machine. After passing selection training, it was off to Ringway for the two-week basic parachute course. Here, the first week was devoted to ground training which involved learning how to exit the aircraft, the control of the parachute during a descent and mastering the correct drills for landing. Attention here was very important, just as it is today, if 'twists' were to be avoided. 'Twists' are often caused by a bad exit from the aircraft.

By now the fuselages of Stirlings, Halifaxes, Albemarles and, later, Dakotas had been positioned in the hangars at Ringway. In just a couple of years the Whitley had been abandoned as a suitable aircraft for paratroopers. However, the Stirling, Halifax and Albemarle also had floor exits and it was not until the Dakota arrived at Ringway that troops could enjoy door exits.

Following their parachute training the volunteers were on the move again, this time back to Hardwick Hall for battle training. From the very start it was appreciated that airborne troops would have to be capable of fighting and surviving against larger and more heavily armed formations until link-ups with infantry or armoured formations could be effected. What they lacked in armour and firepower had to be compensated by extremely high standards of physical fitness and individual military skills such as weapon training and fieldcraft. The aim was to make sure the paratroopers were capable of taking on superior forces and could be self-sufficient until such time as the ground forces could rendezvous with them.

Paratroopers fit parachutes on 5 June 1944 in readiness for the invasion of Europe. The men are all wearing oversmocks which were worn over the top of their webbing equipment. These prevented any straps from the parachute catching on the soldier when he landed, ready for action.

3. THE INVASION OF EUROPE

OPERATION 'OVERLORD': THE AIRBORNE ASSAULT

Airborne troops led the D-Day landings in a combined parachute and glider assault on 6 June 1944, their mission to secure and protect the left flank of the seaborne assault and seize strategic objectives, to help protect the British landing force from attack. The main force would then sweep ashore and advance into Europe. Planning for the operation was immense: the south of England was packed with military formations and almost seemed to be sinking under a massive arsenal of weapons and munitions made ready for the invasion. In the first sixteen hours of the assault 132,715 men, supported by an air armada and a fleet of 5,339 ships, would be hurled against 50 miles of enemy defences.

Preparation for the invasion had started several years earlier. It involved Allied air, sea and land units in North Africa, Italy and the Middle East who were brought home and slotted into the complex plan. In addition new units and formations were formed, including the 6th Airborne Division which was raised on 18 May 1943. The number '6' was chosen to mislead the enemy as there was at that time only one other British airborne division, the 1st.

Late in 1941 the War Office had made investigations to see if civilian companies had the capacity to produce hundreds of gliders for this potential new concept of delivering troops into battle by glider. Manufacturers of railway carriages were commissioned to produce component parts for the gliders which were initially constructed by the RAF to maintain the new project's secrecy. As development progressed a secret test took place on 17 April 1942 at Netheravon in Wiltshire to demonstrate the ability of the Horsa glider. The passenger list included Admiral Mountbatten and General Browning, both of whom were impressed, and full-scale production of the Horsa was soon under way. Factories and carpentry workshops that normally produced furniture were signed up to support the huge demand for gliders required to mount the airborne invasion of Europe, but secrecy was still paramount in an effort to ensure that the Germans did not get any indication of the build-up of military equipment in the UK.

Throughout 1942 discreet preparations continued for the invasion and in May 1943 Prime Minister Churchill met President Roosevelt, this time in Washington, where they confirmed their decision to undertake a full-scale invasion of north-west Europe. The operation, codenamed 'Overlord', had an initial invasion date of 1 May 1944, but this would slip by a month as the planning staff highlighted a shortage of equipment which influenced the postponement. Later it was agreed that General Eisenhower would be appointed as the Supreme Allied Commander for Operation 'Overlord' and the

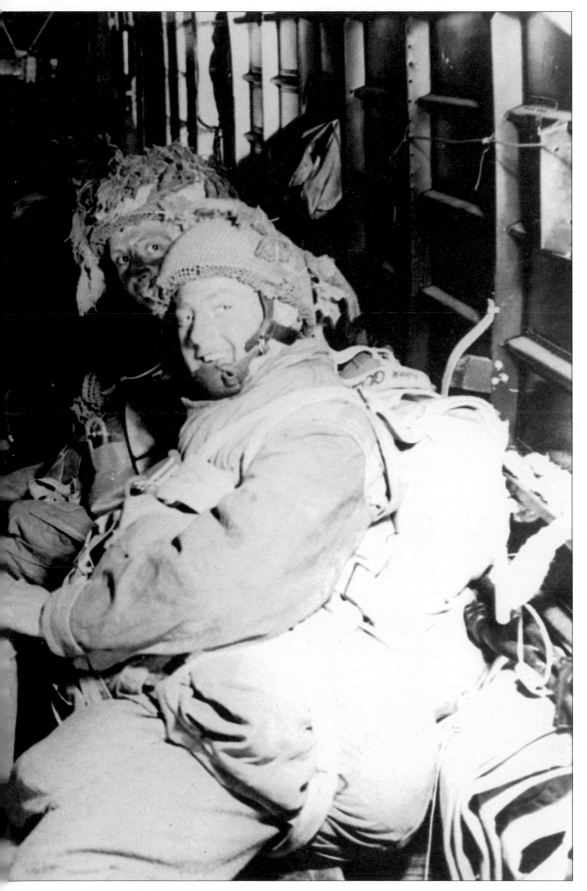

Men of the 6th Airborne Division en route to Normandy. The division was formed in 1943 and the number '6' chosen to mislead the enemy – there was in fact only one other airborne division. The man on the right is holding an airborne flask which was taken aboard so the Paras could enjoy a cup of tea during the flight.

President announced the news to the American public in his Christmas Eve speech. General Montgomery, later Field Marshal Viscount Montgomery of Alamein, was to command the British forces.

At the end of 1943 the 1st Airborne Division, minus the 2nd Independent Parachute Brigade, was in England. It was composed of Brigadier Gerald Lathbury's 1st Parachute Brigade; Brigadier 'Shan' Hackett's 4th Parachute Brigade; Brigadier 'Pip' Hicks' 1st (Air-Landing) Brigade; 1st Battalion, the Glider Pilot Regiment; 1st Battalion, the Border Regiment; 2nd Battalion, the South Staffords; and the 7th Battalion, the King's Own Scottish Borderers. The division was commanded by the 43-year-old Major-General R.E. Urquhart DSO.

The 1st and 6th Airborne Divisions made up General Browning's 1st Airborne Corps, and the organisation of the two divisions was broadly similar. This new force needed to develop its warfare role, particularly in the area of tactical organisation and procedure. In addition they had to develop tactics for a formation based on a totally new concept of warfare.

The accurate delivery by pilots of paratroopers to the drop zone (DZ) was of crucial importance, and the Pathfinders of the Independent Parachute Company were given the task of being in position before the drop to plant Rebecca–Eureka air-to-ground radio devices. Eureka issued signals from the ground which were picked up by Rebecca on board the aircraft. At night aircraft dropping paratroops were guided by two lights on the ground placed several hundred yards apart. The aircraft flew to the drop zone on a precise bearing, and the troops jumped as the two ground lights appeared at 90° to port and starboard on the line of approach.

For the gliders the Pathfinders laid out three electric lights 75 yards apart at the head of the landing strip, with five more, positioned 50 yards apart, forming the stem of the 'T'. The lights were masked to shine upwards only, and a flashing beacon was positioned 300 yards from the foot of the flare path to indicate the glider release point.

Divisional artillery was made up of the three batteries of the Air-Landing Light Regiment, plus two separate anti-tank batteries and a light anti-aircraft battery. The guns themselves were American 75 mm pack howitzers. Each airborne division also had a Reconnaissance Regiment comprising Tetrarch tanks, jeeps and motorcycles.

At the beginning of 1944 there were four airborne divisions assembled in the United Kingdom: the 1st and 6th British Airborne Divisions, and the 82nd and 101st US Airborne Divisions. All were available, if necessary, to take part in the invasion of north-west Europe. It was the largest formation of airborne forces ever achieved. As training increased the statistics recorded by the various units were already starting to form military history. At the RAF's No. 1 Parachute Training School at Ringway the total number of jumps recorded between January and May 1944 was 58,990. In addition, during this period the 200,000th jump since the school opened was made and more than 700 glider pilots completed their training.

Former Ringway trainee, Private Jack Wilson, was one of the men who were put

Men of the Air-Landing force smile for the camera before taking part in the airborne invasion. Their task was to secure the left flank for the ground force which would land by sea.

through their paces at the Manchester base in readiness for action in Europe. Wilson, who went on to serve with the 8th Battalion, recalls: 'It was very exciting at the time, I had some great friends, we were very close.

'We were all nervous, I know I had a pair of lucky socks which I always wore. Some people carried lucky charms or just prayed. Jumping out of an aircraft required maximum guts, but once the course was finished we felt special, we were paratroopers.'

The expansion of the RAF's 38 Group continued throughout the early months of 1944 and operational squadrons were established at Brize Norton, Harwell, Keevil, Fairford and Tarrant Rushton. To assist in the airlift 46 Group had been formed on 17 January 1944 and, while it was not dedicated to airborne operations, it was to come under the command of 38 Group and would support the lift of men and supplies for Operation 'Overlord'.

Large-scale exercises to rehearse and practise procedures were carried out in early February 1944. The biggest of these was Exercise Bizz 11. This involved the entire force of the 6th Airborne Division who were dropped by parachute or air-landed by glider. Later, in mid-April, another exercise, codenamed Mush, involved a major rehearsal over similar ground for 6th Airborne Division's task in the invasion of north-west Europe, although this was not known to those taking part in the manoeuvres.

In the initial stages of the invasion the British 6th Airborne Division would protect the left flank and the American 82nd and 101st would secure the right flank.

The initial tasks for the 6th Airborne Division included the capture of the bridges at Benouville and Ranville over the River Orne, and the destruction and neutralisation of the coastal artillery battery at Merville (this had to be completed by dawn minus 30 minutes, before the seaborne force came within range of the guns). In addition the Division was to destroy the bridges over the River Dives at Varaville, Robehomme, Bures and Troarn in order to impose the maximum delay on enemy reinforcements coming from the east. The destruction of the Merville battery was vital: the guns of this coastal artillery unit dominated vital ground overlooking the landing beaches and

A Hamilcar glider is towed into the air over England by a Halifax tug. Hundreds of troop-carrying Horsa gliders and the larger vehicle-carrying Hamilcars formed the backbone of the airborne invasion force.

A runway full of Hamilcar gliders and Halifax tug aircraft sit prepared and ready at Tarrant Rushton a few hours before take-off, June 1944.

would present a major threat to the seaborne landings if they were not seized by the 6th Airborne Division and put out of action.

As soon as resources allowed they were to secure the area between the rivers Orne and Dives. This was to include the capture of the towns Sallenelles and Flanceville Plage. In order to assist the 6th Airborne Division to carry out these tasks the 1st Special Service Brigade (Commandos) was to be placed under command of the Airborne Division, after it had landed by sea.

The airborne spearhead of the D-Day operation was to be the American 82nd and 101st Airborne Divisions, which would land astride the River Merderet near Ste Mère Eglise to help the advance of the US Army's 7th Corps. While this was happening the British 6th Airborne Division would land 40 miles to the east to secure the Allied left flank between the Orne and Dives rivers. Major-General Richard 'Windy' Gale, Commander of 6th Airborne Division, tasked 3rd Parachute Brigade with neutralising the Merville Battery and committed the 6th Air-Landing Brigade to the task of capturing the two bridges at Benouville and Ranville. His plan was to seize the bridges in a surprise raid using glider troops. Owing to the limited number of aircraft available from 38 and 46 Groups, 5th Parachute Brigade would have to be flown in on a second lift, together with the 6th Airborne Armoured Reconnaissance Regiment and other divisional troops.

Intelligence reports in April indicated that the Germans had erected anti-glider defences on the landing and dropping zones selected by Gale and his staff. At first it was feared that the invasion plans had been compromised, but it was then realised that similar defences had been erected along the coast of France and Belgium. As a mass glider landing was no longer feasible, Gale altered his plans. The task of capturing the bridges at Benouville and Ranville was now given to the 5th Parachute Brigade, although the *coup de main* operation would still be carried out by 'D' Company, 2nd Battalion the Oxfordshire & Buckinghamshire Light Infantry, who were assigned to the 5th and had been undergoing intensive training for the task.

While the Germans had strong forces, including Waffen-SS and the 711th and 716th Infantry Divisions in the Normandy area, the immediate concern for the 6th Airborne Division would be the 12th SS Panzer Division, the 352nd Infantry Division and the 21st Panzer Division – all of whom were deployed in a counter-attack role and posed the biggest threat. Altogether 6,000 British paratroopers were to be landed by 450 Albemarles, Stirlings, Halifaxes and Dakotas of 38 and 46 Groups, which would also deliver 3,000 men of the main glider force later the same day.

After being briefed on their operational tasks the the unit commanders of the 6th Airborne Division commenced specialist training. Day after day gliders practised spot landings for the attacks on the bridges and the battery. The 9th Parachute Battalion was tasked with silencing the Merville Battery and, with sub-units from the 4th Anti-tank Battery RA, 591st Parachute Squadron RE, 224th Parachute Field Ambulance, the Glider Pilot Regiment and the Royal Navy, the men went into a special camp for a fortnight where they built a replica of the Merville Battery and carried out secret rehearsals. Meanwhile, the 7th Parachute Battalion and six platoons of the 2nd Battalion The Oxfordshire and Buckinghamshire Light Infantry, who would be under their command for the capture of the Orne bridges, went to Exeter, where they carried out intensive training on the bridges over the River Exe and the canal immediately south of the city.

On 19 May 1944 the 6th Airborne Division was visited by the King and Queen and Her Royal Highness the Princess Elizabeth. A week later General Montgomery visited the force as it waited to move into transit camps prior to the invasion. By the end of the month all units were camped in isolation, awaiting orders to move. Security was very tight: contact was forbidden with anyone outside the camp and letters could be written but not posted until the invasion had started. On 31 May detailed briefing sessions commenced with models, photographs and outline orders. Morale was high and the formation was ready to 'Go to it', to use the divisional motto introduced by Major-General Gale. He said: 'This motto "Go to it" will be adopted by the 6th

Light guns, jeeps, ammunition and medical equipment were ferried across to France by glider to support the airborne forces already on the ground. Here a 6-pounder AT is loaded aboard a glider. In the background can be seen a Halifax tug aircraft.

Airborne Division and as such will be remembered by all ranks in action against the enemy, in training and during day-to-day routine duties.'

After almost three weeks of intense preparation the final orders were issued and the operation launched. In the early evening of 5 June 1944 sixty Pathfinders of the 22nd Independent Parachute Company prepared their parachutes and equipment at Harwell in Oxfordshire ready to jump ahead and mark the drop zones. At 2203 hours their Albemarle aircraft lifted off. Shortly after, six gliders carrying a party of Ox & Bucks and Royal Engineers, set off for the Caen Canal and Orne bridges, to be followed by the 3rd and 5th Parachute Brigades.*

*A memorial marks the spot at Harwell, now the Atomic Energy Research Establishment, where the first gliders left for D-Day.

Next in the air was an assault party from the 9th Parachute Battalion in three gliders, who were to make a crash-landing by the Merville Battery. Just after midnight the sky was filled with over 1,000 aircraft carrying British and American troops to storm Hitler's Fortress Europe.

The Pathfinders landed on three drop zones, north-east of Ranville, west of Troarn and between the Merville Battery and Varaville. The glider-borne troops of the 5th Parachute Brigade, who left Harwell airfield shortly after them and were instructed to seize the bridges over the Caen Canal, landed exactly on time at 0200 hours. Aboard the gliders were six platoons of the 2nd Battalion the Ox & Bucks Light Infantry and a detachment of Royal Engineers, commanded by Major John Howard. Five of the gliders landed near their objective, the sixth put down on a bridge near the River Dives, seven miles away.

Sergeant John Wilson of the Glider Pilot Regiment took off from Harwell at about midnight on 5/6 June. He recalls:

My glider was loaded with a jeep, trailer, two motor bikes, ammunition and rations and we were tasked to support the attack on Pegasus Bridge.

We were the third to cross the coast and ran into very heavy anti-aircraft fire over Le Havre and got badly shot up. I couldn't say for sure when we cast off from the tug aircraft, but we were very badly positioned for flying and seemed to be nose heavy. We could see a cluster of red and green flares. We should have landed from green to red, but we didn't have enough height, so we just went straight for it. As we landed we kangarooed – bounced a couple of times – and the next thing I knew we hit a house.

I can remember a hell of a crash, feeling my legs crushed and losing consciousness. The next thing I knew I was waking up in hospital in England. I learned that I had been trapped in the crash for two and a half days. I was lucky to be alive, I lost a leg, but at least I came back to tell the story. My co-pilot was killed instantly.

At Pegasus Bridge Major Howard jumped from his glider to see that he was just 50 yards away from it, instantly recognising the distinctive tower from the model made in the UK during training preparations for the operation. The surprise of the *coup de main* attack was total and the assault party from the Ox & Bucks, led by Major Howard, raced for the bridge. They ran into German small-arms fire but in true airborne tradition stormed on and overwhelmed the defenders. Very soon both the canal and river bridges were in British hands.

Major Howard has regularly returned to the bridge and recalls:

My main memories today are of Lieutenant Don Brotheridge, who was the commander of my leading platoon. He led the attack and was shot in the neck as he ran across the bridge. He died an hour later, the first casualty of D-Day. I had been sitting next to him in the glider just a few minutes before and I knew his wife was expecting a baby in a fortnight's time. It was very sad.

It was a great honour and privilege of course, to be chosen for Pegasus Bridge. They called it the spearhead of the invasion. We always boasted that we were the best company in the 6th Airborne Division and when we were chosen for this we felt we had been noticed after all.

There were six gliders each carrying 30 men, which gave us a fighting force of 180. One of the gliders, which had my second-in-command, Captain Brian Priday, on board, landed by the wrong river, the Dives, some 10 miles away. He was commanding D Platoon and didn't come into the battle at all.

The 7th Battalion, the Parachute Regiment was our relief. They arrived soon after 3 o'clock and we were very pleased to see them. But they were in very depleted numbers, because they had not had a good landing: instead of 650 men there were only 150. But as luck would have it the enemy hadn't made a proper attack. They sent some tanks down which we had put out of action and that rather stalled them. They might have been waiting for daylight, I don't know, but by the time daylight came the Paras that had arrived were in position ready to meet them. They did a very good job. The bridges weren't attacked from then on and were in our hands right through the battle of Normandy.

British ground forces on the Normandy beaches. The success of the airborne operation ensured that the initial seaborne landings were not subjected to enemy artillery fire from the Merville battery.

Before joining up Howard had served as a policeman and had completed seven years in the ranks before being commissioned. After landing Major Howard and his men found everything exactly as they had been briefed, the training back in the UK proving vital. After capturing the bridge he and his men moved on to take part in the bitter fighting in the Escoville area. Two days after capturing the bridge at Escoville they were surrounded by a German Panzer troop and only 52 of Howard's 100 men survived.

Howard himself was shot in the back of the head by a sniper, leaving a clean hole in his helmet. Luckily it was only a scrape and the Major knew nothing about his injury until his sergeant saw blood covering the back of his shirt and called a medic. Major Howard added, 'Luckily, although I was a strict disciplinarian, my hair was a bit thick at the time and may have help protect me. But I still have a blue scar across my scalp where the bullet grazed me.' Later Major Howard's helmet, complete with bullet hole, was worn by the actor Richard Todd, who portrayed Howard in the the film *The Longest Day*.

The codewords for the capture of the bridges intact were 'Ham' for one and 'Jam' for the other, and after Howard and his troops took the bridge they were greeted in the afternoon of D-Day by members of the Gondrée family, who presented them with a bottle of champagne that they had hidden in the garden of their café throughout the German occupation. Years on, when Howard chats with friends he still ends his conversation with the words 'Ham and Jam'.

Arlette Gondrée was just four years old when Major Howard's men arrived to free her family from the Germans.

> I was sleeping with my mother on the night of 5 June when my father came into the room and told my mother to take the children to the cellar.
>
> I was still in my nightie and was very frightened, not knowing if it was the Germans or the Allies. We heard a loud crash and then footsteps all around the house and a bang on the door. Then we heard people breaking in and Daddy recognised English voices. Daddy opened the cellar door at last and two British soldiers with helmets and blackened faces came in.
>
> From his rations Captain Dan Thomas of the Oxfordshire and Buckinghamshire Light Infantry gave me the first chocolate I had ever had. It was the most wonderful feeling. We all rejoiced and Daddy went upstairs and dug up his champagne from the garden for our liberators.

Arthur Brock, a Royal Engineer serving with the airborne forces, was in one of the gliders which landed at Pegasus Bridge. He owes his life to his pay book: 'Initially we came across a fair bit of fighting and it seemed to go on for ages. I was showered by shrapnel from a shell blast which whacked me in the chest. I couldn't believe it – the splinter had gone straight into my pay book. I was very lucky,' said Arthur.

The drop of the 7th Parachute Battalion, who had the Ox & Bucks under command, was scattered around Ranville and the 2,000 men of the 5th Parachute Brigade encountered heavy enemy flak. Once on the ground Lieutenant-Colonel Pine-Coffin moved off to relieve Howard as Royal Engineers cleared the area of 'Rommel's asparagus' – wooden spikes placed in the ground to hinder glider landings – before the main glider force arrived. As they did so the 12th and 13th Parachute Battalions secured Le Bas de Ranville and Ranville in the face of heavy enemy fire. Lieutenant-Colonel Terence Otway's 9th Parachute Battalion had the Merville Battery in its sights. The journey had been a nightmare: of the eight gliders taking part in the assault several parted their tow lines and crashed into the sea and just two made it to Merville, one which actually crashed near the battery, killing many of the men on board. The paratroopers of the 9th Battalion who jumped into Normandy fared little better. Many of the pilots and aircrew in this massive armada normally flew bombers and had little experience of dropping troops. Many missed the dropping zones and troops were dropped in wrong areas. Once on the ground Otway could only find 25 per cent of his battalion, but resolved to storm the battery anyway.

An advance party had been able to reconnoitre the battery and marked a route through a minefield ready for the main assault but, as they prepared to attack, Otway's force came under heavy fire. Sergeant-Major Sid Knight and another soldier moved forward and silenced three machine-guns and in the battle that followed the force fought its way forward to the four casemates and damaged them in any way they could. A distant German artillery unit then started to lay down an artillery barrage on Merville, which they apparently considered they had already lost to the Allies. Many years after the action at Merville, Colonel Otway said: 'My orders were to destroy or neutralise the battery before the rest came ashore and that's what we did. Because of the efforts of my men the first waves arrived [on the beaches] without a single shell being fired from Merville.' Otway's men had spiked the four main guns before daybreak. After lighting yellow 'success' flares they moved off to launch an attack on Sallanelles.

Brigadier Hill's 3rd Parachute Brigade, like the 9th Battalion, had been widely scattered as a result of the failure of the Eureka beacons, but nevertheless managed to capture Varaville and destroy the road bridge, then do the same at Robehomme. Hill himself was injured within hours of the drop but continued to direct the brigade operation.

The landing of the 8th Parachute Battalion completed the drop of the 3rd Parachute Brigade but it was also scattered, many men landing in the 5th Brigade's area, and the commander, Lieutenant-Colonel Alastair Pearson, was left with a reduced force and few engineers. But at Bures advance elements of the battalion met up with the sappers and destroyed both bridges successfully.

In the sky, meanwhile, more gliders approached their landing zones. The latter had been cleared of spikes and were marked by flares. Once on the ground glider troops would reinforce Lieutenant-Colonel Pine-Coffin's beleaguered men at the Bénouville and Ranville bridges. The 21st Panzer Division had been alerted and was moving towards Ranville, which meant the Paras had to link up with forces from the beaches quickly.

By daybreak 'B' Company, the 7th Parachute Battalion, was under heavy enemy pressure at the Caen Canal bridge, and repulsed eight German counter-attacks during the course of the day. It looked as though the Paras would have to yield in the face of

British paratroopers drop in at Ranville in June 1994 to mark the fiftieth anniversary of the original Normandy drop.

savage enemy attacks, but at 1300 hours a lone piper came into view, followed by Brigadier the Lord Lovat marching at the head of No. 1 Commando of the 1st Special Service Brigade, who had linked up with the Paras.

During the same afternoon 250 gliders landed south-east of Ranville, bringing in the bulk of Hugh Kindersley's 6th (Air-Landing) Brigade, the Armoured Reconnaissance Regiment with light tanks, Bren carriers and motorcycles, and the guns of the 53rd (Air-Landing) Light Regiment. The weather had improved and the sappers had managed to clear four landing strips, three for the Horsas and one for the Hamilcars. The gliders in general made good landings, and by 7 June the whole of the 6th Airborne Division was deployed in Normandy. That day units of the 3rd Division took over the Caen Canal and Orne bridges, the canal crossing being officially renamed 'Pegasus Bridge'. The division held a V-shaped area of land pointing south-east to Troarn with its base on the River Orne at Longueval and Sallanelles. To the north-east were scattered elements of the 3rd Parachute Brigade.

The overall position was precarious, and indeed by 10 June the German 711th, 346th and 21st Panzer Divisions were attacking the Para positions. Heavy enemy attacks occurred against Le Plein and on the high ground south of Bréville. The defenders – the 3rd Parachute Brigade, 5th Battalion, the Black Watch, and the 12th Parachute Battalion – withstood a furious assault. Two days later the German 346th Division tried again, and again the Scots and Paras came under pressure. The 8th Battalion were moved up from the Bois de Bavent to plug the gap, and finally the Germans were forced back when Hill himself led a counter-attack.

The 6th Airborne's commander, Major-General Gale, knew he had to eradicate enemy concentrations at Bréville to consolidate east of the Orne, and so a night attack was launched from Amfréville. The troops were made up of a battalion of Devons, the 13th/18th Hussars with their Sherman tanks, and Paras of the 12th Battalion and the 22nd Independent Parachute Company. The attack started disastrously, as friendly covering shells fell among the British troops, killing some and injuring many others. The German fire was just as intense, and the 12th Battalion lost half its strength in the operation to close the Bréville gap. However, the attack was eventually successful and the Orne bridgehead was secured. As the Normandy bridgehead was consolidated and expanded, the 6th Airborne Division was reinforced by various ground units, and after the action at Bréville it remained in the Calvados area until August. Gale was then ordered to form a pivot of the Allied arm sweeping across France to the River Seine, though he was told not to offer battle. The operation was codenamed 'Paddle', and commenced at 0300 hours on 17 August, with Pearson's 8th Battalion leading Hill's 3rd Brigade. They reached Bures before dawn. As the advance continued the sappers were fully employed repairing bridges destroyed by the retreating enemy and clearing minefields. The 1st Canadian Parachute Battalion moved through the Bois de Bavent and crossed the Dives.

The 3rd and 5th Brigades conducted a leapfrog operation, though German armour and small-arms fire inflicted many casualties on the Paras. At Dozulé the 13th Battalion was thrown back during a fierce battle with the Germans. Then Poett's brigade came up against enemy guns and tanks in the steep-sided Touques valley. The fight to gain the town of Pont Leveque was a tough one, and Pine-Coffin's 7th Battalion was rushed up to hold it. The capture of Beuzeville was equally hard, with the 8th Battalion spearheading the assault. The 6th Airborne was then ordered to stand down on a line from Honfleur on the coast to Pont Audemer. Resistance in this sector was not as stiff, but there was still some fighting to do, made more hazardous by the presence of mines and booby-traps.

The airborne Belgian Brigade, under command of the 6th Airborne, bridged the Dives at Cabourg, while the Devons and Ox & Bucks drove east towards Branville, and by 30 August enemy resistance west of the River Seine had ceased. The result of the airborne division's efforts after D-Day was impressive – the liberation of 400 square miles of France. Of course, such a prize did not come cheap, and the casualty list numbered 821 killed in action, 2,709 seriously wounded and 927 missing. The commander of the division, Major-General Gale, wrote an open letter to his men in early August, in which he summed up the qualities that set his airborne troops apart from many others, and which epitomises the airborne spirit: 'We have fought for ground and gained all we fought for: all we have gained by skill and guts we have held with courage and determination. Our reputation stands high in the 21st Army Group and at home. Let us see to it that none of us lets the side down.'

The following story shows that the airborne troops were very loyal to the cause. Prior to D-Day Lieutenant-Colonel Alistair Pearson's fiancée, Joan Niven, had planned their wedding but all along the officer knew he would not be able to make it. He had been summoned to a secret meeting and told of his unit's mission in the D-Day plan, although he could say nothing to Joan. In May she had indicated to him that she would like a short engagement and would like to arrange the marriage in four weeks' time – the exact point her future husband was to be in Europe. The highly decorated officer who rose to the rank of Brigadier said, 'I knew I wouldn't be there but it would have been fatal to say a word.' Pearson's colleagues even kept quiet when Joan passed them wedding invitations. But when the order came to depart he left in the middle of the night. The first Joan knew of it was when a neighbour called in and asked if she had heard the news. By that time Pearson had been parachuted behind enemy lines in Normandy.

When Pearson returned from Europe in the autumn he discovered that his fiancée had secretly fixed everything while he was away and most of his battalion turned up to watch Joan, a cousin of the actor David Niven, become Mrs Alastair Pearson at Marsden in Kent.

Britain often used wardogs in Normandy. They were used to sniff out enemy positions, locate explosives and lead escaped prisoners-of-war out of enemy territory. The dogs were trained, but not forced, to parachute and jumped into action on Operation 'Overlord'. In the British Military Cemetery at Ranville a gravestone there reminds visitors of the price paid by wardogs and their handlers.

One stark grey headstone states that Private Emile Corteil of the Parachute Regiment was just nineteen years old when he joined 2,238 others who lost their lives in the battles for Normandy. 'Had you known our boy,' says the carved epitaph, 'you would have loved him too.' There is also a very British footnote: 'Glen, Paratroop dog, was killed with him.' Emile and Glen also lie together; the authorities decided that Emile's dog should join him in consecrated ground and share forever the exclusive fellowship that men of the Parachute Regiment call 'The Brotherhood'.

The men of the 6th Airborne Division had learnt to expect anything from another group of dedicated people who have received little recognition. These were the nurses who flew to Normandy in specially equipped Dakotas, ready to administer drugs and other medical help to men traumatised by their injuries, and help to evacuate them back to England. But because they flew out in aircraft packed with ammunition and other war material the Government decided that they could not qualify for the protection of the Red Cross insignia. Nearly 10,000 sick and wounded soldiers were flown back to Britain, and within five months of the first operation the number had risen to almost 50,000. The nurses continued to follow close behind the action, into Holland, Arnhem, Belgium, then into Germany itself after the bloody crossings of the Rhine.

OPERATIONS IN THE SOUTH OF FRANCE AND GREECE

As well as the operations in Normandy, British airborne troops were involved in the invasion of southern France – Operation 'Dragoon' – as part of the American 1st Airborne Task Force, commanded by Major-General R.T. Frederick. The British component consisted of Brigadier Pritchard's 2nd Independent Parachute Brigade Group, whose task it was to seize the area between La Motte and Le Muy, destroy the enemy there and prevent him reaching the coast.

D-Day was 15 August 1944, but the weather was poor and the Eureka wireless beacons were not totally reliable, and of the 125 aircraft involved in the operation only 73 dropped their troops accurately. Only around half of the men of the 4th and 6th Parachute Battalions managed to rally at the drop zone. The glider landings were somewhat better, the 6th (Royal Welch) Battalion captured Le Muy, and by nightfall the 2nd Brigade was in control of all three roads into the village.

Having taken all their objectives and linked up with the ground forces, the brigade returned to Italy on 26 August to prepare for their next operation in Greece. On 12 October 1944, the 2nd Independent Parachute Brigade launched Operation 'Manna', the airborne landing in Greece. The 4th, 5th and 6th Battalions landed at Megara airfield, which is only a short distance from Athens. Pritchard then led his men into the Greek capital, where airborne units were engaged in pursuing German forces in Thrace, Salonika and on the Bulgarian frontier. The 2nd Independent Parachute Brigade was dispatched back to Italy in January 1945, and thus ended its service in the Second World War.

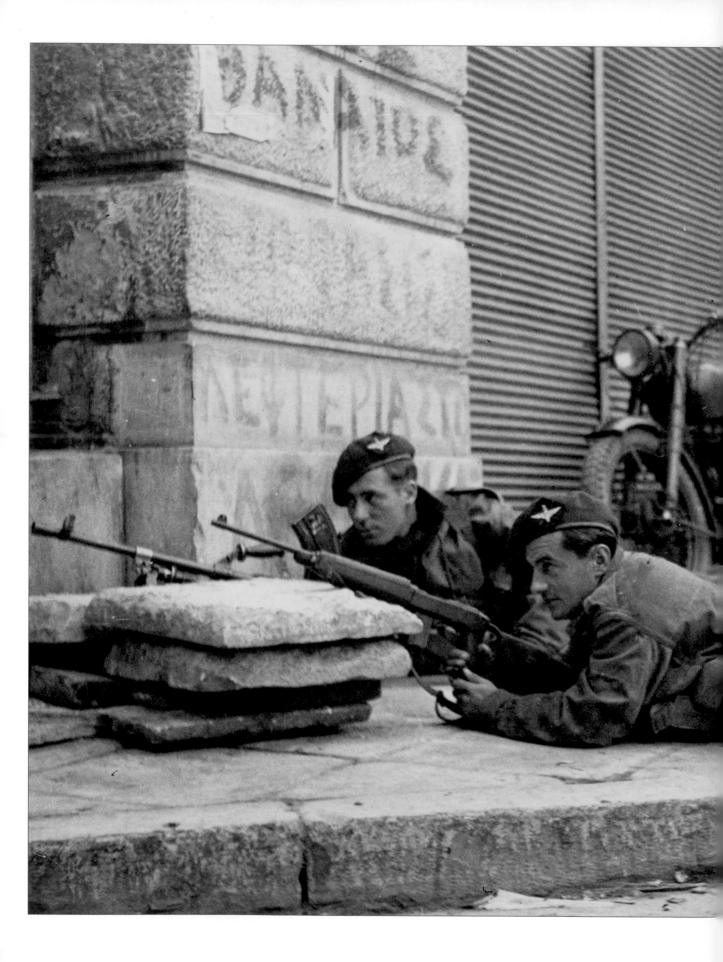

On 12 October
1944 the Paras
launched Operation
'Manna' – the
airborne landings in
Greece. The men
landed at Megera
and advanced into
the city of Athens
where they pursued
the German forces.

General 'Boy' Browning, pictured left, discusses plans for the air invasion with Air Chief Marshal Sir Arthur Tedder, centre, and a senior American officer before Operation 'Market Garden'.

4. Arnhem: 'A Drop Too Far'

Operation 'Market Garden': an 'Airborne Carpet of Soldiers'

In August 1944 General Montgomery proposed an Allied offensive based on one final powerful thrust through Holland and into the Ruhr. The plan involved dropping by parachute and glider an 'airborne carpet of soldiers' who would seize key objectives to secure a route across the Rhine, allowing ground forces to advance across the plains of northern Germany and strike at the heart of the Third Reich. Such an operation presented the opportunity to isolate and occupy the Ruhr, thus depriving Germany of more than half of her industrial might and crippling the supply lines to Hitler's war machine. It was an ambitious plan and General Eisenhower, the Supreme Allied Commander, rejected the initial proposal partly because it required almost all of the Allied logistic support in Europe and partly because he regarded such an advance as too risky.

Instead Eisenhower agreed to a modified scheme in which the 21st Army Group would attempt a narrow thrust to and beyond the Rhine, supported by its own resources. The concept was bold and simple, and involved the capture of five key river and canal crossings, with Arnhem as the ultimate prize as a bridgehead into Hitler's heartland. By seizing the five crossings the airborne forces would open up a 60-mile long road corridor between the front line of 30 Corps on the Maas–Scheldt Canal and the town of Arnhem. But they would be lightly armed and would have to operate for 48 hours unsupported, before the advancing ground forces of the British 2nd Army could link up with them. That was the plan.

By early August the German front in France had collapsed and the landing of British, French and American troops in the south of the country had liberated vast areas. The Allied advance was quick: Paris was liberated on 25 August and by early September British forces had reached Brussels. The opportunity now arose to finish off the enemy and end the war before the winter. On 17 September 1944, Operation 'Market Garden', the Allied operation to outflank the Siegfried Line, was to be put into effect. A force of 10,095 men would be dropped by parachute and gliders to seize the vital objectives along the Eindhoven–Arnhem road, allowing 30 Corps of the British 2nd Army to move swiftly across the Rhine. It was an awesome task, and many senior officers had reservations about its chances of success.

During August and September there had been a host of potential airborne operations to support the 21st Army Group, but all had been turned down or cancelled at the eleventh hour. At the beginning of September senior officers were asked to examine the possibility of an airborne operation against the Walcheren islands; this would assist in opening up the

British paratroops land at Arnhem, while elements of the glider force can be seen already on the ground.

port of Antwerp by cutting off and hastening the German retreat across the Scheldt estuary. But the potential operation, codenamed 'Infatuate', was rejected owing to the heavy enemy defences and the lack of dropping zones. Also in early September the 1st Airborne Division had been tasked to plan Operation 'Comet'. The objective was to secure the bridges over the River Rhine from Arnhem to Wesel in order to facilitate the advance on the Ruhr basin from the north. Only the 1st Airborne Division and the 1st Polish Parachute Brigade were available for this mission and D-Day was listed as 10 September – but yet again the mission was cancelled just hours before the airlift was due to start. 'Comet' had been overtaken by events. General Eisenhower had assigned US airborne units to Field Marshal Montgomery's plan and Major-General Urquhart, commanding officer of the 1st Airborne Division,* was

---

* The 1st British Airborne Division included the 21st Independent Parachute Company, the 1st, 2nd and 3rd Battalions of the Parachute Regiment (of the 1st Parachute Brigade), the 10th Battalion Parachute Regiment, the 11th Battalion of the Parachute Regiment and the 156th Battalion Parachute Regiment (of the 4th Parachute Brigade). The 1st Air-Landing Brigade included the 1st Battalion the Border Regiment, 7th Battalion the King's Own Borderers, and the 2nd Battalion the South Staffordshire Regiment. The Division also included the Glider Pilot Regiment (Army Air Corps), 250 (Airborne) Light Composite Company Royal Army Service Corps, 89 Parachute Security Section Intelligence Corps, the Royal Military Police 1st (Airborne) Division Provost Company, and 15 Parachute Field Ambulance Royal Army Medical Corps.

In addition, there were the following units, all of the Royal Regiment of Artillery: 1st (Airborne) Divisional Ordnance Field Park Royal Army Ordnance Corps, 1st Airborne Divisional Signals, 1st (Airborne) Division Workshop Royal Electrical Engineers, Corps of Engineers, including 1 Parachute Squadron, 4 Parachute Squadron, 9 (Airborne) Field Company, 216 (Airborne) Park Company, 1st Reconnaissance Squadron, 1 Air-Landing Anti-Tank Battery, 2 Air-Landing Anti-Tank battery, 1st Air-Landing Light Battery and 1 (Air-Landing) Forward Observation Unit.

busy preparing fresh plans to upgrade 'Comet' into Operation 'Market'. The ground forces who would link up with the airborne troops at Eindhoven, Uden, Grave, Nijmegen and Arnhem would form the 'Garden' part of the operation.

The tasks facing the British 1st Airborne Division, with 1st Polish Parachute Brigade under command, were to capture the bridges at Arnhem and establish a bridgehead around them so that the land formations could continue their advance northwards. The 82nd US Airborne Division was to capture the crossings at Nijmegen and Grave and hold the high ground between Nijmegen and Groesbeek. The headquarters of the 1st Airborne Corps was to land with the 82nd US Airborne Division. In addition, the 101st US Airborne Division was to seize the bridges and areas between Eindhoven and Grave while the 878th US Aviation Engineer Battalion and 2nd Air-Landing Light Anti-Aircraft Battery were to be flown in by glider, if the situation permitted, to prepare and defend landing strips north of Arnhem. Finally, 52 (Lowland) Division would be flown into the prepared landing strips in Dakota aircraft.

As with any airborne operation, success at Arnhem was dependent on the element of surprise, enabling the lightly armed airborne troops to seize their objective before the defenders had the chance to bring their superior forces and fire power to bear. If the enemy had the opportunity to quickly direct its forces, especially artillery and armour, against the assault force, then the initiative would be lost and the paratroopers left at an overwhelming disadvantage.

British paratroops take German prisoners shortly after landing at Arnhem.

British troops advance after being dropped into Holland on Operation 'Market Garden'.

For the Arnhem operation there were insufficient aircraft available to lift the entire division on the first day. Only the 1st Parachute Brigade, the 1st Air-Landing Brigade, plus Divisional HQ, could be carried in the initial lift. The remainder would follow on D+1 and D+2, resulting in only half the division benefiting from the element of surprise. In addition, the Air-Landing Brigade, whose initial task was to protect the dropping zones rather than push forward to the bridges, had been included in this initial lift, thus reducing the number of effective troops still further.

Potential dropping zones were found to be waterlogged and crossed by 8 foot wide irrigation ditches, making them unsuitable for glider landings and parachute drops. In addition, intelligence reported that there were strong anti-aircraft defences in the area of Arnhem. On the best available information, therefore, Major-General Urquhart, the commander of the 1st Airborne Division, selected several landing zones, the furthest of which was 8 miles away. Again the key element of surprise was lost.

Allied intelligence was confusing: it had been reported that there was the threat of a German counter-attack by a brigade-strong force supported by tanks and self-propelled guns, but initially it was not known that the 9th and 10th Battalions of the 22nd Panzer Corps were refitting east of Arnhem. Further information indicating a much larger enemy force and supporting armour was passed to the 2nd Army HQ, although it was discounted as unreliable. On the ground the 1st Airborne Division was to discover that they faced an entire Panzer Corps.

The confident perception was that the Airborne Reconnaissance Squadron, followed by

1st Parachute Brigade, would reach the bridge quickly and capture it. The remainder of the division would then take up blocking positions on the approaches on D+1 and the Polish Brigade would relieve the 1st Brigade on D+2, which would create a Brigade reserve. Such a plan could only work if everything went smoothly and the level of opposition remained on the small scale suggested by the intelligence available. If the airborne division met strong opposition it could slow down their advance and cripple the aim of the operation, worse still it could trap them before they had time to advance on Arnhem.

On the morning of 17 September 1944 Lieutenant-Colonel Frost rose from his comfortable bed at the transit camp at Stoke Rochford, where he and his battalion had prepared for Arnhem. There was no sense in rushing: the first sticks would be ready at 0800 hours, and so Frost read his newspaper and enjoyed breakfast – it might be his last decent meal for some time. The battalion had prepared their equipment and parachutes the day before, and after breakfast Frost wandered along to the mess to find everyone else reading and smoking, all in the best of spirits and no worries anywhere. He made a final check of his equipment with his batman, Wicks – including golf clubs to follow. There was a foggy mist outside which would delay the second lift. A final cup of tea and it was off to Saltby, where the airfield swarmed with Dakotas, and convoys of lorries were moving slowly round the perimeter track. Small groups of men were busy by each aircraft, checking containers and readjusting parachutes. Officers in jeeps were driving in all directions. Frost's aircraft was No. 16 and before he boarded it he walked along the battalion line to have a few last words with his officers. For the men of the 1st Parachute Brigade waiting for the aircraft to take off was perhaps the worst time. For the parachutist, the transition from peace to war is always a nervous period.

Frost himself was confident. In the light of past experience, his men had prepared and planned well, and he was sure that the battalion had reached its maximum readiness. The 2nd Battalion had been selected for the most important task, and there was determined confidence within the unit that they would succeed. If the people of Grantham had looked into the misty sky that Sunday morning they would have seen a mass of aircraft. Dakotas took off and circled overhead, waiting for other aircraft in their formation to join them, and then they headed for the coast.

Tension inside the aircraft was no doubt beginning to mount by now, but there was some good news for the troops: low winds, which meant happy landings for paratroopers at the drop zone in Arnhem. The first aircraft had taken off at 0945 hours and the drop was scheduled for 1300 hours. At ten minutes to H-hour (the military term for the hour a specific operation begins) the men aboard Frost's aircraft were called to readiness and began their equipment checks.

As the aircraft passed the Waal, and finally the Lek, bridges they were later to battle for, the red light glowed. Suddenly it was 'green on, and go'. Canopies filled the skies, but there was no sound of enemy action, just the steady continual drone of approaching aircraft, then an increase in engine noise as the aircraft wheeled for home at speed, leaving rows of parachutes across the sky. The battalion landed with practically no trouble, and there was no difficulty in finding the way to the rendezvous. En route local Dutch people greeted the Paras and passed on what they knew about the enemy. For the moment everything was going according to plan. The operation had got off to a good start as parachute and glider troops reached their first rendezvous, but not all the news was good. Several gliders had crashed, among them those containing the armoured jeeps of the reconnaissance squadron. Then an appreciation of the enemy forces confirmed the worst: they were much greater than had been indicated at the final briefing. As they moved away from the dropping zone the leading elements of the battalion came under fire from a wood. It was a small party of Germans who had driven up in a lorry with one armoured car as escort. They were quickly dealt with and several prisoners were taken.

The 1st Brigade set off on foot. The 3rd Battalion the Parachute Regiment advanced on the main Heelsum–Arnhem road to approach the bridge from the north. The 1st Battalion initially remained with Brigade HQ in reserve while the 2nd Battalion advanced to Heelsum and then on by the southern road running close to the north bank of the lower Rhine. In Heelsum itself the 2nd Battalion ambushed a small patrol of German vehicles, taking twenty prisoners.

Members of the Dutch Resistance informed the commanding officer, Lieutenant-Colonel Frost, that there were few Germans in Arnhem itself, which was 6 miles away, and the battalion pressed on. They arrived at the railway bridge only to find it had already been destroyed, and then met stiff opposition from enemy forces occupying the high wooded ground called Den Brink. 'B' Company was sent to clear the enemy and the CO pushed on with 'A' Company into Arnhem town.

Air-land troops of the Border Regiment fire a 6-pounder anti-tank gun, nicknamed 'Gallipoli II' (Gallipoli I was lost en route to Sicily), as they engage a German position some 80 yards away.

Back at the landing zones troops poured out of gliders, although some never made their planned objectives. Dispatch rider Dennis Clay had volunteered for 'special service' and, having completed parachute training at Ringway, found himself serving in RASC Airborne Light Company. He was detailed to fly into Arnhem by glider, ready to get access to his jeep. But the glider cast off from its tow and crashed 10 miles short of Arnhem. 'The wings were ripped off and the aircraft turned over, everyone was killed. I was the only one alive,' recounted Private Clay. He was helped by a Dutchman, who told him there were five Germans in his home, who wanted to surrender. Clay took them all prisoner and marched through the woods until he met up with men from the Staffordshires of the 1st Air-Landing Brigade.

'I'll never forget it! There I was, on my own having just survived this crash and a bunch of Germans give themselves up to me,' he added.

Sometime after 1500 hours Brigade HQ gave the order to move on with all possible speed and the battalion headed for Arnhem. As they moved off a man and a woman on bicycles tried to pass the front of the column and were ordered to turn back in case they alerted German forces ahead.

'A' Company led the advance under Major Digby Tatham-Warter. As the forward element of the battalion, they were to come under fire numerous times from small pockets of German forces. As they approached the small village of Heveadorp, they came under fire again, suffering light casualties but as they passed through the village they could not believe the welcome they received: local people gave them a heroes' welcome, handing over fruit, jugs of milk, and even flowers.

The 3rd Battalion had also come under attack and at Oosterbeek they had ambushed an enemy staff car. Among the dead was General-Major Kussin, the Commandant of Arnhem, who had been visiting the 16th Panzer Grenadier Depot situated between Oosterbeek and the nearby village of Wolfheze.

When the advance began again the battalion came under heavy fire, suffering more than a dozen casualties. The commanding officer, Lieutenant-Colonel Tony Fitch, spoke to Brigadier Lathbury by radio and was told to press on, which he did. But no communications could be established with either the 2nd or the 1st Battalion.

On the outskirts of Oosterbeek the 2nd Battalion faced more fighting. Here Frost learned from prisoners being passed back down the line that there was a company of SS troops in Arnhem who were now expected to be covering the entrances to the town. Moving through Oosterbeek, Major Victor Dover was ordered to take 'C' Company down towards the river in order to capture the railway bridge over the Lek. His men managed to capture it, but before they could rejoice at their success the Germans blew the bridge up. This caused major problems for the battalion who would now have to cross the river by means of a small pontoon bridge in order to seize Arnhem bridge from both sides. If they couldn't do so, they faced the difficult task of assaulting it from one side only.

'A' Company now came under fire from Germans on the high ground at Den Brink. This high ground overlooked the railway which swung round from the bridge into Arnhem, and all attempts to move forward along the roads were met by fire from

Parachute troops of the 1st Battalion engage in close-quarter battles as the airborne force pushes its way closer to its objectives.

patrolling armoured cars. Major Tatham-Warter called for an anti-tank gun to keep the armoured cars in order while he tried his luck through the back gardens of the houses. Meanwhile Major Douglas Crawley's 'B' Company moved to the left flank under cover of the railway embankment.

Before his death, Frost recounted his memories of the events that followed.

Suddenly I realised that the hindermost parts of 'A' Company had disappeared. Everyone in the area by the railway was engaged, so I went on ahead with 'Bucky' Buchanan, our Intelligence Officer, to find out what had happened.

Some three hundred yards beyond the railway I found a party of ten German prisoners guarded by one of 'A' Company's men, who wasn't sure what the situation was, but had seen the company moving on fast. I surmised that Digby's back garden manoeuvre had been completely successful and that he had rushed on again as the way was open, leaving the information to reach me by wireless.

We ran back to the railway and soon had the battalion on the move again. It was now getting dark and though at times bursts of fire swept across the road, we could afford to ignore them.

At increased speed the leading group of the battalion swept on through the streets of Arnhem to reach the pontoon bridge – but found the centre portion dismantled and useless. Leaving part of the support group to wait for 'B' Company the remainder of the battalion marched on towards the main Rhine crossing.

The advance elements of the battalion reached the bridge just before 2100 hours on 17 September. They quickly secured the northern end of the bridge and Lieutenant Grayburn was ordered to lead his patrol across. The Germans opened fire immediately; there was no cover and the young officer was hit several times.

The Germans were in fact well established at the bridge, with machine-guns and two heavy calibre 20 mm guns firing straight along it. 'A' Company were already taking up positions on the embankment leading up from the town and a house on the corner overlooking the bridge was deemed perfect to monitor activity; the owner was invited to allow the battalion into his home, but by all accounts he was not too impressed with the idea.

Headquarters Company took over a government building next door and were joined by Brigade Headquarters who arrived in force, but without the brigadier. With them was

Air-landed troops from the Border Regiment fire a Vickers machine-gun. The picture is believed to have been taken near the northern area of the Hartenstein Hotel, which was used as the divisional HQ.

Airborne troops, believed to be from the Border Regiment, man a 3-inch mortar during Operation 'Market Garden'.

Major Freddy Gough with part of his reconnaissance squadron. They had also brought with them a captured German lorry full of ammunition from the drop zone. Major Gough's jeep-mounted squadron had planned to by-pass the town from the north and approach the bridge from the east, but this proved to be impossible and several jeeps had been shot up in the attempt. So Gough had left his squadron with Divisional Headquarters and followed the 2nd Battalion on the route they had cleared. Both the 1st and 3rd Battalions had been held up on other routes and this allowed the Germans valuable time to close the gap, and eventually resulted in the 2nd Battalion being isolated at the bridge.

In the darkness of this September evening 'A' Company moved on to the bridge and ran straight into trouble. As they started to move across they were met by withering fire from a machine-gun mounted in a pillbox and an armoured patrol car. After putting up illuminating flares of various colours, then lobbing over a few mortar bombs, the men attempted to rush straight in, but this cost them dearly. It was stalemate. Communications were still out of order and a report on progress so far was written and dispatched via a homing pigeon, which should have flown to London. The pigeon was reluctant to start at first, but took to the air after some abuse from the RSM.

During the next three days the fighting at the bridge was intense as each side sent patrols across the bridge to test the other's defences and if possible to try to storm the bridge. But neither side could gain the upper hand. The Germans brought in a 150 mm gun, firing a shell weighing nearly 100 lb, which they aimed at the battalion's main building. The house was pulverised and casualties increased. Then, as the Paras started to run low on ammunition, they learned from a prisoner captured in one of the skirmishes that among the Germans were several troops from the 9th SS Panzer Division. Previously, it had been thought that the renowned 9th and 10th SS Panzer Divisions had been written off in the Falaise battle on the bank of the River Seine in France, but the Paras now discovered from their prisoner that these Panzer Divisions had been in the Arnhem area re-equipping and absorbing reinforcements.

Approximately four battalions were trying to reach the 2nd Battalion, with the enemy besetting them on all sides, and the men were spread out from Oosterbeek, the village outside Arnhem, back to the original landing zones. The abundance of cover provided by the woods and buildings made the area ideal for ambush, so that quite small bodies of enemy, armed with machine-guns and supported by tanks, could interfere with and even paralyse movement along the roads leading into Arnhem. For the time being, the 2nd Battalion was on its own.

More German weapons, including tanks, were brought to the bridge to finish off the Paras, and on more than one occasion the German commanding officer called on Frost to surrender, but there was no question of giving up. The tanks mounted a constant barrage against the remains of the battalion's buildings and as the second night

British paratroopers clear buildings of snipers around the Oosterbeek area. It was here that the 10th Battalion the Parachute Regiment suffered heavy casualties.

approached the town of Arnhem was on fire: two great churches were burning and clouds of dense smoke rose into the night sky.

Soon after first light on Wednesday morning, the third day, the shelling began again. Buildings on both sides of the bridge had been destroyed and their rubble was still smouldering, and most of the surviving men of the 2nd Battalion were concentrated round the remains of the headquarters buildings. Determined not to be beaten, the Paras had found a limited water supply in one of the houses, sufficient for one more day at any rate. At last Divisional Headquarters came on the air and Frost was able to speak to the General, but he could tell him nothing more than he did not already know about 30 Corps. They were obviously having great difficulty in getting through.

That day Frost was injured in the legs but he tried valiantly to continue his command in order to maintain morale. Dazed and exhausted, he was eventually carried to the cellar where the casualties were being treated. The situation was desperate, but it was to get worse. Major Tatham-Warter came in and told Frost about Lieutenant Jack Grayburn. This brave young officer had assaulted the bridge with his platoon several times and, despite being injured, he refused to leave his men and died in action with them. His outstanding leadership and courage would win him a posthumous Victoria Cross.

Having run out of ammunition and with almost every surviving man wounded, the battalion could do nothing but wait for the Germans to arrive. They came in and evacuated the seriously injured and marched away the walking wounded. Frost was bitter as he recalled what happened:

> The SS men were very polite and complimentary about the battle we had fought, but I felt bitter at the way the battle ended. The battalion did not have a chance without ammunition, no rest and with no positions from which to fight. No body of men could have fought more courageously and tenaciously than the officers and men of the 1st Parachute Brigade at Arnhem bridge.

Frost, along with the other members of the 2nd Battalion, was taken prisoner. Later in his career he was promoted to Major-General.

At his Surrey home he joked that the war had played havoc with his golf and remembered that, before flying out to lead the 2nd Battalion in their finest hour, he ordered his clubs to be sent to him, 'so I could enjoy myself after beating the Germans'.

But the hero of Arnhem found himself playing a different kind of game, grimly defying the might of a German SS Panzer Division. Frost held no bitterness towards his old commanders, confining his criticism to the fact that 'our generals had an off day'. He believes the worst mistake was the failure to take Nijmegen bridge 17 miles to the south, on the route of a relieving Guards armoured brigade. By the time the Guards arrived, Nijmegen was in German hands.

> A US unit should have taken that bridge. Wasn't their fault, they were only acting on orders. Instead the Americans were sent to some high ground where they were totally out of things.

It was a waste of resources. It slowly dawned on us that no help was coming. By the time we surrendered we had 250 wounded, including myself. I'd been hit in the feet by shrapnel. In war there are two things people always forget: how to care for the wounded and how to supply ammunition. We'd got only the bullets we'd carried with us.

The 2nd Battalion had sustained terrible losses at the Bridge and the rest of the brigade had fared little better. Both the 1st and 3rd Battalions had encountered fierce fighting, as had the units of the 4th Parachute Brigade. The men of the 7th Battalion the King's Own Scottish Borderers, the 1st Battalion the Border Regiment, and the 2nd Battalion the South Staffordshire Regiment all suffered losses.

On the afternoon of 21 September the western sector of the perimeter was attacked but the Border Regiment drove the enemy back. At the same time an assault was made on the Lonsdale Force in the south, while at the northern end the 7th Battalion the King's Own Scottish Borderers were forced out of their positions. Fixing their bayonets, the Lowlanders counter-attacked and routed the enemy, although by the end of the battle the battalion's strength numbered just 150.

On the eastern side of the perimeter the 10th Battalion the Parachute Regiment were attacked by enemy tanks at Oosterbeek. The commanding officer, Lieutenant-Colonel Ken Smyth, was killed in the action and the battalion were forced to withdraw. One of the fast-dwindling number of 10 Para officers was Captain Lionel Queripel, who gathered the remnants of the three companies to form a composite company which he helped to lead into Arnhem. But the group came under heavy enemy fire and Queripel, already wounded in the face, crossed and recrossed a road in front of enemy fire to rally survivors and carry an injured sergeant to the regimental aid post. As the fighting continued, Queripel was wounded in both arms and when their ammunition was almost finished he ordered his men to try and save themselves while he stayed behind, facing certain death, to cover their withdrawal. He was awarded a posthumous Victoria Cross for his courage and leadership and today the headquarters building of the 10th Battalion (V) at the Duke of York's HQ in London is called Queripel House in his honour.

No account of Arnhem would be complete without mentioning Kate ter Horst, a mother of five who helped to treat hundreds of wounded British soldiers brought to her house beside the Osterbeek church. She prayed with the dying and men of the airborne forces remember her actions with great respect and affection. At the end of the battle, the garden of her house, which was destroyed in the conflict, contained fifty-seven graves of airborne soldiers.

On 22 September the 1st Polish Independent Parachute Brigade moved up to the southern bank of the Lower Rhine. They were to cross the river in inflatable boats, but the enemy illuminated the river and pinned them down – only fifty men crossed to the other side. It was all too clear to their commander that their objectives could not be achieved and the decision was taken to withdraw. On the night of 25 September an artillery barrage commenced on the German positions, which was to provide cover while the remains of

Arnhem bridge – the objective for the 2nd Battalion the Parachute Regiment. This picture was taken shortly after the British troops arrived at the bridge.

the division pulled back. Diversionary attacks were mounted to distract the enemy's attention and by the time the operation was complete 2,120 men had been evacuated.

The order to evacuate had been passed on to survivors on Monday afternoon and for many of the weary airborne soldiers it was a huge relief. Glider pilot Peter Fletcher was absolutely delighted at the news.

> I was frightened throughout the battle. Almost from the beginning to the end we had been at the mercy of the Germans with hardly any fighting cover. The times our fighters attacked the Germans it worked and their guns fell silent, but it wasn't enough.
>
> Most of our supply drops went to the Germans, so the valiant efforts of the many bomber and transport crews were in vain. A lot of British aircraft were shot down trying to drop supplies to us.

Paddy McMahon was sent back down the Rhine with other airborne engineers to help oversee the evacuation crossings. He worked alongside soldiers of the 43 Wessex brigade and Canadian engineers. After dark the 2,000 British airborne soldiers able to walk were told to cover their boots with rags to muffle their steps and tie down any equipment which might rattle – torrential rain also helped muffle any noise. Each group were escorted down the river throughout the night, under a barrage of fire from 43 Wessex's artillery.

Paddy McMahon was in the water for hours as he helped load wounded soldiers into dinghies. 'It was all very solemn. Groups of soldiers patiently waited, there was no talking, everyone was exhausted.' British wounded who were left behind contributed to the covering fire and as the walking wounded were evacuated some were killed by shrapnel and gunfire from British and German guns. Paratrooper Stan Turner fought at Arnhem with a detachment of the Royal Electrical and Mechanical Engineers, and kept a diary of events during Operation 'Market Garden', before spending nine months in a prisoner-of-war camp.

September 16 We are briefed about the Arnhem operation and told it will be a success because there are only remnants of German divisions there. Some of us had a drink in Cirencester.

September 17 – We didn't go with the first lifts, but our thoughts are with those who do. We are told we will be going tomorrow morning

September 18 – Our take-off is scheduled for 11.30 am and everyone is sat around having thoughts of their own. At 2.30 pm we cast off from our tug aircraft and make a steep dive to land. There is a mass of gliders on the ground, some burning, some overturned. We are told to dig in near the Hartenstein Hotel, firing can be heard in every direction.

September 19 – At 10 am fighter planes appear overhead, around thirty of them. At first it is presumed they are ours, then one dives down to machine-gun a position and we can see the black crosses. Bren guns all around me open fire at the aircraft.

September 20 – The noise is unbelievable as we are shelled for the first time. Orders are given for us to move inside the grounds of the Hartenstein Hotel to act as defence troops for the divisional headquarters. This confirms our feeling that things are not going well.

September 21 – Early in the morning a jeep which has been adapted to carry wounded is brought to us to repair its shrapnel-pierced radiator. This we do in between breaks from the shelling. During the morning a good friend of mine is killed by shrapnel. Later we are ordered into slit trenches between the hotel and Oosterbeek.

September 22 – During the day I go in search of food and am almost killed when a German machine-gunner opens fire at me. I take cover in a nearby trench.

September 23 – We had heard rumours of tanks and self-propelled guns. Today they become a fact. Looking up the hill from our position we see a very large tank. We say to ourselves what can we do against it. There is a lull in the German shelling because they don't want to hit their own tank. Luckily it moves off, then the shelling starts again.

September 24 – We see the first Polish paratroopers who have been ferried across the

Major-General Urquhart, Commanding Officer of the 1st Airborne Division outside the Hartenstein Hotel.

Rhine. They are not pleased to have been landed in a very poor situation. The latest rumours are that 30 Corps has been held up.

September 25 – We are all feeling tired and are ordered back into the grounds of the hotel. Everyone is shattered.

September 26 – I wake up and it is daylight. I immediately know something is wrong because British troops always stand-to before dawn. The grounds of the hotel look deserted compared to how they have been over the past couple of days. I go over to the German PoWs in the tennis courts hoping one of them can speak English and one of them tells me 'Tommy, they have all gone.' Scarcely able to believe what has happened myself and the other REME soldier who shared my trench wander over to the hotel building. We are astounded to see a pile of British dead, all of them very young. It is a sight I will never forget.

We meet a medical officer who tells us the 1st Airborne Division was evacuated in the night, he has been left to look after the wounded and tells us we will be taken prisoner.

The failure of the Arnhem operation did not detract from the determination and outstanding performance of the 1st Airborne Division which held on for nine days, although the plan had stated that 30th Corps would link up with them after 48 hours. Casualties numbered 7,167 killed, wounded or missing out of a total of 10,095 men dropped or landed at Arnhem as part of the 6th Airborne Division. Among the dead were two chaplains, while another two were taken prisoner.

Five Victoria Crosses were awarded to men who took part in the Arnhem battle, four of them posthumously. These were awarded to Lieutenant Jack Grayburn, who fought with the 2nd Battalion at the bridge, Captain Lionel Queripel of the 10th Battalion Parachute Regiment, who ordered his men to withdraw while he remained to face the enemy, and Staff Sergeant John Baskeyfield, who continued to take charge of his gun crew despite serious injury, then crawled to another six pounder and fired it alone. The Victoria Cross was also awarded to Flight Lieutenant David Lord RAF who was delivering supplies to Arnhem when his Dakota was hit by fire and set alight; he bravely remained at the controls to allow his crew to bail out, but it exploded in flames – only one member of the crew survived. The fifth VC was awarded to Major Robert Cain, who charged a German Tiger tank single-handedly and forced the Germans to withdraw. Major Cain survived to receive his decoration from King George VI.

After Operation 'Market Garden' Field Marshal Montgomery, the architect of the whole operation, told the Paras: 'So long as we have officers and men who will do as you have done, then we can indeed look forward with complete confidence to the future. In years to come it will be a great thing for a man to be able to say, "I fought at Arnhem."'

Thirty-six years after the epic battle, Frost returned to Arnhem, this time as a military adviser to the makers of the film *A Bridge Too Far*. Frost instantly disliked Anthony Hopkins, who was playing his character. And it was mutual. Frost said: 'I told the director, Richard Attenborough, that it wasn't working. Attenborough told me to stick close to him, watch every move and tell him where he was going wrong. At the end of the two weeks we had worked so closely together that we became the greatest of friends.'

The thrill-seeking General had 'one last bash' at parachuting with his men twenty-five years ago . . . and it almost cost him his life. 'I'd been looking forward to it,' he recalled. 'I remember hurtling through the air aware that something was very wrong. Above me people were shouting that I'd got a thrown line. That was serious because it meant the parachute wasn't behaving properly. There was nothing I could do but hope for the best. Luckily, I landed in a rabbit warren which was as soft as thistledown. I walked away without a bruise. The rest of them couldn't believe it. I just swore it was my last jump.'

General Frost – 'Johnnie' to his men – believed that the shared fear of jumping into battle is what makes the Paras special. 'With soldiers it's the mental attitude that makes the difference. The very act of jumping with your friends means you all have a certain amount of fear. There's an invisible bond that's still there when you're on the ground. In the early days of the war the Ministry sent a psychiatrist to study us. Afterwards he told me: "Sir, it's an extraordinary thing but 80 per cent of your men

British airborne troops who made it to Nijmegen after being pulled out of Arnhem in the evacuation operation on 25 September.

Personal belongings of a soldier in the Ox & Bucks which were retained in the UK during deployment in Europe. If captured, no proof of identity would be found on the soldier.

have an inferiority complex." Maybe he was right. Paras do need to prove themselves – like they did at Arnhem.'

In his later life Frost worked on his farm at Milland but maintained his links with the Paras and hosted yearly reunions for his officers. 'There is a very special bond in the regiment,' he said. 'Pride, friendship, call it what you will. It has served us well all over the world. And in the end it's what the enemy thinks that counts. It wasn't for nothing that Hitler nicknamed us the "Red Devils".' General Frost often returned to the battlefield at Arnhem, to the bridge he and his men had fought so hard to capture. It was eventually re-named 'John FrostBrug', the John Frost Bridge, in his honour. A legend within the Parachute Regiment Frost fought in Africa, Sicily, Europe and then went on to serve in Palestine after the war. Here he met his wife Jean MacGregor who had been badly wounded by a bomb there. He went on to command 52nd Lowland Division and ended his career in 1967 as the GOC in Malta at the rank of Major-General. He died at his farm in May 1993, aged eighty-one.

In September 1994 more than 200 Arnhem veterans and 100,000 Dutch and British spectators braved high winds and driving rain to watch 800 paratroopers mark the 50th anniversary of the 1st Airborne Division's role in Operation Market Garden. The mass airborne landings from seventeen C-130 Hercules were to be on the original wartime drop zone at Ginkel Heath. These drops were spearheaded by paratroopers from 5 Airborne Brigade, including the 10th Battalion – now a reserve battalion – who had fought so gallantly at Arnhem, the Parachute Regiment and the Special Air Service. Airborne troops from New Zealand, South Africa, Canada, Poland and America also jumped.

The weather was appalling and twenty-one Paras were injured – fortunately none seriously – and a drop by fifty-eight Arnhem veterans, the oldest aged eighty-four, was cancelled because of the conditions. One veteran, 76-year-old former sergeant Tex Banwell, did parachute, as he has done for many years at the Arnhem anniversary, from a private aircraft. Twenty-four hours later the veterans did get to jump and one of the first out of the door was George Sheldrake, who jumped in tandem with AAC helicopter pilot Sergeant Dick Kalinski. One of those who returned to pay his respects was former Para Phil Banks, who served with the 10th Battalion the Parachute Regiment in the battle at Arnhem.

At the Airborne Cemetery in Oosterbeek Phil found the grave of his best friend, Peter Poupard, who was killed in the fighting at Arnhem. 'This is our spiritual home. All of us in the 10th Battalion of the Parachute Regiment, the finest in the world. I came to find Peter's grave and when I did I cried my eyes out. I put flowers on it and said "Never forgotten".'

Phil has already made plans to join his old comrades when he dies.

They will bring me here and scatter my ashes and I will be with my mates again. I can remember parachuting on to Ginkelsheide. They were shooting at us all the way down. This was my first time in action and it was very scary. I was just nineteen.

We were trying to break through to Arnhem where 2 Para were trying to hold the bridge. There was fighting in Oosterbeek and more than ninety of the battalion were killed here. I was captured and sent to a German ore mine, but I escaped with a Royal Engineer – although not for long, we were recaptured and the guards knocked my teeth out.

I escaped again and linked up with the Americans. I fought with the best. The men lying here, Corporal Wally Dunkley and Captain Queripel, who won the Victoria Cross.

THE POLISH PARACHUTE BRIGADE

After the overrunning of Poland by German and Russian forces in September 1939, the Polish Army was reorganised under General Sikorski in France and elements of this force reached Britain after its fall in 1940. Once in Britain these elements were reformed into new Polish units which included the Polish Parachute Brigade. This brigade, which was raised and trained in Scotland, was commanded by Major-General Stanislaw Sosabowski and formed part of 1st Airborne Division for the Arnhem operation.

On 19 September 1944, after two delays due to poor weather conditions, the Polish Parachute Brigade was finally dropped as part of the third lift in drop zones K & L. As reinforcements they were, through no fault of their own, 'too little, too late', but they fought with the grim determination and professionalism that was the hallmark of all those who fought at Arnhem.

Polish airborne hero Lieutenant Zbigniew Gasowski needed all the courage he could muster to confront history again. Visiting the Airborne Forces Museum at Browning Barracks, Aldershot, the veteran of the ill-fated Arnhem conflict came face to face with his old wartime uniform. 'It wouldn't fit me now. It's at least four inches too small,' he said.

Lieutenant Gasowski lives in London after retiring from eighteen years of lecturing at the city's University College. He was born in Warsaw but escaped to the West after the German occupation in 1939. He made his way to France through Hungary, Yugoslavia and Italy and joined the Polish army in exile. After the collapse of France he escaped again in the Dunkirk evacuation and re-joined the free Polish forces in England. He served first with the 2nd Battalion of the 1st Polish Infantry Brigade and, after his commission, he volunteered to transfer to the 1st Polish Independent Parachute Brigade.

Gasowski dropped at Arnhem and later fought with the Polish Paras through to Germany. After the war he served with the British Army for a further two years and has lived in England ever since. 'His story is typical of the thousands of Poles who braved every hardship to join the free Polish forces and continue the fight for freedom against Nazi Germany and who, for political reasons, have been denied the fruits of victory they fought so hard to achieve – the right to return to their homeland,' says a note alongside his uniform in the Aldershot museum. It should remain a constant reminder for future generations of all nations of the price exacted to preserve and cherish the fundamental human right of liberty.

Dropping from a Dakota. British troops first used the Dakota in North Africa, but as the war progressed more aircraft were delivered into the UK to airlift the British force. The paratrooper is wearing a Sorbo rubber helmet and is jumping at Tatton Park, near Manchester.

5. THE FINAL PUSH

OPERATION 'VARSITY': AIRBORNE ASSAULT INTO GERMANY

The last and most successful large-scale airborne drop of the war marked the beginning of the end for the Germans. After their defeat in the Ardennes, it was necessary for the Allies to strike quickly before the German forces could regroup. On 24 March 1945 the Allied Airborne Corps formed a spearhead for the British and American armies that breached the formidable enemy defences on the River Rhine at Wesel. Operation 'Varsity' involved the 6th Airborne Division and the American 17th Airborne Division. They were tasked to drop in the Wesel area to secure and deepen the 21st Army Group's bridgehead east of the Rhine, then they were to occupy the high ground of the Diersfordter Wald, the village of Hamminkeln and certain bridges over the River Issel.

During the winter of 1944/5 the 6th Airborne Division were rushed across the Channel, not by air but by ship, to help counter the German Christmas offensive in the Ardennes. The Germans had thrown all their resources into the battle, but it failed and by March 1945 the shortage of weapons, ammunition and fuel, largely due to the success of Allied air attacks against Hitler's war economy, was crippling the German withdrawal.

Field Marshal Montgomery, who had been appointed Colonel Commandant of the Parachute Regiment in January 1945, now introduced a new airborne tactic. Instead of landing *ahead* of the ground operations his plan was to drop *after* the amphibious crossing of the Rhine had begun. Both British and American divisions would land at full strength in one full-scale tactical airborne assault, timed to overwhelm the German defences and link up immediately with the ground forces.

The tasks set for the 6th Airborne Division were crucial. 3 Parachute Brigade Group, commanded by Brigadier Hill, would parachute on to dropping zone 'A' at the north-west corner of the Diersforder Wald and seize the high ground of the Schnappenberg feature to prevent the Germans maintaining observation posts overlooking the Allied bridgehead. They would then mount patrols westwards and link up with Brigadier Poett's 5 Parachute Brigade Group which was to drop on to dropping zone 'B', north-west of Hamminkeln to clear and hold an area astride the main road between their dropping zone and Hamminkeln itself. They would also mount patrols to link up with 3 Parachute Brigade Group. The 6th Air-Landing Brigade, under the command of Brigadier Bellamy, would land in company groups aboard their gliders. The 12th

Field Marshal Montgomery meets senior officers of the 6th Airborne Division in the Ardennes, in spring 1945. On the left is Major-General Bois, Montgomery, Brigadiers Flavell, Hill and Poett. Lieutenant-Colonel Crookenden is in the background.

Battalion the Devonshire Regiment were to land on landing zone 'R', south-west of Hamminkeln, and capture the town. The 2nd Battalion the Oxfordshire & Buckinghamshire Light Infantry were to land on landing zone 'O', north of Hamminkeln, to seize and hold the rail and road bridges over the River Issel between Hamminkeln and Ringenberg, while the 1st Battalion the Royal Ulster Rifles were also to land on landing zone 'O'. Their task was to seize and hold the bridge over the River Issel on the main road from Hamminkeln to Brunen. Divisional Headquarters would land on landing zone 'P', north-east of the Diersforder Wald adjacent to Kopenhöf and establish itself there. Supply points for heavy drop and additional resupply would be made on dropping zones 'A' and 'B'.

Field Marshal Montgomery's bold plan also called for a crossing to be made north of the Ruhr, between the towns of Wesel and Emmerich. The assault would be carried out on a two-army front, with the 9th US Army on the right and 2nd (British) Army on the left. A bridgehead would be established beforehand from which the divisions would fan out and advance into northern Germany.

On the night of 23 March a massive barrage was brought down on the German positions as 3,500 guns opened fire. During the previous two days more than 5,000 bombers mounted round-the-clock sorties to drop 15,100 tons of bombs on defensive positions, roads, railways and airfields. The crossing of the Rhine by Allied ground forces began shortly after nightfall on 23 March 1945, and at dawn the next day 1,696 transport aircraft and 1,348 gliders brought in 21,680 airborne troops in one single lift. Escorting this massive aerial armada were 1,000 fighter aircraft.

The gliders of the 6th Air-Landing Brigade swept in through the smoke and dust kicked up by the Allied bombardment, with the 2nd Ox & Bucks capturing the key bridges over the Issel. The 12th Devons took the village of Hamminkeln with the help of the US 513th Parachute Infantry Regiment. It was daylight but smoke drifted across the drop zone as enemy gunfire opened up on the 7th Battalion the Parachute Regiment. Many men were hit in the air, others as they landed. Some men missed the drop zone completely and landed almost on top of the German units where they were taken prisoner.

Despite being outnumbered and outgunned, the Germans put up a large amount of flak and some forty-four C–46 Commando transports and eighty gliders were destroyed by anti-aircraft fire. Once they had landed, the British airborne troops started to secure the northern half of the Corps zone, and they moved on, some heading for the high ground of the Diersfordter Wald east of Bergen, others to the town of Hamminkeln and some of the bridges over the River Issel.

Hill's 3rd Parachute Brigade landed north of Schnappenberg and was engaged by the enemy from the start. Casualties were immediate, the commander of the 1st Canadian Parachute Battalion, Lieutenant-Colonel Nicklin, being shot dead by a German marksman as he tried to free himself from his parachute harness while dangling from a tree. In the face of stiff opposition Schnappenberg was captured by the 1st Canadian and 9th Battalions, and during the afternoon the 3rd Brigade linked up with the ground forces advancing from the Rhine. Brigadier Poett's 5th Parachute Brigade (7th, 12th and 13th Battalions) had captured their objectives by late afternoon.

Operation 'Varsity' was thus a success – but it was a costly one. The losses in aircrew were 41 dead, 153 wounded and 163 missing, while the 6th Airborne Division itself lost 347 men killed and 731 wounded. In addition, some 1,000 British and American soldiers were listed as missing, though most of them eventually managed to find their way back to Allied lines.

By early April the battalion was preparing to carry out its mission to seize Lion Bridge at Neustadt; the 12th Battalion was to take other bridges over the River Leine at Bordenau; their orders were to prevent the Germans getting across the river. The 7th Battalion had arrived at Wunstorf aerodrome to prepare to move to the bridge when they came under heavy fire.

Private Brannen Wylie was in one of several trucks the battalion had 'procured' when enemy fire opened up. He recalled:

I set my Bren up and started firing at the windows of a nearby building, until somebody dropped down alongside me and told me that the Germans were in fact dug in in front of the building. Then someone shouted tanks, and I thought they were enemy tanks, but they were ours that were moving in support of us.

It was hectic, everyone was nervous. Preparations were being made to charge the enemy and the RSM came over and gave me four extra magazines for the Bren and told me to stay where I was and provide covering fire.

A few minutes later the RSM and I ran forward to join the rest of the lads. It was only then that I realised how many dead and wounded there were: Lieutenant Pape, a Canadian on loan to us was dead, as was my great friend George Jamieson.

We filled all the Bren magazines we could and Lieutenant Gush gave us a brief about going for the bridge. We were going to take the bridge and consolidate in a large white house on the other side. It seemed straightforward enough at the time.

We set off across country for the bridge; it was a long way and then we came into the town. In darkness we continued our advance and eventually came to the bridge. We assaulted it firing and as a Bren-gunner I was at the front. I saw some charges and someone shouted the bridge is charged.

It seemed as though I had just reached the other side of the bridge when it went up, I don't remember a bang, just a rumble, lots of dust and a flash. I was stunned and as I got up to walk away from the bridge I was convinced I was the only one alive – then I saw Lieutenant Gush and the others at the house.

We lost a lot of men at the bridge and the lady who owned the white house came out to help with our wounded. She spoke very good English and later promised me that she would plant forget-me-nots on the graves and look after them for as long she could. It wasn't until forty-seven years later that I learnt her name was Frau Erika Naujoks, when I attended a remembrance service.

The company who took the bridge lost twenty-four men that day; another eleven would later die of their wounds. Only days later thousands of Germans in massive columns marched down the road with their hands on their heads. They had given up the fight and were handing themselves over to the Allies. The war was almost over. Today there is a plaque at the bridge in memory of the men of the 7th Battalion the Parachute Regiment who lost their lives on 7 April 1945 during one of the last actions of the Second World War.

The Allied drive into Germany was accompanied by men of the 6th Airborne Division, though the Paras operated more as infantry than airborne troops. And despite the assistance of the 4th Tank Battalion, Grenadier Guards and additional artillery, the parachute and glider soldiers covered much of the 350 miles to the Baltic on foot.

Now that the final barrier to Germany had been crossed the Paras, who were trained to fight with only light support, exploited the situation, mounting swift and deliberate attacks as the Allies pushed their way across Europe. Many of the attacks were at night and on one occasion the 3rd Parachute Brigade pushed forward 15 miles in just twenty-four hours, fighting continuously for eighteen hours. The brigade also eliminated a Panzer Grenadier training battalion, capturing most of its vehicles. On a separate occasion the 5th Parachute Brigade marched 50 miles in seventy-two hours, during which period they mounted two night operations.

Between 26 March and 2 May the 6th Airborne Division had advanced from Hamminkeln to the Baltic coast. The 3rd Parachute Brigade captured Lembeck, while the 1st Canadian Parachute Battalion took Greven during a night assault. In April 1945 the division was given a spearhead role in the advance towards the River Elbe and Wismar, largely as a result of General Dempsey's promptings to repair its shattered pride after the Arnhem failure. However, the 11th Armoured Division had been allocated the privilege of actually linking up with the advancing Russians. This appeared to be the end of the matter but, true to the airborne spirit, the Paras turned their berets inside out and draped their Sherman tanks (they had been reinforced by the 4th Tank Battalion the Grenadier Guards) with camouflage netting to hide their tactical signs. Unaware of their real identity, the military police let the vehicles through, and on 2 May 1945, eleven tanks carrying members of the 1st Canadian Parachute Battalion arrived in Wismar on the Baltic. The Russians arrived before nightfall but the Paras had won the race to the sea by eight hours.

Thus ended the 6th Airborne Division's war in Europe, a campaign that had cost them 1,520 dead, 3,459 wounded and 1,302 missing. The 1st Airborne Division ended the war in Scandinavia, overseeing the surrender of the German garrison in Norway. On 21 May General Urquhart's headquarters was redesignated HQ Norway Command. His 6,000 Paras served in Norway until 24 August 1945, being officially disbanded two months later.

The history of the 1st Canadian Parachute Battalion, who served throughout the war with the 3rd Parachute Brigade, was so closely bound up with the regiment as to be part of it. The story of the Parachute Regiment is also inseparable from that of the Glider Pilot Regiment, the Indian Parachute Regiment, and those other arms and services that supported the regiment in battle. In total, 188 officers and 2,004 men were killed in action while serving with the Parachute Regiment. All their names, together with those of 10 officers and 120 men of the 1st Canadian Parachute Battalion who served so closely with the regiment, are recorded in the Roll of Honour lodged in the Royal Garrison Church of All Saints at Aldershot in Hampshire.

Gliders played a key role throughout the war, particularly in Operation 'Varsity' – the Horsa being the main workhorse. However, the Hotspur was the first military glider to be built by the Allies; the first one flew on 5 November 1940, just four months after the order had been given to investigate the value of glider operations. There is no doubt that the design was heavily influenced by the civilian sailplane. The specification called for an

NO VICTORY ROLLS PLEASE
RGINS ROOST
FIRST AID
IVE GOT YOU NOW
IS THIS THE WAY IN
DUFF ?
HA. HA.
IS OUR JOURNEY
REALLY NECESSARY
RIBS
ANY TIME

Paratroopers, glider troops, glider pilots and RAF aircrew check a map of Europe before the final major airborne assault of the war – Operation 'Varsity', the crossing of the River Rhine.

8-seater, the equivalent of an infantry section, and capable of a very long approach flight so that it could cast off at a respectable altitude and glide in to its target in silence, the tug having returned for home before being detected. A gliding angle of at least 24:1 was called for, and operationally the machine would be used for one flight only.

The glider needed to be both cheap and expendable, yet it also had to exhibit considerable aerodynamic refinement. The General Aircraft Company was remarkably successful in interpreting this difficult requirement, and the first Hotspurs performed very well. The pilot was housed in a glass cockpit in the nose, and the passengers sat astride a long bench running up the centre of the fuselage. Later models changed the seating to a side bench. The glider was mid-winged, which meant that the main spar cut the passenger compartment in two, but the Mark I had no doors and the passengers entered and exited by lifting the top half of the fuselage clear of the boat-shaped bottom half.

The Hotspur Mark II was introduced soon after the Mark I. It was different in that it

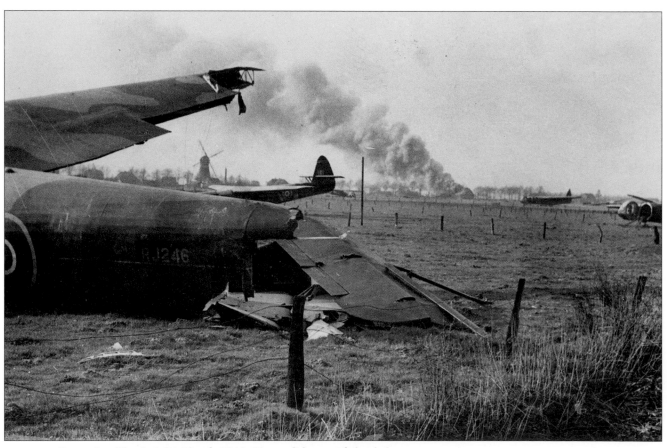

Operation 'Varsity', 24 March 1945. Many gliders crash-landed.

had small doors in the fuselage allowing passengers to parachute from it and the lifting lid was abandoned. Another change was a smaller wing and a much stronger construction, leading to greater weight but the loss of its good aerodynamic qualities. However, this did not matter. It was soon realised that the best way to use these gliders was to make a dive approach to the landing zone and not try to glide for a long distance. Another factor in the change was the fact that it was difficult to train pilots for one flight only.

Finally there was the Mark III, a trainer pure and simple. This constituted a complete change in the specification since a trainer has to be very strong to cope with continual landing and take-off, and once again the construction was different. Hotspurs were only used for training and as far as it is known no operational flights were ever made with them. In 1944 there was a scheme to use the remaining ones as a freight train for a quick re-supply of the Normandy invasion, but it was never carried out. The little glider rapidly faded out of sight as the wood and fabric deteriorated when it was stored out in the open.

The Horsa was the proposed 25-seater operational glider. The idea was that it should increase the capacity of a bomber on the approach to a parachute assault, and then both bomber and glider would drop their men together. The men from the Horsa were to jump from two doors simultaneously, a brave idea in June 1940, and two doors were cut in the fuselage. In flight these doors would open to allow troops to fire a machine-gun from each door against counter-attack. There were also two other positions for defensive guns: one a round hole in the roof just aft of the wing, and the other a hole in the lower floor of the tail to deter attack from below the belly. These were never used.

Apart from the two doors there was also a freight-loading door on the port side, just behind the cockpit. This was quite ingenious in its application as it was appreciated that all loading would be with the wheels in place, and so the floor line would be high. For loading the door hinged downwards and all cargo was run in on two long ramps. When unloading the glider would be on its skids, the door was dropped down and two short ramps taken from the floor and laid on it, making a short and wide ramp down which all the cargo could be taken. It ruined the door but for an operational flight this did not matter.

The cargo door was not large as it was intended that only motorcycles and combinations be taken on airborne assaults – a direct copy of the German concept. The jeep fitted round the doorpost, however, and could be pushed in, but it was too slow getting it out for an operational landing zone and a modification was made to allow the removal of the tail and then the cargo could be run out over the sill. The earliest method of doing this was to blow the tail off with cord explosive but the RAF Technical Development Unit devised a way of holding the tail section on with six large bolts. These could be released quickly without damaging the structure. The Horsa Mark II overcame most of the loading difficulties by having a hinged nose, which allowed very rapid loading and unloading. The entire cockpit and controls was swung to one side but as it was apparent that the nose gets the worst of any rough landing, the removable tail was kept for emergencies.

The Horsa was built in much the same rapid way as the Hotspur. The mock-up was produced in January 1941 and the first production models were issued in June 1942 – by the end of the war more than 5,000 had been built. Some were flown to North Africa in November 1942 and others were shipped to India. As the wood shrank in the tropical heat 'renovation kits' were made up by the manufacturers to keep them airborne.

Horsas were used in all the British airborne assaults after 1941 and many were used by US airborne divisions. They were both strong and practical and without them the great airborne missions on Normandy, Arnhem and the Rhine would have been very different.

The Horsa was a plywood high-wing monoplane of very plain appearance. The fuselage was long and cylindrical with an angular glasshouse nose roughly rounding off the front. The tail was a plywood cone, bolted to the cylinder. The wing ran out from about half way along the top of the fuselage. A tricycle undercarriage stuck out from the centre of the fuselage and there was a large and prominent rudder. The feature that surpassed all others in size and effect, however, was the glider's flaps. They were huge and controlled by compressed air carried in bottles. On the dive approach to the landing zone, the pilot lowered these large flaps and the entire glider seemed to stop dead in the air, and then simply flop on the ground in the most docile manner. Viewed from the landing zone itself there are few more terrifying sights than a Horsa with full flap whistling in to land, the air shrieking around the whole structure. The Horsa carried either twenty-eight fully equipped men, a jeep and trailer, a jeep and 75 mm gun, two jeeps, or 3.6 tons of cargo.

The Mark I was towed by a single rope attached to the underside of the nose. The Mark II had to change this because of the opening nose, and the tow rope was a 'Y' shape and ran to the wings. One or two were fitted with engines and tried as transports but these were not a success. This was perhaps because the only engines that could be spared, and ones which the wing could accommodate, were Armstrong-Siddeley Cheetahs of 375 hp (278 kw) and 750 hp (556 kw) which was scarcely enough to pull the large structure through the air.

The Hengist was the back-up 15-seater ordered in 1940. Only eighteen were built since it was quickly seen that the Horsa was going to be the workhorse. The contract for the Hengist was given to Slingsby, the only large-scale manufacturer of gliders in Britain before the war. The resulting machine was graceful and smooth, despite the fact that most of the surfaces were either flat or straight. It towed well and flew easily, calling for little effort on the controls. Once it was seen that the Horsa design was a success the remaining Hengists were broken up.

The Hamilcar was the designated British tank-carrier and the Germans decided that they too needed to fly tanks in gliders. Hamilcar was the largest glider built by the Allies, and the only one that actually carried an armoured vehicle. It closely resembled the German Messerschmitt Me 321 in general outline, although it was only just over half its size and carried one-third of its load. On the other hand it had the great advantage of being able to be towed by existing RAF bombers and did not need the complicated and expensive tug arrangements that the Me 321 called for. The design was not settled until early 1941 and the contract given to the General Aircraft Company, who set about building it at their Birmingham works.

The whole idea was a novelty and two half-scale models were made first. The first one flew so well that the second model was never built and the next version was the first full-size Hamilcar. The entire structure was made of wood, and in order to gain necessary strength and aerodynamic efficiency the loading had to be higher than any previous glider – it was even higher than the Whitley. The entire glider was covered with plywood and on the fuselage the ply was used as a stressed skin to take some of the load off the floor. The big square cargo compartment was reached through the nose, the entire front of it swinging to starboard. Passengers could enter by small doors at the rear but the main load was either driven in or pushed over the sill. The two-wheeled undercarriage was suspended on oil-damped struts and these could be released to allow the fuselage to sink down on to its skids and bring the floor closer to the ground. A vehicle could then bump over the sill without needing ramps. In fact the vehicle was usually started up while the glider was still on the approach, the exhaust gas being piped out through the side. As soon as the glider had stopped the lashings were released by pulling wires and the vehicle was moved forward. A mechanical catch released the door lock and pushed it open and the vehicle ran out, barely stopping at the sill. It was reckoned that a vehicle could be in action within twenty seconds of the glider stopping on the landing zone if this method was used.

The two pilots were in a long glasshouse above the cargo space and they had no direct communication with the passengers. They reached their 'office' by climbing up the outside and had to use telephones to communicate. They had a difficult job because the controls were anything but light but they were not as tough as those in the German Me 321 glider. However, an hour or two was all most crews could take without becoming tired.

The first prototype flew in March 1942 and was found to be a success without modification. Production on a modest scale began shortly afterwards and over 400 were completed by 1945. They only ever flew in Europe and were not shipped overseas. The chief reason for this was that the tugs were all UK-based four engined bombers and the overseas bases were not equipped to service them. Another reason was the fact that, by 1944, when the Hamilcar was available in numbers and when suitable light tanks were also available, these same tanks were becoming less and less useful on the battlefield. The size and effectiveness of battle tanks and other armoured vehicles steadily improved and light tanks found themselves at more and more of a disadvantage.

FAR EAST

Airborne operations in the Far East during the Second World War never approached the scale of those conducted in the European theatre, though they were, as usual, carried out with courage and determination. In early 1944 Major-General Orde Wingate wished to force the Japanese to withdraw from the whole of Burma north of the 24th Parallel. To do this he wished to fly the 3rd Indian Division behind enemy lines to the three landing strips nicknamed 'Broadway', 'Piccadilly' and 'Chowringhee'. This would be done in two stages, with twenty-six gliders flying to each airstrip in the first part and fourteen to each in the second.

On the day of the operation intelligence reached Wingate that 'Piccadilly' had been blocked with felled trees by the Japanese. His plans were immediately revised, and the number of gliders reduced from eighty to sixty. The first troops to arrive at the landing strips were the Pathfinders. At 'Broadway' Colonel Alison USAAF and his team were followed fifteen minutes later by Brigadier Calvert and Advance Headquarters, 77th Indian Infantry Brigade, who set oil-burning lamps to guide the gliders in. As the main body arrived the second body of gliders swung round and blocked the landing strip; the next group then crashed into them, killing two men and seriously injuring six others.

The strips at 'Broadway' and 'Chowringhee' were quickly secured and expanded, and very soon gliders and Dakotas were off-loading their contents inside enemy territory. By 11 March the first airborne landing was complete, 'Chowringhee' having been evacuated just before an aerial attack by Japanese Zeros and light bombers. By the middle of March three Long Range Penetration Brigades were established behind enemy lines.

It was now time for Phase 3 to begin: the airlift of the 14th British Infantry Brigade and 3rd West African Brigade to the Meza Valley. On 22 March the first six gliders landed on the new airstrip, codenamed 'Aberdeen'. However, owing to the Japanese offensive against the 4th Corps there was a shortage of transport aircraft, so the airlift into 'Aberdeen' dragged on for twenty days. Though the Japanese strafed the strip, the damage was fairly minimal. A much more serious loss was the death of Wingate himself on 24 March, which depressed everyone enormously. The 77th Indian Brigade had established a stronghold codenamed 'White City', which was now reinforced, including the extension of its airstrip. Throughout April supplies were flown into 'White City' while the Japanese tried in vain to destroy the site.

Regarding actual parachute drops in the Far East there is little to tell. One operation, codenamed 'Dracula', involved the clearing of the River Rangoon before an Allied amphibious assault against Rangoon itself. The parachute force was assembled from the 1st Indian Parachute Battalion and the 2nd Gurkha and 3rd Gurkha Parachute Battalions. The first drop was made 5 miles west of Elephant Point, and was completed in the early hours of 1 May 1945. There were no Japanese at the drop zone and thus the force was soon assembled. They were 3,000 yards from the target, but that did not prevent them from being bombed by the US Strategic Air Force, which inflicted some forty casualties.

The second drop went like clockwork, and the leading company reached Elephant Point at 1600 hours, and came under fire from an enemy machine-gun bunker and some small ships. The latter were knocked out by aircraft, but the bunker required an assault and a flamethrower before it succumbed.

On 3 May, leaving a detachment at Elephant Point, the battalion group moved up to Sadhaingmut, halfway up the west bank of the river. This march, in heavy rain and over paddy fields, took eleven hours. Three days later they were sent to Rangoon, and on 17 May embarked for India. The battalion had killed forty-three enemy soldiers and taken one prisoner. It had lost one officer and three other ranks killed, with the largest number of injuries being inflicted by Allied aircraft.

The 50th Indian Parachute Brigade was formed in Delhi in October 1941. It was later expanded until, by November 1944, it formed the nucleus of 2nd Indian Airborne Division with 77th Parachute Brigade and 14th Air-Landing Brigade. Units of this division were to play a vital part in the final defeat of the Japanese Army but outstanding in its heroism and in its consequences was the battle fought in March 1944 by 50th Indian Parachute Brigade in North Burma. Two divisions of the Japanese Army unexpectedly crossed the Chindwin river and marched against Imphal and Kohima as the first stage of their planned invasion of India.

Although on a training exercise in the Naga Hills at the time, the 50th Parachute Brigade, commanded by Brigadier Tim Hope Thomson, was hastily thrown into battle, with orders to delay the Japanese advance while Imphal and Kohima were reinforced. Although heavily outnumbered and wholly unsupported, Hope Thomson's brigade held out at the hill village of Sangshak for six days until ordered to fight its way out. This it did. The brigade paid its own very heavy price but in the course of its near destruction it had exacted a fearful toll on the enemy. Moreover the contribution it had made to the disruption and eventual defeat of the Japanese advance into India was of huge importance. In a special order of the day Lieutenant General 'Bill' Slim, General Officer Commanding 14th Army, wrote,

> There is not a division or brigade in the Fourteenth Army which has not proved its superiority over the enemy and knows it. Your Parachute Brigade bore the first brunt of the enemy's powerful flanking attack, and by their staunchness gave the garrison of Imphal the vital time required to adjust their defences.
>
> To the Officers and Men of the 50th Parachute Brigade I send my congratulations. The Fourteenth Army has inflicted on the Japanese the greatest defeat his army has ever suffered. He is busily trying to build up again and reinforce his broken divisions. He will fight again and viciously, but we have paid him something of what we owe. There still remains the interest. He will get it.

Post-War Operations: Palestine

Only a few months after the war in Europe had ended, the Paras found themselves in action again, this time manning a 'peace line' against Jewish terrorists whom, ironically, they had helped to liberate. The 6th Airborne Division went to Palestine in 1945 as an integral part of the Imperial Strategic Reserve for the Middle East, but the men soon found themselves deployed to the streets on internal security duties as violence flared up between Arab and Jewish communities.

With the Holocaust over, thousands of Jews sought refuge in Palestine, but a British White Paper, drawn up in 1939, had limited Jewish immigration to 75,000, a figure which was soon exhausted. To the Jews, the decision by the British to impose a restriction on the

Paratroopers make an arms find during operations in Palestine after the Second World War.

number of people entering their 'homeland' was inhuman and could only lead to conflict, with extremist groups committed to armed attacks against the security forces.

To the Paras, it was unbelievable: only months earlier their actions had helped to liberate the Jewish prisoners of war, and now they were being spat at and insulted by those very people. In November 1945 Jews in Tel Aviv organised a huge and ugly riot during which the 'Red Berets' were forced to return fire, causing casualties. It seemed a deliberate attempt to discredit the Paras and make them appear oppressors.

Several active terrorist groups, of which the Stern gang later became the most violent, began to ambush police patrols using the 'hit and run' tactics of guerrilla warfare. Bitterness deepened when the Stern gang shot dead seven paratroopers of 5th Parachute Battalion, gunning them down in cold blood. The Jews hated the 'Red Berets' and labelled them anti-Semitic. They also called them 'Karionets', their word for poppy . . . a red flower with a black heart. No Para enjoyed Palestine. As one officer recalled, 'It was very unrewarding and unreal for soldiers, most of whom had taken part in heavy fighting across Europe, to find themselves being attacked by these people. It should not be forgotten that the actions of airborne troops helped to secure the liberation of many Jews, yet they suddenly turned on us. I think that is what hurt most. So much of their hatred was directed at the soldier in the red beret. Yet we were not violent with them, in fact we went out of our way to calm the situation.'

After Palestine, in 1948, airborne forces were subjected to a major reformation, which resulted in a single parachute brigade being retained, comprising the 1st, 2nd and 3rd Battalions. It was named the 16th Independent Parachute Brigade, in respect of the wartime roles of the 1st and 6th Airborne Divisions, whose numbers formed the title of the new unit. A year later, all three battalions returned from Germany and established a permanent base at Aldershot. The depot was eventually named 'Browning Barracks' after the general of airborne forces. The first battle colours were presented to the regiment on 19 July 1950 by King George VI to all three battalions at the same time – this is believed to be a first in the history of the British Army.

MALAYA

Between 1948 and 1956 Communist terrorists had infiltrated into Malaya; they soon dominated the jungle terrain and 'brain-washed' whole communities. The Special Air Service was formed from Malayan Scouts to fight this new enemy at his own game. When in 1954 the SAS completed its tour of duty, General Sir Geoffrey Bourne recommended that a parachute battalion be invited to supply a force of volunteers to fight in the jungle.

The War Office agreed and the eighty officers and men of the Parachute Regiment formed the Independent Parachute Squadron and served with distinction until April 1957, when they sailed home on the SS *Nevasa*. This was a busy period in the regiment's history, for trouble also flared up in Cyprus in January 1956, when the EOKA terrorists began their campaign of terror to free the island from British rule.

Only months after the end of the war paratroopers found themselves in Palestine facing hostile abuse from people they had helped liberate.

The 3rd Battalion prepare for Operation 'Musketeer' in Cyprus as RQMS Chippy Robinson, left, and Lance-Corporal John Morrison fit parachutes on the night of 4/5 November 1956.

6. THE SUEZ CONFLICT

OPERATION 'MUSKETEER'

The Suez crisis saw the first postwar operational drop by the Parachute Regiment and it highlighted the value of maintaining a highly trained force that could move swiftly into action, at a time when the political agenda was focused on a reduction of airborne forces and their assets. Operation 'Musketeer' would remind the decision-makers that the airborne capability was a role that should be retained within the British Army.

In July 1956 President Nasser of Egypt nationalised the Suez Canal and denied free access to ships of all nations. This was Nasser's response after Western powers withdrew their offer to fund the Aswan Dam project in Egypt. (Following the closure of the canal, Nasser impounded the Suez Canal Company, which was jointly owned by Britain and France and generated $35 million a year, and used its funds to finance the Aswan Dam project.) The West had expressed concerns about Soviet influence in Egypt and had become convinced that the Egyptians, who were already receiving arms from Eastern Europe, were about to join the Eastern Bloc.

Then the Israelis mounted a successful offensive against the Egyptians, pursuing them across the Sinai desert, where an Israeli parachute battalion dropped to cut them off at the Mitla Pass. It was clear that the fighting would soon affect the Canal Zone and both the British and French governments, the principal shareholders in the Suez Canal Company, issued ultimatums for both sides to draw back. The Israelis, still in hot pursuit, agreed, but the Egyptians refused. Consequently the British and French governments informed the United Nations that if fighting broke out around the canal they would be forced to intervene.

The growing tension in the region had resulted in the 2nd Battalion Parachute Regiment and the remainder of the 16th Parachute Brigade being flown to Cyprus in July to join the 1st and 3rd Battalions who were already on the island, deployed on internal security operations. In August the 1st and 3rd Battalions were flown back to the UK for parachute training as neither battalion had jumped for eleven months. When they returned to Cyprus ten days later they took with them a number of reservists who had been called up to face the threat of action in Egypt. Further training took place in Cyprus to prepare for any deployment and in late October 1956 plans for Operation 'Musketeer' were ready. The plan was based on an amphibious assault, supported by relatively small numbers of British and French parachute troops. The problem for the British force centred on the lack of aircraft:

On the ground at El Gamil airfield men of 'A' Company the 3rd Battalion the Parachute Regiment prepare to clear buildings around the airport.

in just ten years since the end of the Second World War the neglect of airborne forces was apparent.

On 31 October 1956, the British and French air force began attacks on Egyptian air bases and virtually destroyed her air wing in forty-eight hours. The seaborne landings were timed to begin on 6 November and were to coincide with the airborne drop, but at the last moment the parachute assault was brought forward by twenty-four hours. This meant that the joint Anglo-French drop would not be able to call on naval gunfire support, and instead Royal Navy strike aircraft would be available for fire missions, if required.

In the early hours of 5 November, the 3rd Battalion Parachute Regiment fitted their parachutes and boarded their aircraft. At 0415 hours they lifted off from Nicosia airfield in Cyprus bound for Egypt. Headed by Lieutenant-Colonel Paul Crook, 660 men jumped at Suez. Although they were well trained and ready for action they were at something of a disadvantage. There was a lack of good equipment: the outdated Sten gun and bolt action rifles were still in service and their 106 mm recoilless anti-tank guns were elderly. The RAF still did not have a suitable fleet of transport aircraft for parachuting and as such the thirty-two aircraft assigned to the operation included a combination of eighteen Valettas and seven Hastings transporting the troops, and another seven Hastings carrying the heavy drop. The Hastings had been designed in 1939 while the Valetta was not suitable for parachuting because its main spar ran across the fuselage creating a small barrier inside the aircraft, which the last half of the stick had to scramble over before they could jump.

The jeeps were loaded on to platforms and secured under the Hastings, where they were rigged to a beam in the bomb bay. This external load system, which hung in the slipstream, was very crude and cut down the flying endurance of an aircraft. In addition it made it difficult for the dispatch crew inside the aircraft to release palettes from the beam cleanly.

Operation 'Musketeer' involved about 80,000 men, spearheaded by the British 16th Independent Parachute Brigade, commanded by Brigadier M.A.H. Butler DSO, MC, and 3 Commando Brigade, Royal Marines. The French forces were troops from the 10th Parachute Division and 7th Mechanised Division, both fresh from service in Algeria.

The British force would jump on to El Gamil airfield near Port Said, while the French 2nd Colonial Parachute Regiment (2 RPC) was to seize the two bridges at

The airfield from the air at El Gamil where 3 Para dropped in November 1956.

Paratroopers of the 3rd Battalion seize the airfield at El Gamil during Operation 'Musketeer'.

Raswa, connecting Port Said with the Egyptian mainland. On the next day, an amphibious assault spearheaded by 3 Commando Brigade, Royal Marines, and the 1st Foreign Legion Parachute Regiment (1 REP) would land on either side of the canal and forge inland to reinforce the paratroops.

The drop zone on which the battalion would land was to present problems for the commanding officer and the RAF. Gamil airfield lay on a narrow spit of land with beaches and the sea on its northern edge and a large inland lake to the south. This clearly indicated the need to approach on an east/west axis, but a mile to the east there was a small dockyard which was, according to intelligence reports, packed with anti-aircraft units. No pilot wanted to fly at low level over such a threat. An alternative was to approach from the west at dawn, flying in tight formation, but this meant flying straight into the sun – a tactic not favoured by pilots. But the commanders favoured this option, and in an effort to camouflage the aircraft from the bright rays of the rising sun a large quantity of gentian violet – a blue-coloured medication – was procured from a local hospital and painted on the aircraft – and it worked very well.

Tactically it was a key requirement of the plan to get the entire force on the ground within four and half minutes, but this was an unusual drop zone. The strip of land was just a mile long and very narrow, therefore aircraft would fly in a tight formation with following aircraft slightly higher than the leaders so as not to fly into parachutists already in the sky. The RAF meteorologist highlighted the danger of cross-winds and it was clear that a drop at 1,000 ft might result in some soldiers drifting into the sea. It was therefore decided that 700 ft would be the ceiling.

A further move which was not popular with the battalion was the decision not to wear reserve parachutes. The reserve parachute had been introduced after the war (in 1955) and many of the battalion's soldiers had never jumped without one, but they only worked if the dropping height was above 1,000 ft – so the commanding officer gave the order 'no reserves'.

Just before Lieutenant-Colonel Crook boarded his aircraft in Cyprus he was handed the latest intelligence report. It indicated that the drop zone was littered with what looked like anti-personnel mines, which could all too easily pin down the battalion at El Gamil. Bravely, Crook opted to go in, and when the men landed they found that the 'mines' were in fact oil-drums. But the beaches *were* strewn with mines, and well-sited machine-guns covered the whole area.

Crook's plan dictated that 'A' Company would drop at the western end of the

Paratroopers strip down a jeep from its platform at the El Gamil airfield.

airfield to seal it off. 'C' Company was to seize the southern perimeter and 'B' Company was to gain control in the east in preparation for the advance into Port Said itself. In support of the companies, Crook had elements of the 33rd Parachute Light Regiment, Royal Artillery, a field surgical team and an RAF forward air control team and teams from the 9th Independent Parachute Squadron, Royal Engineers and the Guards Independent Parachute Company – both of whom also had detachments with the French at Raswa. Defending the airstrip was a battalion of Egyptian troops and a number of National Guardsmen with four SU-100 self-propelled guns. All were believed to be dug in and El Gamil was expected to be well defended.

The normal procedure of inserting a Pathfinder force to locate and mark the beginning and end of the drop zone was clearly not possible on an occupied airfield. Instead a Canberra aircraft was to adopt the role of Pathfinder aircraft and would drop a smoke flare to mark the jump point of the first wave of paratroops before circling around to lead the main force into the DZ. Inside their aircraft the men of the 3rd Battalion were no doubt anxious about what to expect on the ground. All were mindful of the last advice given to them by their parachute jump instructors: 'keep your feet and knees together.'

Men of 3 Para pictured minutes after they had seized the airfield.

Lieutenant-Colonel Paul Crook, commanding officer, with TAC HQ pictured on 6 November. A captured Egyptian tank can be seen in the background.

P-hour, the exact time that the parachute drop commences, was 0715 hours and as the assault started and the drop began anti-aircraft fire hammered into the sky. Of the twenty-six aircraft carrying the battalion nine were hit by fire. The medical officer, Captain Sandy Cavenagh, was hit in the eye by a splinter of shrapnel when a shell came through the equipment container hanging below him, cutting its suspension cord. Major Geoff Norton, commander of the support company, found himself all but entangled in severed rigging lines as machine-gun fire slashed through his canopy. One sapper's parachute was shredded by an anti-aircraft round and he broke both legs on landing. Another soldier, Private Neal from Medical Section, landed in the sewage farm and a third man, Private Lamph, landed in the sea. (Lamph's landing was later used in a humorous context when the battalion claimed that as well as being first in by air, they were first in by sea – Private Lamph having achieved an amphibious landing.) However, the force was on the ground and forming up well within seven minutes. On the drop zone the Egyptians reacted swiftly, directing firepower on to the Paras who went straight into action and within fifteen minutes of P-hour the first of the planned Fleet Air Arm air strikes came in against prearranged targets.

As the buildings burned thick black smoke choked the sky over the DZ and by 0745 hours the airfield was in British hands. 'A' Company had quickly occupied the control tower as Sergeant Legg led the assault. This team came under fire from an Egyptian machine-gun position at the western end of the airfield. A platoon commanded by 2nd Lieutenant Peter Coates attacked the position, killing two Egyptians and taking nine prisoners. 'B' Company had landed almost on top of an Egyptian position and encountered an immediate and fierce firefight. Several soldiers were hit by enemy fire but Major Dick Stevens, the company commander, quickly rallied his men and they launched an immediate assault on the Egyptian positions.

Private Looker had been near the end of his stick and drifted dangerously close to the Egyptian troops. As he headed straight for an enemy position one particularly keen defender climbed out of his slit trench to get a better shot at the helpless paratrooper as he swung below his canopy. But Looker was saved as his container, oscillating like a 120 lb pendulum, knocked the Egyptian back into his hole just in time for the British soldier to land on top of him. The story made headline news in the British Army's *Soldier* magazine.

While 'B' Company cleared the buildings and the water-tower at the eastern end, smashing the heavily defended pillbox on the south-eastern perimeter which had caused so many casualties at the start of the drop, 'A' Company, who had taken the control tower, secured their area while the south side of the airfield was cleared by 'C' Company. Headquarters and 'D' Companies (the latter consisting of an assortment of cooks, clerks and storemen formed into a fighting reserve force, in accordance with the regiment's insistence that every man in the battalion should be a trained paratrooper) collected the heavy drop equipment and set up both Lieutenant-Colonel Crook's headquarters and a rudimentary headquarters for Brigadier Butler, the brigade commander who had also jumped with the battalion.

With the initial objectives secured, 'B' Company, with 5 Platoon in the lead and supported by a medium machine-gun section, advanced forward towards the area of the sewage farm. 4 Platoon, led by Lieutenant Chris Hogg, advanced through an area of thick reeds and cleared some snipers before occupying a group of farm buildings. As the platoon continued its advance it came under fire from Egyptians dug in around the cemetery. The men were ordered to withdraw and as they did so two French Mystère fighters saw them below and made a strafing run which had the platoon diving into the sewage for safety. The pilots had not realised the Paras had advanced so far forward and the French liaison officer quickly directed them to engage ordered targets only.

6 Platoon advanced to the left-hand side of the farm while plans were made for 'C' Company to attack the cemetery. At 1028 hours an air strike by Sea Venoms and Sea Hawks was launched against the enemy position in and around the cemetery. Two minutes after the air strike 'C' Company, supported by mortars and machine-gun fire, attacked. The fighting was intense and at one point the CO came close to being shot dead, when an Egyptian stood up from behind a gravestone and aimed his rifle at him. But before he could take aim Ray Issit, the CO's bodyguard, opened up with his Sten and fired a burst, killing the Egyptian instantly. During this action Major Stevens had been wounded twice, once in the hand and in the leg. But it was not until his leg was shattered that he agreed to be evacuated – he was later awarded the Military Cross for his leadership and courage.

Back at the airfield's control tower, despite an Egyptian SU-100 self-propelled gun that had found the range, the Headquarters staff set about organising the next stage of the assault. Naval helicopters had already flown casualties out of the airfield and 9 Parachute Squadron had cleared the runways of the empty oil-drums used by the Egyptians to block them. Colonel de Fouquières, the French commander's liaison officer, now arrived in a Dakota, ignoring the mortar and machine-gun fire which periodically raked the airfield; after a short conference with Brigadier Butler, he took off again for Akrotiri bearing eight more casualties and 3 Para's medical officer, Sandy Cavenagh, who had been ordered to leave.

As 'C' Company fought eastwards it came under fire from a block of flats on the outskirts of Port Said. However, repeated air strikes had eroded Egyptian morale, and the four SU-100 self-propelled guns which had shelled El Gamil and were based in the defended apartment block had been abandoned by the crews. But machine-gun fire from nearby flats was holding up the company's advance. Lieutenant Mike Newall, commanding the Machine-Gun Platoon, spotted both the guns in ground-floor flats and noticed an abandoned Bren-gun carrier lying in no-man's-land. Leaving his platoon, for whom he had been scouting out better fire positions, he ran to the carrier through a storm of fire and, assisted by a 'C' Company sergeant, got the vehicle started. The two men drove straight at the machine-gun post, overran it and returned in triumph to what they thought was the front line. But the company had been under sniper fire for some time and knew that there was no British armour for miles; on hearing the carrier coming down the road, 'B' Company's anti-tank detachment prepared for action, the first ranging shot from their spotting rifle hitting the carrier fair and square. Only a quick-witted NCO prevented two men being killed.

As D-Day came to an end, 'C' Company pulled back to the airfield, leaving 'B' Company to hold any Egyptian attacks at the sewage farm. Next day the Paras expected to see a major naval bombardment to mark the beginning of the second stage of the operation, the amphibious assault on Port Said. All the 3rd Battalion's objectives had been secured, and their comrades in the French 2nd Colonial Parachute Regiment had completed their tasks at Port Fuad with typical panache.

Their commander, Colonel Conan, had made telephone contact with the Egyptian commander, El Moguy, and was confident that a surrender could be negotiated without further military action. Conan therefore ordered all air strikes to cease at 1700 hours. Brigadier Butler took a helicopter to join Conan in the French positions, and from 1800 to about 2030 hours an uneasy peace reigned. During the night the Paras remained in a high state of readiness, sentries were posted and patrols mounted, but the Egyptians were quiet and this gave the Paras their first opportunity to grab a meal and get some sleep.

The Egyptian commander had been able to speak to President Nasser on one of the lines the Paras had not destroyed and had been told not to surrender. Nasser had in fact told El Moguy that the Russians were coming to assist him and they would counter the Anglo-French assault.

Post Suez, the
Paras continued to
operate in the
Middle East. Here,
men of 'B'
Company the 3rd
Battalion the
Parachute
Regiment in the
mountainous
terrain of Radfan.
The regiment
fought here in the
early 1960s and
was the last British
Army regiment to
leave Aden in
November 1967,
ending 127 years
of British rule.

Men of 'B' Company 3 Para in Radfan. One member of the section can be seen using the 'scope of his sniper weapon to view down the valley. After Suez, the Paras would face operations in the Middle East as well as the mountainous terrain of Radfan and Aden.

At first light the next day, 6 November, 3 Para was attacked by a Russian MiG fighter and one soldier was injured. It was a 'one-off' incident regarded as little more than a show of strength by the Russian Air Force against world opinion.

Later that morning the battalion deployed in support of the amphibious invasion of the port. Following a series of air strikes and a naval bombardment of the beach-head, 40 and 42 Commandos Royal Marines hit the beaches just before 0700 hours, with 3 Para's medium machine-guns helping to give the Marines a clear run from their craft.

A little later, 45 Commando Royal Marines landed by helicopter in the town, while the 1st Foreign Legion Parachute Regiment came ashore alongside Port Said's eastern breakwater. Elements of 3 Para were in action throughout the day, patrolling and securing areas, and, as night fell, the 2nd Battalion the Parachute Regiment came ashore with a squadron of Centurion tanks. Joined by the brigadier, 2 Para forged out to El Cap, 19 miles down the Suez Canal, and at 2359 hours the Egyptians agreed to a ceasefire.

World opinion against the invasion force now forced Britain and France to withdraw. The men of the 3rd Battalion the Parachute Regiment had achieved everything that had been asked of them and the mission had been a total military success. The battalion sustained forty casualties and lost four men in the assault against a force which was equipped with much better weapons and equipment. Fortunately the Paras were well trained, very fit, well led and highly motivated.

THE MIDDLE EAST

The continued unrest in Cyprus called for increased internal security duties against EOKA in February 1957, with the 2nd Battalion Parachute Regiment remaining on the island while the 1st and 3rd Battalions returned to Aldershot. In 1958, 16 Para Brigade was flown at short notice to Cyprus as civil war broke out in Lebanon. In the event,

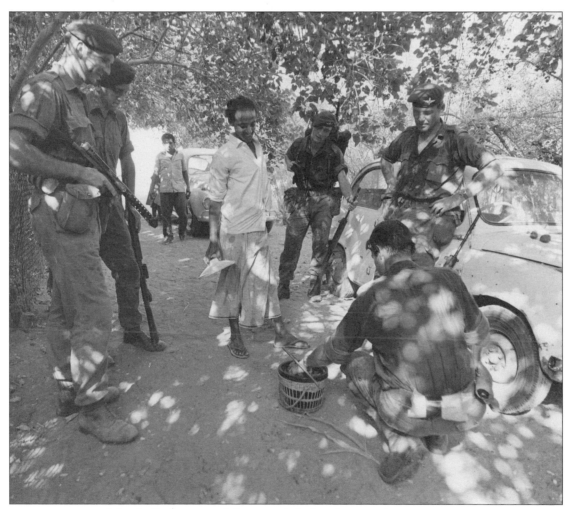

Paratroopers search local villagers around the area of Sheik Othman, Aden, 1967.

American forces were deployed in Lebanon, but within days King Hussein of Jordan asked Britain for assistance following a *coup* in Iraq which threatened Jordan. The brigade was flown into Amman to secure the airport and support King Hussein, and they remained there for three months. Their presence alone had averted further trouble.

In June 1961 the Paras, together with their cousins in the Royal Marines, were deployed as a deterrent force on the border of Kuwait, after Iraq threatened to invade the oil-rich country. Again, their presence was enough to avoid conflict and for the next six years, until 1967, parachute battalions were to be based in the Persian Gulf area as a 'fire brigade' force, ready to react to any conflict in the region. For the first time the Paras were able to take their wives and families with them, based in sunny Bahrain.

Earlier, in 1964, an escalation of trouble in Cyprus, now an independent state, saw 1 Para move in to support a United Nations peace-keeping force, the men replacing their red berets for the first time since 1942, with the light blue of the UN. The battalion was awarded the UN medal and today British troops are still supporting the United Nations force in Cyprus.

Para engineers on United Nations operations in Cyprus, where British troops are still serving today, wearing the blue berets of the UN.

The pack howitzers of 7 Para the Royal Horse Artillery in action in Radfan.

ADEN AND RADFAN

The small British protectorate of Aden on the southern tip of Saudi Arabia first saw conflict in 1964, when the people of Radfan, a tiny state some 60 miles north of Aden, became increasingly influenced by the nationalist Arab movements going on around them. In Radfan, Quteibi, Ibdali and Bakri tribes traditionally supplemented their income by ambushing travellers on the Dhala road which connected Aden to the state of Yemen. Now, with the support of extremists known as the Aden National Liberation Front (NLF), the tribesmen were armed and willing to join the struggle to force the British to withdraw from the colony.

Their activities provoked a swift response. Men of the 'B' Company 3rd Battalion the Parachute Regiment joined 45 Commando Royal Marines and the Federal Regular Army in an operation known as 'Radforce', which set out to dominate the Dhanaba Basin and secure the village of El Naqil.

The initial plan called for a night drop by 'B' Company on a key feature codenamed 'Cap Badge'. But the jump was cancelled and instead they spent thirty exhausting hours marching and fighting to take their target. In recognition of their success, they renamed El Naqil 'Pegasus village' and then, along with 45 Commando, they withdrew to Aden.

This was the first of many assaults into the mountains to put down the Arab rebellion. A reserve brigade was flown into Aden as well as the remainder of 3 Para – then based in Bahrain to counter Iraq's threatened invasion of Kuwait – to support the success of 'B' Company and the Royal Marines. In one brilliantly planned operation, Lieutenant-Colonel Farrar-Hockley led the 3rd Battalion to capture Bakri Ridge in May 1964. His battalion included 105 mm guns from 7 Parachute Regiment, Royal Horse Artillery, sappers from 9 Independent Parachute Squadron, Royal Engineers, and medics from 23 Parachute Field Ambulance.

But by 1964 the terrorist attacks had spread to Aden, south of Radfan, and the 1st Battalion Parachute Regiment was deployed on security duties throughout the areas of Crater and Khormasker, to protect British service families living in those areas. Here they mounted security patrols, escorted British service children to school and manned observation posts, called 'sangars'.

Later, in January 1967, the 1st Battalion the Parachute Regiment was back in Aden, this time on an emergency tour to relieve the Royal Anglian Regiment at Sheik Othman, the key entry point to Aden from the mountains of Radfan. By now terrorist attacks were at their height and all military families had been sent back to England. Military married quarters had been bombed, cinemas blown up and schools shot at, resulting in many British casualties. A large part of the British forces in the province had also been sent back to the UK as plans were laid for the eventual withdrawal of British forces from Aden.

At Sheik Othman, the men of the 1st Battalion found themselves under a hail of fire within days of the battalion officially taking over on 1 June – a day which was to become known in the regiment as 'the glorious first of June'. That day Arab gunmen had launched a substantial assault against the unit to test the Para's resources and attempted to overrun Sheik Othman, but they had not taken into account a series of concealed observation posts heavily manned by Paras. In the battle that followed, the Paras killed sixteen terrorists, destroying the plans of both guerrilla groups – National Liberation Front (NLF) and the Forced Liberation of South Yemen (FLOSY) – to take control of Sheik Othman. Shooting, bombing and rocket attacks continued right up until the battalion was given the order to 'pull out'; they marched six abreast out of Radfan camp, with their weapons still loaded, on 27 November 1967, ending 128 years of British rule in Aden.

Earlier in 1964 the 2nd Battalion had been sent to Singapore for jungle warfare training, after Indonesia had threatened to invade the Malaysian state of Borneo. The remainder of the unit followed in March 1965, and moved direct to the Indonesian border.

A month later one of the biggest battles of the war took place when an Indonesian battalion attacked 'B' Company of the 2nd Battalion Parachute Regiment. More than

In the early part of 1969 trouble broke out on the island of Anguila in the Caribbean, when elements of the population objected to their country joining a federation with other islands in the area. The 2nd Battalion the Parachute Regiment, commanded by Lieutenant-Colonel Richard Dawney, was sent to the island with 120 members of London's Metropolitan Police to restore order. The battalion, less 'B' Company, was flown to Antigua where it boarded two frigates and landed by Gemini assault craft just before dawn on 19 March. Peace was quickly restored and the battalion later returned to the UK.

Paratroopers with a GPMG and lines of ammunition ready for action during the conflict in Radfan.

A Parachute Regiment patrol returns to its base camp in Radfan.

fifty Indonesians were killed, and the Paras lost two men with seven injured. This short but intense Far East deployment ended in July, the battalion having been awarded eight decorations including two Military Medals.

In the same year the 3rd Battalion was sent into Guiana on internal security duties as the country prepared for independence. The next operation for the Paras was to be in 1969, when the 2nd Battalion was sent to Anguila after an armed insurrection on the Caribbean island. The men had been briefed to expect an opposed landing, but there was no resistance and instead the battalion spent six months helping the local community, for which they won the Wilkinson Sword of Peace – an achievement award made by the Wilkinson company every year to the regiment who most helps the community in humanitarian operations or peace work.

'P' Company test. A snake of recruits pictured during the 10-mile run makes its way across the Yorkshire countryside at Catterick.

7. THE MAKING OF A PARA

The philosophy of success for airborne troops is based on the belief that there is nothing they cannot achieve. This self-confidence is developed during the physical selection process to serve with airborne forces, and instils a determination to win alongside the knowledge that their training will sustain them for the physical challenges of combat. There are no second chances in battle and the Parachute Regiment's high standards of military professionalism and physical fitness have ensured success throughout the regiment's history. Airborne troops are used as an advance force to parachute ahead of the ground force and secure key areas. As such they must be self-sufficient in the early days of the operation and resolute in their attack until the battle is won.

This tenacious fighting spirit was recognised in North Africa during the Second World War by the Germans, who feared the British paratroops and dubbed them 'Red Devils'. Throughout the postwar years the reputation and capability of the Parachute Regiment ensured that it was deployed across the globe, playing key roles at Suez as well as in Malaya and Aden. Its ability to deploy at short notice anywhere in the world and mount effective military operations in remote and rugged areas where armour cannot be deployed were key factors in airborne forces being selected as a major player in the battle group tasked to retake the Falkland Islands in 1982, Operation 'Corporate'. Physically fit and well-trained personnel react well under pressure and the high professional standards maintained by the Airborne Brigade to meet any global crisis ensured that it was selected as a core component of the Joint Rapid Deployment Force (JRDF).

'P' COMPANY AND THE PRE-PARACHUTE SELECTION COURSE

Before any officer or soldier can serve with the airborne forces he must pass the ultimate litmus test of military fitness within the British Army – the pre-parachute selection training course which decides whether he's got what it takes to become a paratrooper or not. The Pre-Parachute Selection Company, better known as 'P' Company, has its roots in the wartime Training Company of the Depot School Airborne Forces, which was established in 1941 at Hardwick Hall in Derbyshire. Commanded by a major, 'P' Company is a small organisation, comprising a company sergeant major and four instructors: four NCOs from the Parachute Regiment and one from 7 Parachute Regiment, Royal Horse Artillery.

During the 1960s and up to the early 1990s 'P' Company training took place at the

The training starts to prepare recruits to Catterick for the 'P' Company selection course. Here a recruit ploughs through the assault course.

Parachute Regiment Depot in Aldershot. Here new recruits enlisted straight into the Parachute Regiment and as such could be 'groomed' from day one and physically prepared for the demands of test week. If any recruit showed insufficient physical ability for selection he was invited to re-badge into another regiment. Following the Conservative Defence Minister's 'Option for Change' announcement in 1992 regimental depots across the UK were reorganised; the Parachute Regiment's Depot at Aldershot was closed and training of soldiers centralised. In June 1993 580 Platoon made history as the last course to pass out at Browning barracks and marched off the parade ground to join the 2nd Battalion on active service in Northern Ireland. Lieutenant-General Sir Michael Gray, then Colonel Commandant, took the salute at the last parade, ending an era for the regiment. New recruits to the Parachute Regiment now arrive at the Army Training Regiment in Lichfield in the Midlands where they join 'B' (the Parachute Regiment) Company and complete the Common Military Syllabus (CMS), the basic skills required of all soldiers. The final parade was attended by hundreds of veterans including Brigadier James Hill, the Second World War commander of 3 Parachute Brigade. Former Para John Morrison, who trained at the regiment's original Aldershot

Recruits pictured during a 10-mile tab. A tab is the Parachute Regiment term for covering distances at speed on foot. Carrying their bergan backpack and fighting order, which contains rifle magazines and personal equipment, these recruits are taking a 30-second break. Recruits have to run like racehorses to meet the qualification times set by the instructors, there are no prizes for the 'winners' and little sympathy for those who fail to make the time.

The ultimate test of courage. Two recruits are put into the ring and ordered to box for 1 minute. Maximum aggression is required to obtain good marks.

depot in Maida Barracks and jumped into Suez in 1957 with the 3rd Battalion, said he was very much saddened at the closure of Browning Barracks as the training depot.

At Lichfield the instructors at 'B' Company have adapted the syllabus to take into account the special training of airborne forces and after ten weeks the successful recruits move on to the Infantry Training Battalion at Catterick where they join the Parachute Regiment Company to complete the Combat Infantryman's Course (CIC) of eleven weeks.

At Catterick the aim of the 'P' Company staff is the same as it was at Hardwick Hall in the 1940s and the Commanding Officer tells every new squad in simple terms what the course is all about: '"P" Company is designed to test physical courage, military attitude, fitness and determination under stress to determine whether a soldier has the self-discipline and motivation to become an airborne soldier.' During their time at 'P' Company the recruits will probably clock up several hundred miles training for the

'P' Company test. Pass or fail this is the ultimate confidence tester. Recruits must climb to the top, then stand on the scaffolding bars and walk across the shuffle bars.

'P' Company. All aspects of the confidence course demand courage and confidence from the student.

Tabbing – marching and running at speed with a bergan over rough and hilly terrain – is a basic element of the parachute selection course. These recruits are nearing the top of Penn-y-fan in the Brecon training area.

At the 7-mile mark these potential recruits are tired and exhausted. No matter how physically fit they are, the mental ability to keep running when others might give up is vital.

An officer on the pre-parachute selection course carries out 'running repairs' to his feet after a long tab.

selection tests – but spare a thought for the instructors who run the courses and complete the same routes week after week. In 1997 it was pointed out that one instructor at Catterick went through seventeen pairs of boots and clocked up 2,300 miles in two-and-a-half years – the equivalent of running eighty-eight marathons.

Official records show that since 1955 more than 20,000 officers, NCOs and soldiers have passed through 'P' Company, joining a small and distinguished club for those who have passed the course. The course at Catterick is held in three different packages for recruits, all arms and the Territorial Army – but the tests are the same. The gruelling selection standards of 'P' Company are designed to teach soldiers to fight beyond what may be regarded as the basic acceptable standards, to push men to their physical limits and develop individuals with the inner confidence and mental strength to keep going even when exhausted.

The 'P' Company package is split into two sections, the build-up and

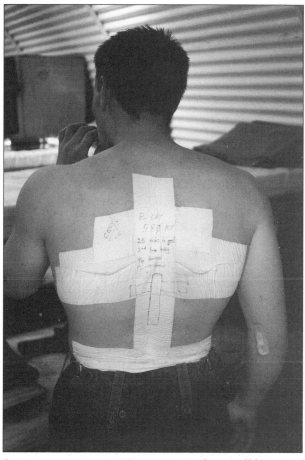

Injuries are common. Here a recruit shows off his taped back which has suffered from skin burn where his bergan has rubbed during long runs.

the test phase. In the initial stage trainees run every morning, followed by a session in the gymnasium to build up their strength and stamina. During the afternoon they carry out a 'tab' with a rucksack (known to the recruits as a bergan), as well as carrying a rifle. Tabbing is a Parachute Regiment term for covering distances by running on the flat and downhill and walking uphill as fast as possible. During 'P' Company training the word 'tabbing' is used regularly and is never forgotten by recruits, many of whom suffer 'bergan burns' on their backs and blistered feet during long tabs.

Each student on the course is given a number and recruits wear red T-shirts while officers wear white. Each morning they must appear on parade immaculate. Some crafty recruits only half-fill their water bottles in a hopeless attempt to carry less weight – forgetting that the instructors know all the tricks! Instructors always encourage the recruits, but for those who are caught attempting to cheat the system

'P' Company test. The log race is a vital event on the course which demands maximum effort.

The pain starts to show as recruits push themselves on the 10-miler.

Pass or fail. The course Sergeant Major makes a few notes at the end of the assault course phase. Nobody will know how they have done until the last day of the course.

there are penalties, such as having to carry a couple of bricks for the day. This tough lesson will, it is hoped, ensure that the entire squad is primed and ready for test week.

In the 1970s and '80s training teams were tough with recruits and it was commonplace to see recruits being yelled at; one officer remarked that this was a form of 'expressive encouragement'. As society changes in the 1990s the Parachute Regiment has modified its attitude towards training, and today encouragement is still there but in a quieter form. A senior Parachute Regiment officer said:

> Society has changed and as such we are recruiting people who have totally different values and attitudes to those young men of the 1970s and '80s. Young men sign up to serve with the Parachute Regiment and if we can we want to give them every encouragement to get through the course.
>
> If someone has not got the potential then they will probably not get past the initial selection, but in the 1990s recruits are in short supply and we can no longer afford to sack a man just because he falls out of a run. Recruits today do not appear to have the same mettle as those who joined ten and twenty years ago.
>
> Having said that, we cannot afford to lower our standards – if a recruit refuses an obstacle on the *tranasium* then he will fail. We can encourage and help, but we cannot do the test for them. If a man refuses to tackle part of the training, he could refuse to jump and that could threaten a parachute operation.

Success for 580 Platoon, the last selection course to complete training at the Parachute Regiment depot in Aldershot. Here they prepare to toast the Queen and the Colonel-in-Chief, Prince Charles.

The Colonel-in-Chief of the Parachute Regiment, HRH Prince Charles, during his parachute training at Brize Norton in the mid-1980s.

There are ten tests to be faced in selection test week and while recruits may become aware of the routes, the optimum time for each event is a closely guarded secret. The reason for this is that points are awarded in respect of each man's time and, in the time-honoured phrase, 'points win prizes'. If a man does not achieve sufficient points he fails. To add to the psychological stress, the men's watches are removed before the start of test week and everyone is warned not to wear one during the timed tests. During the the 'P' Company test week recruits constantly run against the watch, so taking watches off trainees simply adds to the mental pressure of not allowing them to judge time and distance. They have no idea how long they have been running or how

The new low-level parachute (LLP), developed by Irvin. The bulb-shaped canopy is in full operational service with Britain's airborne forces and provides the capability to deploy a force from a height of just 250 ft, sufficiently low to allow the aircraft to evade radar. In training and brigade-level exercises the parachute is used at 800 ft but trials have taken place to prove that the lower capability is effective. In the late 1990s Britain was the only country in the world to pioneer such a system.

far. Each man's bergan must weigh 45 lb and at the start of test week they will be carefully weighed, with random checks throughout the week.

To reveal the times would reduce the mental stress deliberately put on the recruits, but one former 'P' Company instructor made a point of telling his trainees to get 'plenty of sleep and cover your feet in Vaseline before a run or long tab – it will prevent blisters. Some people used to soak their feet in white spirit to harden the soles, but if they crack open you have got serious problems.'

The tests include a 10-mile battle march wearing helmets and carrying bergans and rifle. The carrying strap is removed from the weapon to ensure that soldiers hold the weapon in the 'ready' position as they would do in combat. The confidence test in which recruits climb across a scaffolding tower 48 ft above the ground, called the *tranasium*, is a vital pass or fail test. Having crossed a series of aerial 'runways' the recruit finds himself standing at the apex of the obstacles. Here, alone, he must climb up on to two bars and shuffle along them. In the middle his feet will hit a small obstacle which forces him to hold his balance and lift his feet; then he must shout his name, rank and number to the instructor. The 'shuffle bars' have been the downfall of many potential Paras, no matter how fit, since mental confidence is what is required. One instructor described the shuffle bars as a simple test of nerve. 'It is not hard and it's not painful, you just need to show a little "bottle". If you fail the shuffle bars then you are not much good to the Parachute Regiment.'

Another important test is the assault course. Recruits wearing helmets, in fighting order with weapons, face a combination of climbing frames and obstacles as well as water-filled ditches around a course which must be completed several times within a set period. There is also a sprint around two laps of a cross-country course, carried out in running kit, again within a set time.

Milling must be faced by all officers and men alike. It requires students to put on a pair of boxing gloves, get into the ring and hammer each other for one minute. An aggressive and determined attitude scores points here. Airborne troops are a 'first-in force' who may need to use personal aggression to succeed without any supporting arms to call on. In the Falklands the Paras were on their own and their aggressive spirit ensured their victory.

Teams of eight recruits are pitted against one another for the log race. The route is hilly and across open countryside. The aim is to develop team work as the men race as fast as possible over the 1½ mile course – despite the overwhelming desire of every team member to lie down and quit. Another team event is the stretcher race. Teams of twelve carry a 160 lb metal stretcher for 6 miles. This is the final event and it illustrates the black humour of the Parachute Regiment instructors who first introduced it. Initially designed to simulate carrying ammunition from the drop zone to the front line, in reality most recruits feel they need a stretcher themselves at the end of the event.

The big 'tabs', the 12 and 18 mile battle marches, must be completed within set times. They represent approach marches to a target by airborne soldiers who have just parachuted on to a drop zone. Both 'tabs' encounter hilly countryside and cover ground at a fast pace. In 1996 one determined recruit whose Achilles tendon was inflamed strapped his ankle for the 18-miler, which happened to be his last event.

> I can recall after what I thought was about ten minutes this burning sensation started eating up my left leg. I knew my tendon was about to go, but if I dropped out I would have had to start another course from the beginning. I could feel every pebble on the ground as my foot pounded the deck then, after a period of immense pain, perhaps twenty minutes, the heat disappeared and I can only presume my body had reacted to the pain. I couldn't feel a thing.
>
> Then at the end of the tab, I felt as though my body was on fire. I had to cut the laces to get my boot off, and I limped around for some weeks. But I passed, and that was all that mattered at the time.

All recruits to the territorial battalions of the Parachute Regiment are required to undergo the same tests in the same times as the regulars, and their selection takes place over several training weekends before they depart for two weeks at Catterick.

THE JUMPS COURSE: NO. 1 PARACHUTE TRAINING SCHOOL RAF

In life there are times when you should listen and learn, and others when perhaps you can afford to ignore some of the details. At the RAF's Parachute Training School recruits need to absorb *everything* they are told and ensure they understand it fully. This is reinforced by the unit's motto – 'Knowledge Dispels Fear'.

In 1946 No. 1 Parachute Training School (1 PTS) moved from its wartime location at Ringway to RAF Upper Heyford in Oxfordshire, and four years later it moved again to RAF Abingdon, where it remained for twenty-six years. Then the reserve parachute was introduced in 1955 and during the same period the Beverely transport aircraft entered service and became a workhorse for parachute training. Formal military freefall training began at PTS in 1959 and was taught to selected troops of the SAS and Parachute Regiment. In the late 1960s the C-130 Hercules was introduced and is used to this day by the RAF. In 1976 the school relocated to RAF Brize Norton. By then it had trained approximately 112,000 parachutists, who had carried out some 1,115,000 training descents. The one-millionth descent was made at Abingdon in 1969 by Private Norman Blunn, a recruit at the Depot of the Parachute Regiment and Airborne Forces, during Regular Basic Course No. 701.

When Course 819 formed up at Brize Norton in May 1976, as the first parachute course at the new location, they were surprised to see that their instructor appeared to be an elderly gentleman. He wore no special badges to impress the young Paras and if anything his approach was rather relaxed. As the course divided into groups, this instructor took his team to one side and spent the best part of an hour talking to them about the course and what they could expect. In a very deliberate, but calm manner he advised if they got into difficulty they must always keep their feet and knees tightly together and lock their elbows in.

Then, as the remainder of the course proceeded to carry out 'side left' and 'side right' landing drills, the elderly flight sergeant, whom several students were convinced had

'Fat Albert', the RAF's Hercules C-130 transport aircraft, which is the key form of transport for the UK's airborne forces. For those who have jumped, the smell of aviation fuel combined with the warm atmosphere generated by an aircraft full of paratroopers is the first thing that springs to mind when they see the plane.

spent so much time briefing them because he could not bend his legs, demonstrated the parachute position and a 'side left'. Those who had mocked him couldn't believe it. This man, who looked like a pensioner, was as supple as a baby. Then, just as the lesson was finishing, an SAS officer came across and thanked the Flight Sergeant for the assistance he had given them. Later, the course learned that Flight Sergeant John Carney was one of the RAF's most experienced parachute jumping instructors (PJIs), having taken part in the trials programme for the reserve parachute and been involved in the development of military free-fall. At the end of the course the Royal Marines in his class presented Sergeant Carney with a Commando dagger.

Commanded by a wing commander, PTS comprises four squadrons. The Static Line Training Squadron conducts basic parachute courses for regular and reserve forces personnel of all three services, as well as training RAF PJIs. In addition, the squadron conducts courses in the use of steerable static line parachutes for specialist personnel. The Free-Fall Training Squadron provides training in tactical free-fall techniques for special forces personnel of the Special Air Service and the Royal Marines' Special Boat Service, as well as for 5 Airborne Brigade's Pathfinder Platoon and RAF PJIs.

An RAF Parachute Jump Instructor at Brize Norton guides a recruit through his parachute drills. The instructors all serve with the RAF's No. 1 Parachute Training School which started life training wartime paratroopers at Ringway.

The Support Squadron provides support in the form of training co-ordination, programming, logistical support, parachute packing and the servicing of ground training equipment. Finally, the PTS Ops Squadron is responsible for the co-ordination of the aircraft required for parachute training, the ambulances for stationing on dropping zones, and transport and movement of trainees.

In addition to its four squadrons, 1 PTS also has detachments deployed in support of regular and territorial SAS regiments and the Royal Marines, while another performs a similar role for the territorial battalions of the Parachute Regiment. The largest detachment is based at RAF Pitts Road, Aldershot, and is responsible for providing synthetic training facilities and support for 5 Airborne Brigade.

The basic parachute course is of four weeks' duration for regular troops. During that time trainees are instructed in exit, flight and landing techniques. They are required to complete eight descents, one at night, to qualify for their 'wings'. Training is carried out from full-size mock-ups of C-130 Hercules fuselages inside the hangar at Brize Norton. Every course is split into groups, each having its own dedicated PJI, who trains students in the techniques of both jumping individually and in 'sticks', with or without equipment.

Course students are taught flight drills while suspended in parachute harnesses hung from the hangar roof on cables. Here they learn to control their parachutes while descending, and to carry out emergency measures such as untwisting their rigging lines, taking the necessary action after a collision with another parachutist, and landing in water. By the end of the first week the well-used airborne phrase, 'feet and knees together', is familiar to all students. Forwards, side and backwards landings are practised using a six-sided trapeze from which trainees hang while being swung in the air.

The next stage involves the fan trainer. Wearing a harness connected to a cable wound round a drum fitted with fan blades, trainees jump from a platform located near the roof of the hangar – as they fall, their rate of descent is controlled by the fan to simulate a drop with a parachute. More advanced training comes with the exit trainer, designed to simulate the effect of a slipstream as the parachutist exits the aircraft. The trainer consists of a wooden cabin, mounted on a structure of girders and equipped with doors representing those on the port and starboard side of a Hercules. On either side cables run from above the trainer to a point near the ground some 55 yards away. Wearing harnesses suspended from the cables, trainees jump from the trainer and travel the length of the cables in a gradual controlled descent towards the ground, where their progress is arrested by an instructor.

Until 1996 a parachute descent from a balloon was the next stage of training for all students: a chilling 'clean fatigue jump' – without equipment – from the basket of a balloon 800 ft up. As previously described, the drop has been compared many times to committing suicide off a bridge: the fall is straight down and it requires almost 200 ft before the canopy fully deploys. But the financial costs of maintaining the balloon resulted in the system being retired in 1996 and replaced by the Shorts Sky-van from which trainees now make several jumps. It is cheaper to run than a balloon and more readily available than the C-130 Hercules.

The students must then make an equipment drop from a Hercules in single sticks and 'sim sticks' (simultaneous exits) in which troops exit the aircraft by port and starboard doors. On successful completion of their eight descents, trainees are presented with their 'wings' by the Officer Commanding No. 1 Parachute Training School, and return to their respective units as qualified parachutists.

The course for members of Territorial Army units lasts only two weeks, and trainees are required to complete only seven descents, all in daylight. Before taking the course, however, they will already have undergone a considerable amount of synthetic training to enable them to be of a sufficiently high standard to successfully pass the course.

The value of good training was highlighted in August 1994 when a reserve paratrooper jumping with the new low level parachute found himself hooked up below a C-130 Hercules. In all its years of operation the Parachute Training School had always trained for this worst case scenario but it had never happened since the Second World War.

Private Ron Millington found himself trapped under a C-130 Hercules as it flew 1,000 ft above Salisbury Plain at 120 mph. It was a situation that every paratrooper is briefed about but hopes it will never happen to him. As Ron Millington left the door he tripped or fell awkwardly. Carrying his main parachute weighing 35 lb, his reserve weighing 25 lb, as well as a bergan and rifle weighing 80 lb strapped to his leg, it would have been easy to lose balance as he waited in the doorway. He was the seventh man in a nine-strong stick of paratroopers and as he left the aircraft 10-stone Ron fell forward and possibly somersaulted through his rigging lines as the canopy was deploying. He suddenly found himself hanging upside down, the rigging lines from his parachute wrapped around his legs. As the slipstream caught him the extension strap to his bergan wrapped itself around his neck.

The static line strop was still attached to the inside of the aircraft, as the rigging lines had prevented it from deploying, and it held Ron firmly gripped below the tail of the Hercules. The pilot reported nine Paras out but the ground crew reported only eight. The PJIs quickly realised what had happened and began the rescue using a system called HUPRA – Hooked Up Parachutists Release Assembly.

Hanging below the Hercules, Ron was being choked by exhaust fumes and battered by the slipstream. As the aircraft banked every few minutes it hurled him towards the propellers of one of the four engines, then swung him back the other way. The instructors pulled out the HUPRA kit and connected a fresh parachute to a second steel static line inside the Hercules, at the same time looping a wire through the D-ring of the original static line held on the running lines inside the aircraft. Then, with a pair of bolt croppers, a PJI cut the running line inside the aircraft and the fresh parachute shot out of the doorway and quickly deployed.

The Red Devils pictured air-to-air.

A lone member of the Red Devils, now regarded as the premier Army free-fall team.

Ron was now falling head first towards the drop zone and knew he had to try and release his equipment bergan or face serious injury.

I was desperate as I got closer to the ground. I made a grab for anything above me and managed to pull my head up.

Then I was on the ground. I landed on the small of my back and my backside. I lay there entangled with all the kit and all I could see was faces above me shouting 'don't try to move'. I can't explain how relieved I was – I felt no pain.

There is a saying in the airborne that if your main chute fails use your reserve. If that fails – become a milkman in your next life. But I enjoy the life and I joined the TA Paras for the challenge, it hasn't put me off.

After the incident an RAF inquiry panel studied the video footage and concluded that there was nothing wrong with the parachute. They believed the near-tragedy was caused by a clumsy jump combined with the 120 mph slipstream from the plane.

The team pours out of the back of an RAF C-130 Hercules. On average the team makes 120 public displays per year.

The low level parachute (LLP), designed and produced by Irvin Aerospace of Letchworth, Hertfordshire, is the standard equipment used by British airborne forces. It was developed to give airborne troops the unique ability for rapid deployment at low levels on to restricted dropping zones. Jumping out at 250 ft, the paratrooper is on the ground in just nine seconds.

THE RED DEVILS

The Red Devils are the Parachute Regiment's Free-Fall Team, formed in January 1964 with the principal intention of promoting the regiment at public events, and in 1979 the Red Devils were designated the official British Army free-fall display team.

The early types of parachute and harness were similar to the conventional military static line parachutes still in use today, and consisted of a main pack worn on the back of the parachutist and a reserve on the front, with an altimeter attached to indicate the height above ground. In the late 1960s new types of parachute were introduced. These were of different shapes and included one which was configured like a wing, allowing the parachutist greater control over how and where he could land.

The team has played an active part in the development of military free-fall parachuting and its tactical application as a means of insertion; some of the team's members have even served with the Pathfinders Platoon of 5 Airborne Brigade where their free-fall experience is highly valued.

Based at the Joint Services Parachute Centre in Netheravon, Wiltshire, the Red Devils currently use the latest type of parachute, rectangular high-performance ram-air canopies. Owing to the advances in design over the years, both the main and reserve parachutes are now contained in a compact pack worn on the parachutist's back.

The Red Devils' displays take several forms, and the team constantly strives to improve them. It takes many hours of planning, briefing, rehearsing and debriefing until the various formats are perfected. The displays include 'relative work', which consists of free-fall manoeuvres carried out as the team members plummet earthwards at speeds of up to 120 mph, and 'canopy relative work', which requires a number of parachutists 'docking' together with their canopies to create larger and technically more difficult display formats.

One relatively recent innovation, introduced only five years ago, is the tandem descent. An individual is linked by a harness to one of the Red Devil 'Tandem Masters', who is a skilled and qualified instructor. Pupil and instructor make their exit from the aircraft at a height of 12,000 ft and free-fall to 5,000 ft, at which point the instructor deploys the parachute. During the rest of the descent the pupil is given the opportunity of steering the parachute towards the dropping zone.

The Red Devils play a very active part in media-related events. These have included parachuting into the River Thames to mark the launching of the Airborne Forces Golden Jubilee Appeal, and playing the part of wartime German paratroopers for the London Weekend Television production *Wish Me Luck*, in which they jumped from a Junkers Ju 52 transport aircraft. Other spectacular events in which the Red Devils have taken part include setting the record for the fastest non-powered crossing of the English Channel in August 1980. Sergeant Mark Sheridan was one of a group of parachutists who jumped at 25,000 ft over Dover Castle and flew for twenty-six minutes before landing successfully at Sangatte in France.

Since their formation, the Red Devils have become renowned in many parts of the world for their skill in free-fall parachuting. They have travelled throughout Europe and many other countries, including the United States, Mexico, Kenya, Malaysia, Hong Kong and Cyprus, taking part in international competitions and giving displays for which they are much in demand. Wherever they perform, they make their mark as ambassadors for the Parachute Regiment and for the British Army.

The late Lieutenant-Colonel 'H' Jones, Commanding Officer, 2 Para.

8. THE FALKLANDS CONFLICT

OPERATION 'CORPORATE'

In 1981 the Defence Secretary John Nott recommended savage cuts to the armed forces. One year later, in April 1982, the Falklands conflict gave the Parachute Regiment the opportunity to remind politicians exactly why Field Marshal Montgomery had stated in 1945 that no modern force should be without airborne troops.

On 2 April 1982, Argentine troops invaded the Falkland Islands – a small British dependency in the South Atlantic. For many years Argentina had claimed sovereignty over the islands and when General Leopoldo Galtieri was appointed president in December 1981 one of his main undertakings was to recover the islands, which they called the 'Malvinas'.

In 1978 a Buenos Aires scrap dealer had signed a contract giving him an option to buy redundant machinery at the old whaling station in Leith Harbour on South Georgia which, as part of the contract, he would have to dismantle and take to Argentina. In early March 1982 he took up his option. However, it was the Argentine Navy that landed him and his workers, along with a military escort who promptly raised the Argentine flag. On 24 March an Argentine corvette took up station between the Falklands and South Georgia and prevented the Royal Navy vessel HMS *Endurance* from intercepting the workers at Leith. Then the Argentine Navy sailed 'for exercises' with the Uruguayan Navy; her warships included an aircraft carrier and an assault ship with 1,200 marines aboard.

The Argentine amphibious landing was delayed by twenty-four hours because of bad weather and took place on 2 April. By sheer force of numbers they quickly overran the eighty Royal Marines based in Port Stanley and drove through the streets of the town in their armoured vehicles, claiming to have 'liberated' the island.

The British Government reacted swiftly. By the end of April a Task Force of warships and civilian vessels requisitioned by the Ministry of Defence had set sail on the 8,000 mile trip to the Falklands. The armada of ships included the ferry *Norland* and the cruise ship *Canberra*. Aboard were the 2nd Battalion the Parachute Regiment, commanded by Lieutenant-Colonel 'H' Jones and the 3rd Battalion, commanded by Lieutenant-Colonel Hew Pike. On the way south the Task Force heard that an advance force which had sailed earlier had recaptured South Georgia. For those on *Canberra* weapon training and helicopter drills were the order of the day and as the Falklands got closer more attention was given to the island's terrain and potential objectives.

The 3rd Battalion, which had sailed on *Canberra*, was attached to 3 Commando Brigade Royal Marines, while the 2nd Battalion sailed aboard the *Norland*. On 21

An Argentinian armoured car patrols the streets of Port Stanley minutes after the amphibious invasion of the Falklands.

Argentinian troops patrol through Stanley as smoke billows over the town from an artillery barrage directed on the outskirts of the port.

April 1982 both units were landed in an amphibious assault. At the San Carlos beach-head, which had been secured by the SBS, the men of 2 Para would get wet feet as the landing craft could not get right on to the shoreline. As the ramp went down a coxswain shouted 'Troops Out' – but there was no response until suddenly a senior NCO barked 'Go' and the soldiers poured out of the craft. Soaking wet, the battalion then tabbed 5 miles to Sussex Mountain.

Meanwhile 3 Para had landed and made contact with enemy ground forces on D-Day, the only British unit to do so. They encountered and quickly captured some forty Argentines at Settlement Rocks and Windy Gap. Once ashore and away from the landing craft and ships in San Carlos, which were now under regular Argentine air attack, the men of 2nd Battalion were ordered on to Sussex Mountain.

The British land force was commanded by Brigadier Julian Thompson, a tough Royal Marine officer and 'sharp' academic, who had won respect throughout his career for his no-nonsense approach. He was under pressure from the Ministry of Defence for an early victory. But Thompson was not a man to be pushed and he had no intention of putting his men's lives at risk by attempting a foolhardy operation just to satisfy the wishes of pen-pushing 'Whitehall Warriors' whose civil service priorities were not his concern. Before his force could break out from the bridgehead Brigadier

One of the last photographs to be taken of Lieutenant-Colonel 'H' Jones. He is pictured in a landing craft at Ascension island with two of his staff officers.

The ferry Norland, *requisitioned to take 2 Para to the Falklands, is showered by 1,000-pounders in San Carlos water, but fortunately the bombs missed.*

Thompson needed to secure Goose Green, where intelligence reports had confirmed that at least 400 Argentines were based. Their position would, if ignored, leave them behind the British force as it advanced to Port Stanley, allowing them to attack the bridgehead or counter-attack the rear of the main force.

Thompson had worked with the Parachute Regiment before both on operations and at staff college, and welcomed their involvement. But he was concerned that the units worked within the brigade as 'one force'; there was no place for rivalry. Deliberately not favouring his own units, he gave the first task to the Paras and ordered the 2nd Battalion to Goose Green. Both 45 and 42 Commando, Royal Marines, along with 3 Para, were given missions and moved out of San Carlos, but Thompson's old unit, 40 Commando, was ordered to remain in reserve at San Carlos in case the Argentines attempted a counter-attack with airborne troops.

The men of 2 Para were to mount the first – and bloodiest – action of the land war when they marched from Sussex Mountain for the assault on Darwin and Goose Green. But before the Paras could even get to the objective an almost unbelievable security breach resulted in the battalion's mission being broadcast on the BBC's World Service. It also reported that 3 Para and 45 Commando were advancing on Teal Inlet and Douglas. The commanding officer of 2 Para, Lieutenant-Colonel 'H' Jones, and the force commander Brigadier Julian Thompson were both furious: there had clearly been a gross breach of security which could only have been sanctioned at the Ministry of Defence.

The radio broadcast resulted in an extra 400 Argentine troops being flown into

Goose Green and their positions being turned to face the British advance. It was an act that caused deep anger and resentment towards the media: the battalion felt that they had been betrayed by the BBC and to this day the 'media wound' has never healed for those who took part in the battle.

When the battle for Goose Green was over some officers would compare it to Arnhem. The battalion had four objectives: Burntside House, Boca House, Darwin and Goose Green. After the CO of 2 Para, Lieutenant-Colonel 'H' Jones, was fatally wounded, the commander of 'B' Company, Major John Crosland, heard that another 200 Argentines had been landed at Goose Green; he thought about John Frost's book *A Bridge Too Far* and said to himself 'We've gone an island too far.'

A naval bombardment from the Type 21 frigate HMS *Arrow* signalled the start of the battle at 0630 hours on 28 May 1982. The battalion had been ordered south from its positions on Sussex Mountain where it had been guarding the beachhead at San Carlos. Now it was set to take out the Argentinian forces around Goose Green and secure the important airfield there. Intelligence reports suggested that the Argentinians in Goose Green were at battalion strength but, as events were to prove, this was far from true and 2 Para's resources were to be stretched to the limit. Outnumbered and lightly armed, 2 Para's real strength lay in the professionalism and determination of its soldiers.

From the outset the battle had all the ingredients of a disaster for 2 Para. The Argentine forces outnumbered them, they were well dug in, had both artillery and air support and, thanks to the BBC, the enemy and the world had been told that the battalion was advancing on Goose Green and from which direction.

Major Dair Farrar-Hockley, commander of 'A' Company, opened the land battle at

The amphibious assault at San Carlos; both parachute battalions went ashore by landing craft.

Casualties from Goose Green arrive at the field hospital at San Carlos Bay.

0635 hours and after a brief fight the company took Burntside House, a large building to the left of the battalion's of advance. Their attack was deliberate and fierce, and its success was the signal for 'B' Company, commanded by Major John Crosland, to begin their attack on the enemy defences on the right of the battalion's route. 'D' Company (under Major Phil Neame) acted as the reserve at this stage and was held in the centre of the battalion's line of advance.

'C' Company was acting as the armed reconnaissance team for the battalion and as such had led the advance down from Sussex Mountain and prepared the way forward for the main assault of Darwin and Goose Green. The plan was to hold the company back in the initial stages, ready either to exploit tactical advantages as they occurred or to repulse any Argentinian counter-attacks.

Support Company, with its mortars, Milan teams, an anti-tank missile system and snipers, was deployed on the far side of Camilla Creek and moved round to give direct support to the rifle companies as the battalion moved steadily southwards down the isthmus. 'B' Company moved forward at 0710 hours and made rapid progress. At the centre of the advance 'D' Company had caught up with Battalion Tactical HQ and the commanding officer, Colonel 'H' Jones. It was now that the battalion's battle plan started to fall behind schedule due to fierce Argentinian resistance. In addition company commanders were trying to command their assault and navigate their area of in very poor visibility – it was no easy task.

Colonel 'H' was insistent that 'D' Company should get ahead as quickly as possible. The company was advancing when it suddenly came under intensive small-arms fire from the right flank. The men of Battalion Headquarters (HQ) were also in the line of fire and took cover as best they could by lying in wheel depressions in a track. While 'D' Company dealt with the enemy, the HMS *Arrow* provided naval gunfire support with high explosive (HE) and illumination fire missions. Then the ship's operations room informed the battalion that her 4.5 in gun had jammed. The only other support came from the light guns and two mortars deployed at Camilla Creek House, all of which had little ammunition. Argentinian artillery fire was now raining down on the battalion's positions with considerable accuracy, but the damp peaty ground of the battlefield absorbed much of the impact of the enemy shells and reduced the killing power of the splinters. After the conflict Major Crosland commented that had the terrain had a harder surface casualties on both sides would have been much higher.

'D' Company pressed home its attack, although the proximity of 'B' Company – some distance ahead – made it necessary for considerable restraint to be shown in returning the enemy's fire. It was here that the first Paras were killed, while others suffered gunshot wounds and white phosphorus burns. Any casualties were left where they fell until circumstances permitted them to be treated. The reason was simple: if one man went down, the battalion would lose a second man if someone stopped to help. This was not callous, it was practical; it was the only way that a light force such as a parachute unit could hope to survive on the battlefield. In the event, one man, Private Fletcher, did stop to help an injured colleague, Corporal Cork, and the same machine-gun that had knocked down his friend killed him. He was found with an open field dressing in his hand.

At about 0900 hours the rain stopped, though the sky was still overcast and remained so throughout the day. 'D' Company finished mopping up the enemy and 'A' Company was instructed to pass alongside them and push on towards Darwin, over a kilometre further on and screened from view by a low hill. The Argentinian artillery fire now became more intense and soldiers took whatever cover they could, either in captured enemy trenches or simply lying out in the open in natural hollows. One shell landed directly between the commanding officer and his adjutant, but failed to explode; 'Lucky they're using such lousy ammunition,' the commanding officer commented.

Over to the right, 'B' Company advanced down the side of a shallow valley towards the gorse line, below which were the ruins of Boca House. As they moved down the featureless slope the platoons of 'B' Company all came under fire at the same time. Each platoon attempted to pull back to safety behind the crest of the hill they had just left, or tried to take cover in whatever dead ground they could find.

Field funeral. Members of 2 Para, including a Royal Marine pilot, are buried after the battle for Goose Green.

By now, 'A' Company was also in trouble. As the men approached Darwin Hill, figures were seen moving on the slopes. At first it was thought they might be Falklanders but when a soldier's call was answered in Spanish, recognition dawned on both sides simultaneously. The leading platoon of Paras, followed by the remainder of the company, sprinted towards the hill in an attempt to take the position by surprise. They came under heavy fire from well-placed bunkers along the top of the hill. Five Paras went down before the company found shelter in a gorse-filled gully that ran up the hillside. 'A' Company was now well and truly pinned down and attempts to smash the enemy bunkers using grenades and 66 mm LAW rockets all failed. The Paras, crouching in the gully with machine-gun bullets whistling overhead, were hardly able to move.

Both 'A' and 'B' Companies were now in serious trouble, but since the neck of land on which Goose Green and Darwin stood was so narrow, there seemed to be no opportunity of using the reserves: 'D' Company was therefore told to hold itself in readiness. It was clear that time was on the Argentinians' side. The Paras' ammunition was running low and there was little chance of any being brought forward, casualties were increasing, artillery support had virtually ceased and air support could not be provided because bad weather at sea prevented the Harriers from flying. The enemy were able to mount air operations and the rear areas of 2 Para were attacked by three Pucara ground-attack aircraft at 1155 hours.

Lieutenant-Colonel Jones and his Tactical Headquarters (Tac HQ) inched forward under heavy fire to 'A' Company's position. The CO knew that the momentum of the attack had to be regained, but another attempt on the hill cost the lives of two officers and a corporal, and under a storm of fire the men of 'A' Company were forced back to the point from which they had started. It was during this attack that 'H' Jones and his HQ group moved round to the right and, while the enemy troops were engaging 'A' Company, the colonel made his own assault. He was shot and mortally wounded. Far from lowering the Paras' morale, his sacrifice gave his men new determination; grimly 'A' Company attacked again, this time forcing its way through Argentinian lines to capture an entire position.

When Colonel Jones was killed the battalion second-in-command, Major Chris Keeble, took over. He made his way to Darwin Hill and over the radio spoke to Major Neame to establish what 'D' Company thought it could do. Neame had noticed a low cliff face along the shore by Boca House and, as the tide was not high, he thought he could get his company along the slope under cover of the cliff face to outflank the enemy positions without being seen. Keeble told him to go ahead while 'B' Company kept the Argentinians occupied with small-arms fire.

An important asset had now reached 'B' Company from the Support Company: Milan anti-tank missiles. Several firing posts were set up and began to engage the enemy positions. The Milans' effectiveness was amazing: as missile after missile crashed into the enemy bunkers Argentinian fire began to slacken, allowing 'B' Company to move forward into positions from where they could directly assault the enemy.

One unfortunate Argentinian was seen to leave a bunker that had been struck by a missile, run a few yards and jump into another. As he leapt in, this bunker too was hit

Goose Green, the day after the battle. Hundreds of helmets littered the airfield.

by a missile and disintegrated in a cloud of dust and flying stones. 'Bet that took the edge off his day,' remarked a soldier with some satisfaction.

The end came quickly. As 'D' Company, who had advanced under cover of the small cliffs, stormed up from the beach and 'B' Company continued to pour fire into the trenches, the Argentinians decided enough was enough. White flags began to appear and the position was captured. Barely pausing, 'D' Company pressed on and moved left along a shallow valley, which was sufficiently deep to screen it from enemy forces on the airfield. Their objective was the Goose Green schoolhouse and eventually the airfield. This would leave the Paras in a strong position on the outskirts of the settlement. 'B' Company set off in a wide sweep southwards that would take them to the right of the airfield, and then on for some distance before swinging left in a semi-circular movement across the isthmus until they reached the southern outskirts of the settlement.

Back on Darwin Hill, 'A' Company had secured the position and cleared Darwin settlement. While the bulk of the company set about consolidating its defence and other troops rounded up prisoners, one platoon was detached to join 'C' Company, which then advanced down the long, gentle gradient towards the airfield and Goose Green. To the Paras the scene resembled a First World War battlefield, with an extended line of soldiers advancing across ground that seemed as smooth as a billiard table. Suddenly, some of the Paras noticed Argentinians running across the airfield. The helpless men realised that the enemy troops were racing for anti-aircraft guns. Then then came the ear-splitting crashing and lines of tracer as anti-aircraft guns on the airfield poured a stream of heavy-calibre fire on to the advancing British. The 20 mm double-barrelled automatic Rheinmetal cannon from the airfield were soon joined by 35 mm weapons in Goose Green itself. The men at Major Keeble's command post behind the gorse hedge on Darwin Hill frantically hit the deck as the high-explosive rounds raked along the hedge.

The men of 'D' Company, screened from the airfield, were relatively safe from the anti-aircraft guns, but as they approached the schoolhouse they came under heavy fire from both the school and the edge of the airfield. A brisk firefight was soon in progress, and 'C' Company joined in. The schoolhouse caught fire and, as it contained a considerable quantity of munitions, it burned well. At this point Lieutenant Barry, having seen a white flag in the area of the schoolhouse, went forward to take a surrender but in the process was shot and killed. The result was inevitable: the Paras were not going to be caught by the 'white flag' trick again and hit the enemy with everything they had.

With an end to the fighting around the schoolhouse and the completion of 'B' Company's move to the south of the settlement, the men of 2 Para could breathe more easily. The Argentinian artillery was still in action, however, as was the Argentinian Air Force. Two A-4 Skyhawks made fast runs using cannon against 'B' and 'D' Companies, although one was shot down by small-arms fire. A second attack was made by Pucara aircraft, one of which was shot down by a Royal Marine Blowpipe detachment which had been attached to the battalion.

At last a Harrier attack became possible and for the first time that day the men of 2

Para felt there were others on their side. At about 1930 hours – with the light fading – three Harriers attacked the enemy positions with cluster bombs, and as the explosions echoed over the battlefield a cheer went up from the men of 2 Para.

Just before dark the firing lessened although another Pucara made a run over the battlefield, dropping napalm on 'D' Company. It was an ill-judged attack: every single weapon was turned on the aircraft, and the pilot almost immediately lost control and crashed, showering 'B' Company with fuel. In a final effort to defeat 2 Para, the enemy flew in reinforcements by helicopter and began to put them down about a kilometre south of the settlement. 'B' Company moved to prevent this while artillery fire from the gun line at Camilla Creek House soon scattered the Argentinians.

As night finally fell on the evening of 28 May, so the gunfire died down across the battlefield. Major Keeble ordered no aggressive patrolling and no firing unless necessary. His aim was to give the Argentinians time to think about the diplomatically worded ultimatum of surrender he had sent to them via two prisoners, who were to return under a white flag no later than 0830 hours local time the next day. It was a cold night and the men of 2 Para went about their various tasks and sentry duties in the hope that morning would not bring renewed fighting.

At 0825 hours the prisoners returned under a white flag: the surrender was accepted. For the loss of 15 men killed and 30 wounded, 2 Para took prisoner or killed about 1,300 Argentinian troops – it had been a magnificent effort. Captured hardware included four 105 mm pack howitzers, two 35 mm anti-aircraft guns, six 20 mm anti-aircraft guns and, six 120 mm mortars; two Pucara aircraft had been shot down. The most significant result, however, was the reassertion of an old truth that the side whose will breaks first loses. And 2 Para had not been broken during more than twelve hours of the most intense fighting. Just four days later they would attack Wireless Ridge.

Following the death of Lieutenant-Colonel 'H' Jones a new commander was dispatched from England to the Ascension Islands. There Lieutenant-Colonel David Chaundler boarded a C-130 Hercules and parachuted into the south Atlantic where he was picked up by a Sea King helicopter and flown to the assault ship HMS *Fearless*. His battalion was about to become the most celebrated in the British Army. If the Argentinians had invaded a few days later than they did, the men would have been on their way to Belize for a six month stay. Again, since 2 Para was occupying the southernmost position after landing at San Carlos, it became the obvious choice as the battalion to attack Goose Green. Acting as 3 Commando Brigade's reserve battalion in the assault on the mountains around Port Stanley 2 Para was also chosen to take part in the assault on Wireless Ridge, thus making it the only battalion to be committed twice against the Argentinians. Chance certainly played its part but the battalion's pride, tradition and training all contributed to its success in the Falklands.

By the simple expedient of making a telephone call to a Falkland islander's house in Fitzroy, via the civilian link with Swan Inlet, it had been established that Bluff Cove and Fitzroy were unoccupied by the Argentinians. During the evening of 3 June and the next morning, the battalion flew forward to occupy the two settlements, using the one available

A member of the Royal Marine Air Defence Troop pictured at Goose Green. A small detachment supported 2 Para armed with Blowpipe.

The only Chinook to operate in the Falklands during the campaign. It was used on several occasions to ferry members of 2 Para.

In between battles a company group takes shelter from the weather in a cowshed to cook a meal, or 'scoff' in Para language.

Chinook helicopter. One lift carried eighty-two fully armed soldiers – something of a record.

There then followed nine days of rest to recover from the effects of the cold weather and the fighting at Goose Green. The sheep-shearing sheds of the two settlements provided decent shelter in which the soldiers could dry out, get a good night's sleep and enjoy a meal.

On 6 June the battalion was relieved by the Scots Guards at Bluff Cove and, with the battalion now concentrated around Fitzroy, 2 Para completed its preparations. Rations, radio batteries and medical supplies were issued and ammunition stockpiled. This period of relative quiet was marred, however, by the disastrous attack on the landing ship *Sir Galahad*. This occurred at Fitzroy and not, as was reported by the press, at Bluff Cove. The Welsh Guards were old friends of the battalion and 2 Para had recently served alongside them in Berlin and then in South Armagh: they had the unhappy task of pulling many of them out of the sea. The next day 2 Para were glad to receive orders preparing them to move.

Two days later the whole battalion flew north by helicopter and once again came under the command of 3 Commando Brigade (while in Bluff Cove and Fitzroy the battalion had been under the command of 5 Infantry Brigade). That night the men

Mount Longdon: casualties of 3 Para are carried to a helicopter.

moved forward, leaving bergans, spare food and sleeping bags behind – they did not see them again until Port Stanley. It was a spectacular night. As the battalion moved forward in single file (known colloquially as the 'airborne snake'), weaving its way around the Argentinian minefields and periodic enemy artillery bombardments, they could see 3 Para attacking Mount Longdon and 45 Commando attacking Two Sisters.

Soon after first light the battalion arrived at its assembly area behind Mount Longdon, finally secured by 3 Para. They dug in and waited for further orders. Three hours before last light a Scout helicopter arrived and the brigade liaison officer, Major Hector Gullan, climbed out and ran towards Lieutenant-Colonel Chaundler shouting 'Wireless Ridge tonight, chaps'. The CO quickly devised a plan of action and summoned his officers, but halfway through the conference he was told that the boundaries for the attack were to change. Just as he was about to conclude the new brief a radio message came through to postpone the assault for twenty-four hours.

The next day Chaundler, along with Major Tony Rice RA, the commander of 2 Para's artillery support, flew up to 3 Para's position on Mount Longdon. From here they could see Wireless Ridge. It did not appear on their maps as they had first thought and the CO's plans had to be altered. Then, a group of Argentine Skyhawks came in for the last air attack of the campaign; this grounded the helicopters and the CO's group could not rejoin 2 Para until two hours before last light – the time set for the battalion to move out. The Skyhawks had also delayed the battalion's mortars moving forward – they had only just begun to arrive – and the intensive enemy fire directed on Mount Longdon prevented the artillery spotters of 3 Para from registering their targets. The CO decided there was only one thing for it and sent his company commanders away for a brew, the army's answer to all ills, while he replanned the attack. They were fortunate that the terrain of Wireless Ridge was reasonably flat and open. So far, most of the attacks in the Falklands had been along narrow ridges with little room for manoeuvre; at least on Wireless Ridge there would be enough space for an attack.

The enemy force in this instance was the Argentine 7th Infantry Battalion and intelligence reported it had four companies and a platoon on the ridge. The CO's plan called for an attack in four phases, with each phase coming from a different direction. The battalion's experience at Goose Green had highlighted the importance of fire support. Up to this point in the campaign all Para attacks had been launched in silence to achieve maximum surprise. Mortar and artillery fire had been held back until contact was made. Now the CO decided upon a noisy attack with an extensive preliminary bombardment, believing that the Argentines, essentially a conscript army, would crack under a heavy barrage.

It was hardly surprising that the impact of fire support was generally underestimated. Before the campaign few soldiers had seen or experienced the effects of a bombardment with large quantities of high explosives. On Wireless Ridge the Paras would experience both aspects of this. They had two batteries of artillery, fire support from a frigate and 3 Para's mortars, in addition to their own mortar and machine-gun platoons. But

Men of the 2nd Battalion the Parachute Regiment arrive in Port Stanley – the first troops to arrive in the town.

perhaps the most significant support weapons were Lieutenant Lord Robin Innes-Ker's four Scorpions and Scimitars of the Blues and Royals, which had not yet been seen in action. They made a remarkable journey over the mountains from Fitzroy to join the battalion in their assembly area, and though normally classed as reconnaissance vehicles, were used as light tanks in this conflict. Their firepower was to prove devastating.

At last light on 13 June the battalion moved out. It took four-and-a-quarter hours to reach their forming-up positions (FUPs). The night was exceptionally dark with snow and sleet flurries. The battalion was being tested to the limit. Few soldiers had slept for the last two nights; the previous night had been unbelievably cold and sleep was impossible without sleeping bags. The men had also not seen a ration pack for twenty-four hours and plans were being changed constantly. Also, for most of the soldiers, this was their second time into action. At Goose Green they had not really known what to expect: this time they were under no illusions.

As the battalion moved towards their goal Forward Observation Officers (FOOs) were finding their targets by using illumination shells to spot the fall of shot. This was not an easy task and the battalion was eternally grateful for their skill in completing it. By this time the Argentinians knew they were going to be attacked and they started to shell likely approach routes and forming-up positions. As the Paras moved into their FUPs the CO received a message from battalion main headquarters, who were about 1 km to the rear, that they had something he ought to see. Lieutenant-Colonel Chaundler walked over to the HQ and Major Chris Keeble, the second-in-command, handed him a captured Argentinian map that had just been sent up by brigade headquarters. It showed a minefield laid right across the battalion's main axis of attack. The CO returned to his tactical headquarters and met the officer commanding 'B' Company, Major Crosland. '"John, we've got minefield out there." We just looked at each other and shrugged. We knew it was now too late to do anything about it and we had no option but to cross it. Miraculously, although "A" and "B" Companies and HQ moved across it, no one was blown up.'

By now the softening-up bombardment had started and Major Phil Neame's 'D' Company started phase 1 of the plan. They were supported by artillery, mortars, light tanks and the machine-gun platoon, and with suppressive fire coming from the Argentinians within the second battery and the frigate, they attacked their first objective. It was quickly overrun but the Argentines responded immediately and opened fire on the captured positions. 'D' Company rapidly moved off and reorganised, one soldier taking cover in a trench which had been used as an Argentinian latrine.

'D' Company's firepower was then switched back to support 'A' and 'B' Companies in their attack: this was phase 2 of the plan. Enemy shells had now begun to fall and Major Crosland came up on the radio net – 'It's getting a little hot here. Can we move?' The CO was finally satisfied that all was ready. 'B' Company's two batteries of guns increased their rate of fire to seventy-two rounds per minute and 'A' and 'B' Companies were given

Members of 2 Para advancing along the main street leading into the town.

the order to move forward. As they approached their objective, a position held by an Argentinian company and their regimental HQ, the lines of tracer from machine-guns and Scorpions began reaching out for the enemy. Then, an Argentinian artillery shell homed in on Major Dair Farrar-Hockley's 'A' Company, killing a Colour Sergeant and wounding several soldiers, but the momentum of the battalion's attack did not stop.

The artillery fire of 29 Commando, Royal Artillery lifted as the companies reached the edge of the enemy positions. Illuminating mortar rounds began to burst overhead, casting an eerie flickering light over the battlefield, as soldiers skirmished from rock to rock. The enemy broke and fled, and aided by their night sights, the machine-gunners in the Scorpions drove them from the ridge. Between them 'A' and 'B' Companies had captured thirty-seven prisoners and were now quickly digging in. Except for the Argentinian artillery shelling their old positions there was a pause in the pace of the battle, and the Paras prepared for the next two phases of the assault.

'C' Company, commanded by Major Roger Jenner, who gained the forward positions in the attack and guided the battalion up to them, regrouped his men. Phase 3, their next task, was to capture a position held by an enemy platoon. As 'C' Company approached they heard the sound of weapons being cocked but the firepower proved too much for the Argentinians and they fled. A number of pairs of boots were found left behind, highlighting the enemy's hasty departure.

Back at the regimental aid post the medical officer Captain Steve Hughes was busy with the first casualties. He himself had cracked a bone in his foot at Goose Green but did not admit that he was in immense pain until after the final attack. Though Hughes had only recently qualified, every soldier treated by him, a total of fifty from both Goose Green and Wireless Ridge, survived. These men included Private Gray, whose leg was amputated under the most primitive conditions.

Lieutenant-Colonel Chaundler now took stock of 'A' and 'B' Companies' position. Many had had lucky escapes: a member of the CO's Tac HQ had been hit on the front of his helmet, the bullet passing round inside and coming out the back without grazing him. A shell exploded next to Corporal Curtis of 'B' Company, tearing his clothes to ribbons, yet he escaped without a scratch; Private Phillpot had fallen into a freezing pond and a rapid change of clothing was needed to prevent exposure.

The Blues and Royals and machine-gun platoons had been resupplied and moved up to the CO's position. 'D' Company, having made a wide outflanking movement, was prepared to begin the final phase of the operation. Once again the battalion's firepower swept down on the enemy along the final ridge. Back on the mortar line crews were making Herculean efforts to keep their weapons in action on the soft ground. Trying not to let down their comrades in the forward rifle companies, they had to stand on the base plates when the mortars fired to keep them steady and four men suffered broken ankles. The artillery was also having problems with the ground. One gun had slipped back from its position and its shells were landing on 'D' Company. But the Paras were ready to go again. 'D' Company's movement had gone undetected by the Argentinians who were expecting the next attack to come from the north rather than the west. The CO gave the order to attack. Now began the longest and most difficult part of the operation. 'D' Company was to attack two enemy positions on the final ridge line from the flank.

On the approach the men ran into a minefield and once again there was no option but to go through it. Once more the enemy had abandoned their positions, leaving behind a considerable amount of equipment, including a 106 mm recoilless rifle. The company was beginning to advance along the ridge behind the battalion's artillery fire when disaster struck – in the chaos of battle a forward observation officer had directed fire on to the wrong target and several salvos of shells crashed around 'D' Company. Fortunately no one was killed but the attack was broken up and it took forty-five minutes to reorganise the men. 'D' Company's advance continued, still undetected by the enemy, who were directing their fire towards 'A', 'B' and 'C' Companies and the Scorpions. With just 90 metres to go the element of surprise was lost when a 'D' Company soldier fired a flare by mistake and the company instinctively went to ground. However, with their Company Commander Major Neame very much at the front, the men got up again and resumed the charging of the enemy positions.

By now the mortars and artillery had run out of illuminating rounds so the Royal Navy was asked to provide light for the attack. Soon starshells from the frigate began to light up the night sky as artillery shells crashed all around. The intermittent sound of Milan missiles being fired, the crack of high velocity rounds and 30 mm Rarden cannon

Mount Longdon: casualties of 3 Para are carried to a helicopter.

could be heard as the company sought out Argentinian positions. At first light 'D' Company was well dug in when the Argentinians launched a counter-attack, the only one of the campaign. This, however, was quickly broken up. Just then the CO heard that Mount Tumbledown had fallen to the Scots Guards after some extremely tough fighting. This was a great relief to 2 Para as they were very vulnerable to attack from that area.

It had taken ten hours to capture Wireless Ridge and standing on the final objective as dawn broke Lieutenant-Colonel Chaundler was greeted with the most amazing sight – the complete collapse of the Argentine Army. Like black ants several hundred of them were coming off Tumbledown and Sapper Hill across the valley and out off Moody Brook below and heading for Port Stanley. The break had come: the priority was now to get into Port Stanley before they reorganised.

The CO ordered 'A' and 'B' Companies forward and they began pouring fire down into the valley. The Battery Commander asked for and got additional fire support. The Scorpions and machine-gun platoons were now with the companies and an air strike was requested. This was refused, however, owing to the bad weather. Then Captain John Greenhalgh, the Scout helicopter pilot, appeared with two more Scouts and engaged an artillery battery across the valley with SS11 missiles.

The Argentines were now defeated. The Brigade Commander, Brigadier Julian Thompson, arrived by helicopter and Lieutenant-Colonel Chaundler told him the battle was over and requested permission to advance into Port Stanley. The Brigadier took stock of the situation and immediately gave the Paras permission to go ahead. 'B' Company passed through Moody Brook and 'A' Company took the Port Stanley road. In a completely impromptu gesture the men of the 2nd Battalion removed their helmets and put on their maroon berets and marched into Stanley. At 1300 hours on 14 June 1982 the leading elements of the battalion entered Stanley, the first British troops in the town since the Argentinian invasion. But the battalion's euphoria was dampened by their sadness for the dead they had left behind.

The men of 3 Para also saw intense action in the Falklands under the command of the then Lieutenant-Colonel Hew Pike, later to be promoted to Lieutenant-General. On 27 May, while 2 Para was lying up at Camilla Creek, the 3rd Battalion was also heading out of the beachhead, initially towards Teal Inlet. This advance eastwards was a prelude to the battalion's key mission at Mount Longdon, when it would take part in a brigade night attack. It was at this point that 'D' (Patrol) Company prepared for a parachute operation on to Great Island. But bad weather forced the drop to be cancelled and instead 'D' Company was ferried to the island by a Royal Navy frigate and landed by boat. The battalion would attack Longdon and exploit forward to Wireless Ridge, if possible; 45 Commando would attack Two Sisters and exploit forward to Tumbledown; and 42 Commando would capture Mount Harriet and be ready to move through 45 and on to Mount William. 2 Para would be held in reserve.

Lieutenant-Colonel Hew Pike, the commanding officer of 3 Para, made his attack from the west because other approaches were precluded by minefields. In direct support of 3 Para were 79 Commando Battery of 29 Commando RA and naval gunfire support from a frigate, together with 2 Troop of 9 Para Squadron, Royal Engineers.

Pike had given codewords to the start line and key objectives: the start line would be *Free Kick*; the western summit of Longdon would be *Fly Half*; the eastern summit *Full Back* and the spur running north *Wing Forward*. In the heat of battle there was little time for encoding and deciphering messages and these nicknames could be used in 'clear speech' on the radio net without giving any information to the Argentinians listening in.

From their new positions, the battalion had a clear view of Port Stanley and the airport – looking strangely familiar after all the careful briefings – though, significantly, the western part of the town was hidden behind the fortress-like bulk of a feature quickly identified as Mount Longdon. Within a day or two 3 Para was joined by a number of Falkland islanders from Green Patch settlement with their tractors, trailers and Land Rovers. Terry Peck and Vernon Steen, having taken to the hills from Port Stanley, had already linked up with 3 Para, proving they were valuable not only as guides, but as men more than willing to die for their island's freedom. The new party was led and organised, however, by Trudi Morrison, a most remarkable woman. She did wonders for the commanding officer's morale by addressing him as 'General'!

The weather now took a turn for the worse. It was not until 3 June that an artillery battery could be flown into the area of Mount Estancia in order to support the move forward. From late May until the fall of Port Stanley (14 June), the battalion received regular attention from enemy artillery, especially from long-range 155 mm guns. A high-level night bombing run by Canberra aircraft added to their discomfort but caused no casualties. On 3 June, 'A' and 'B' Companies moved eastwards beneath the shoulder of Mount Kent in order to establish nearer and secure patrolling bases, which was the battalion objective. Extensive patrolling by the patrol company and by fighting patrols from each rifle company was conducted from 3 to 10 June. A number of clashes with the enemy resulted providing valuable intelligence, although unfortunately it was not very detailed. Much of the intelligence was collated by a 'D' Company four-man patrol which was able to close to within a few metres of Argentinian positions on the mountain. They would normally spend two nights out, returning on the second with any information.

The battalion's mortars regularly engaged the enemy in this period, the Mortar Fire Controllers (MCFs) having something of a field day and relishing this unique chance to prove their skills. Meanwhile, 'A' and 'B' Companies were on the receiving end of increasingly accurate fire from enemy artillery, and a Pucara attacked their positions, but without loss of men.

Later, an Argentine map, recovered from Government House, showed the positions of the battalions in red and proved just how accurately the enemy had located the British force from reconnaissance flights. On 10 June the battalion received orders to take Mount Longdon on the night of 11/12 June. Nothing like this had been undertaken by the battalion for at least a generation. Under cover of darkness and moving by independent routes under patrol company guides, the CO's party and the three rifle companies ('A', 'B' and 'C'), closed in on the objective after a three-hour approach. The narrow and broken-up summit of the feature dictated that only one company could effectively fight along it at any time. Outflanking was not a sound option because of known enemy positions on Wireless Ridge to the east and a minefield to the south. (As things turned out, however, there were also mines on the chosen attack route.) The summit of Mount Longdon also dominated the very open ground around it for several thousand metres, adding to the hazards of a flanking approach – even one made during the pitch black night.

Lieutenant-Colonel Pike's plan was for 'B' Company, commanded by Major Mike Argue, to tackle the Longdon summit (composed of the two missions codenamed *Fly Half* and *Full Back*), while 'A' Company, under Major David Collett, would seize the ridge immediately to the north-east (*Wing Forward*), also thought to be held by the enemy. 'C' Company, commanded by Major Martin Osborne, was to hold back out of contact as a much-needed reserve, using what cover it could find in the shallow valleys. Major Peter Dennison led Fire Support Teams – equipped with Milan, anti-tank, missile launchers and GPMGs in the sustained fire role – to a position west of the mountain, codenamed *Free Kick*, for subsequent redeployment as required. The mortars moved independently; Major Roger Patton was in command of the ammunition resupply and casevac teams, who were equipped with tractors and Volvo BV tracked supply vehicles. Unfortunately the battalion lost its troop of Scorpions and Scimitars to 5 Infantry Brigade, but it did have one battery of 105 mm light guns in direct support, and further batteries could be called up if needed. Naval Gunfire Support (NGS) from the frigate HMS *Avenger* was also available to the battalion and was to remain in support throughout the night.

The start line for the assault was along a stream running south from Furze Bush Pass, and the battalion crossed it just as the moon rose to illuminate the dominant, craggy outline of the mountain. The two assaulting companies ('A' and 'B') advanced steadily over the open moorland, shaking out from loose file to extended assault formation as they moved forward in the bitterly cold night. Throughout the advance it was vital that the Paras avoided long waits in obvious assembly areas and forming-up places, for fear of being spotted by Argentinian artillery, and the men remained silent as they got closer to the mountain. 'B' Company, assaulting the summit, moved stealthily over the rocks at the base of Mount Longdon – then, suddenly, the battalion lost its advantage of surprise.

Corporal Milne, a section commander, stood on a mine, and the Argentinian defenders quickly opened fire on both assaulting companies. Mortar and artillery fire was soon being directed on to the Paras and although the shells were landing initially behind the force the enemy quickly redirected their fire. During the subsequent battle, heavy shells pounded the ground around the Paras. Support fire controlled by the Artillery Battery Commander Major John Patrick and his Forward Observation Officers, the Mortar Fire Controllers and the Naval Gunfire Support Officer Captain Willie McCracken, was very accurate and played a crucial part in the battle. Captain McCracken was later awarded the Military Cross for his efforts.

The Argentinians were ensconced in well-prepared bunkers in the rocks. They could only be shifted by combining intensive fire support with an immediate follow up by the rifle sections, using GPMGs, 66 mm light anti-tank missiles (LAWs) and grenades, then a final attack with rifle and bayonet. The battle consisted of a rush forward, a pause, some creeping, a few isolated shots here and there, then some artillery and mortar fire followed by a concerted rush: then the whole process would start again. During this long night of freezing rain and sleet, the weather, the darkness, the terrain and the nature of the task placed great demands on the leadership and stamina of young officers, NCOs and many private soldiers. 5 and 6 Platoons were the first to come under effective enemy fire when the surprise attack was lost. Lieutenant Cox, commanding 5 Platoon, ordered a GPMG team to move up the rock face and engage a position that was holding up his advance. The enemy was finally silenced by LAW and Carl Gustav fire (a large shoulder-mounted anti-tank weapon). But then more automatic fire came from further east of the platoon. Some of 5 Platoon were now high on the ridge and made contact with 6 Platoon to confirm their positions and avoid overlapping. Under covering fire from Lance-Corporal Carver and Private Juliff, Privates Gough and Gray tried to take out the enemy position using a LAW but it misfired twice; finally they charged, using grenades to destroy the enemy. Gray was later shot through his helmet, luckily escaping with only stitches to his scalp as the bullet diverted through the crown of his protective headgear.

Meanwhile, 6 Platoon had gained a foothold on the southern side of *Fly Half* without making contact with the enemy, although they grenaded a number of abandoned bunkers, including a 0.5 in HMG sangar, on their way up. But they had missed one bunker, concealed by the darkness and rocky terrain, in which at least seven Argentinians were hiding. These men engaged the platoon from the rear with great accuracy, and undoubtedly accounted for a large number of dead and wounded. Pressing on, 6 Platoon then came under accurate sniper and automatic fire from further positions; these attacks caused four casualties in quick succession. Attempts to help these soldiers and destroy the sources of enemy fire led only to more casualties. 6 Platoon's position was soon critical because it had advanced into the killing zone of the weapons engaging 5 Platoon. Casualties lay among rocks swept by enemy fire, but the men of 6 Platoon treated them as best they could.

The attack, carried out with such bravery, had created a valuable foothold but now it had stalled. Back on the northern side of the *Fly Half* 4 Platoon was moving up to the left of 5 Platoon, and although its left forward section was in ground sheltered from enemy bullets, the right section was pushing up behind 5 Platoon, and also came under heavy fire. Both platoons had arrived at an area forward of the summit of *Fly Half*, where the rock ridges had started to break up and the ground to slope away to the east. Their immediate problem was how to deal with a well-sited enemy platoon position containing 105 mm recoilless rifles, two 7.62 mm GPMGs and one heavy machine-gun that suddenly opened up on them. This position also included a number of snipers with passive night sights which proved extremely effective, and were soon making things very difficult. In the initial burst of fire the commander of 4 Platoon, Lieutenant Andrew Bickerdike,

Members of 3rd Battalion the Parachute Regiment celebrate after victory at Longdon.

was shot through the thigh and his signaller hit in the mouth; despite their disabilities, however, both continued to fire their weapons and to man the radio until relieved some time later, when Sergeant Ian McKay took over the platoon. 5 Platoon was already under cover among the rocks and fortunately avoided casualties. McKay quickly gathered a number of men from 4 Platoon and led Corporal Bailey's section against the heavy machine-gun fire that formed the core of the enemy position. This HMG was situated in a well-built sangar and protected by several riflemen who covered all approaches. In the attack McKay and Private Burt were killed and Corporal Bailey seriously wounded. Sergeant McKay's body was found later in an enemy sangar. The men of 4 Platoon had displayed great gallantry under McKay's leadership, and enemy resistance was greatly reduced in this area, although heavy fire continued to make progress painful.

By now Company Headquarters was forward with 5 Platoon on the ridge and under heavy fire from the east. Several enemy positions could be identified from their tracer bullets, particularly those firing the distinctive Browning machine-guns. Having heard that Lieutenant Bickerdike was wounded and that Sergeant McKay was missing, Sergeant Fuller from Company Headquarters went forward to take command of 4 Platoon. He gathered them together, with Corporal McLaughlin's section providing fire support, and pressed forward. Although the men cleared several enemy sangars this force was eventually halted by heavy automatic fire which wounded Corporal Kelly and four others. In addition to providing fire support McLaughlin's section also managed, however, to obtain a commanding position dominating areas to the east of the mountain. On their way up they had been temporarily halted by the enemy rolling grenades down the rocks towards them. Fortunately no casualties had resulted. McLaughlin crawled to within grenade-throwing distance of one machine-gun, but despite several attempts to silence it with both grenades and 66 mm LAWs, he was forced to withdraw under heavy small-arms fire.

Attacks were soon supported by the GPMG and Milan teams who had moved on to the mountain under Major Dennison. The GPMGs hammered it out with enemy heavy machine-guns while the wire-guided Milan missiles were used to devastating effect against the bunkers, the operators homing them on to targets at very short ranges. Unfortunately, all three members of one Milan crew were killed by a single round from an enemy 105 mm recoilless rifle during these engagements. Argentinian dead lay in the shadow of the rocks where they had fallen, while others, who had been cowering, were winkled out by follow-up sections.

The fighting had now reached a critical phase, developing into a battle of wills between attacker and defender. The battalion had established a secure hold on their objective but were finding the enemy's resistance much tougher than they had expected. The battalion was also being heavily shelled, and the enemy had no difficulty in adjusting their fire to be more accurate. On the eastern peak (*Full Back*) the enemy's fire held up both the frontal assault and also 'B' Company's repeated attempts to outflank Argentinian positions. Fire from these positions had also effectively pinned down 'A' Company and stopped them fulfilling their initial objective of *Wing Forward*.

By now Lieutenant-Colonel Pike had gone forward with his signaller, Lance Corporal 'Jock' Begg, to the forward groups of 'B' Company and had linked up with Major Argue. The company had been seriously reduced in strength, but was firmly in possession of *Fly Half*, the western end of the mountain. Every attempt to make further progress by outflanking was now being beaten back, with continuing losses. It was also at about this time that the battalion got news on the brigade net of enemy Huey helicopters taking off from Stanley and heading towards Longdon – perhaps some kind of counter-attack. But this seemed unlikely to make things any more difficult than they already were, and, in the event, the helicopters never arrived!

It was clear to the commanding officer that he must use 'A' Company, now closer than 'C', to take the fight through to *Full Back* and to maintain the pressure of the attack. He reported all this to the brigadier, as he crouched next to three bayoneted enemy corpses, and left him in no doubt that they would succeed in the end. While 'A' Company's attack got under way the stretcher-bearer platoon was moving in the darkness, and over the ice-covered rocks, to locate and evacuate the wounded – a most trying and exhausting task, made a hundred times more so by the constant artillery and mortar fire to which they were exposed. Lance Corporal Bassey was wounded by a mine when he tried to reach Corporal Milne (the first man to have been wounded that

The rifle butt of a captured Argentinian soldier.

night), while others were hit by shellfire as they struggled down the rocky slopes with their wounded comrades. These stretcher parties, led by Major Roger Patton, Battalion Second in Command, also humped ammunition forward for the battalion's various weapons, assisted as far as the Murrel Bridge by wheeled and tracked transport. On this lifeline, the battalion's ultimate success in battle was wholly dependent.

'A' Company now fought a slow, systematic battle, well supported by the battalion's GPMGs and artillery, in the face of very heavy and accurate enemy machine-gun fire from the rocks above the grassy saddle between *Fly Half* and *Full Back*. The impact of artillery, mortar and machine-gun fire, and the stunning effect of Milans, Carl Gustavs and 66 mm LAWs at short range, smashed into the enemy's will to fight. But it was daylight before *Full Back* was fully secure. Most of the enemy who had not withdrawn were strewn dead along the tracks and among the rocks – some dismembered by artillery and mortar fire, others shot and bayoneted.

As dawn broke this scene will be perhaps the most enduring and haunting memory of this long, cold fight. Groups of young soldiers, grim-faced, shocked but determined, moved through the mist with their bayonets fixed to check the enemy dead. The debris of battle was scattered along the length of the mountain, encountered around every turn in the rocks, in every gully. Weapons, clothing, rations, blankets, boots, tents, ammunition, sleeping bags, blood-soaked medical dressings, web equipment and packs had been abandoned, along with 105 mm recoilless rifles, 120 mm mortars, Browning heavy machine-guns, and the sophisticated night vision binoculars and sights with which the Argentinian snipers had pinpointed the British troops during the long night.

Lieutenant-Colonel Hew Pike, later to serve as one of the British Army's senior officers, said:

> The sour and distinctive odour of death lingered in the nostrils as we began to dig temporary graves for some of the enemy dead. But it was a slow job, and eventually the task was abandoned when enemy artillery and mortars started again.
>
> Argentine bunkers yielded not only the particular 'smell' of the enemy, but also Camel cigarettes, bottles of brandy, rounds of cheese, bully beef, and mail from Argentina – a poignant reminder that those we had fought against were also men with families at home, awaiting news of them.
>
> The flock of prisoners we now had to move to safety from their own artillery fire were mostly bewildered peasants in uniform, some hardly more than boys, but with professional soldiers made of sterner stuff to organise them and provide backbone and discipline.
>
> From my position on the forward slopes of Longdon, Wireless Ridge looked to be ours for the taking, and I was anxious to continue our advance if at all possible. But Wireless Ridge was beyond the range of our guns until they moved forward, and was dominated by enemy-held Tumbledown. Further exploitation was not now a feasible operation of war.
>
> We held our ground, protecting ourselves as best we could on our hard-won mountain, for the enemy's artillery and mortar fire was to continue to plague us until their collapse three days later, and a number of men who had fought so well and survived through a night of battle were to be killed by sudden barrages of shell fire as they moved out of necessity over the mountain, often to help the wounded.
>
> It was a grim business, and the battalion continued to lose some of its best soldiers – men like Corporal Stewart McLaughlin, who had been in the thick of the fighting during the night and received a nasty shrapnel wound in the back just after first light. Together with his two escorts, he was hit by heavy mortar fire as he was being evacuated. Or again, Private Richard Absolon, a Patrol Company sniper, had come through numerous recce patrols and a night of battle only to be mortally wounded in the head by shellfire as he helped a comrade reach safety.

In the bitter night-fighting and the subsequent shelling among the rocks of Mount Longdon the battalion lost twenty-three men and had forty-seven wounded. Many of the latter, six of whom lost limbs, had reason to be grateful to the professional skills and dedication of Major Charles Batty and the members of his Field Surgical Team who had worked tirelessly in the bunkhouse at Teal Inlet during the long battle to take and hold Mount Longdon.

Lieutenant-Colonel Pike added:

> The headlong gallop into Stanley on 14 June, down slopes upon which a few hours before such movement would have drawn a massive weight of artillery fire, seemed scarcely believable. We had been screwing up our courage for another night battle through Moody Brook; and suddenly here we were, requisitioning bungalows and outhouses along the Stanley waterfront. The sense of relief, and of achievement, was profound.
>
> Self-confidence and the will to win – developed through tough selection and demanding training – had

Memorial at Goose Green to the men of the 2nd Battalion's Battle Group who were killed in the first action of the conflict.

seen us through to victory in a remarkable passage of arms. But the overwhelming emotion was not one of elation in victory but of shock and sadness that so many had been killed or wounded, and deep exhaustion.

'Well, thank God, I don't know what it is to lose a battle,' the Duke of Wellington is said to have remarked to Dr Hume when he was shown the casualty list on the morning after Waterloo, 'but certainly, nothing can be more painful than to gain one, with the loss of so many of one's friends.'

The outstanding bravery of the Parachute Regiment in the Falklands was recognised by the award of two posthumous Victoria Crosses and a significant number of additional decorations including six Military Crosses, twelve Military Medals, five Distinguished Conduct Medals and many officers and soldiers Mentioned in Dispatches. Lieutenant Colin Connor, a young officer in 2 Para, won the Military Cross at Goose Green after he was sent forward on a reconnaissance mission. Connor is a modest man who played down his role but he demonstrated the courage typical of the men of the Parachute Regiment during Operation Corporate.

By the time the battalion had moved off Sussex Mountain for Goose Green, Connor was already stalking the Argentines. In freezing conditions, and without food or water, Connor and his team crawled 5 miles to observe enemy positions. For fourteen hours he lay still as Argentine look-outs scanned the hills for signs of an advance. Finally, disregarding his own safety, he radioed for RAF Harriers to blitz their positions. It was a call that almost cost him his life.

The Argentinian gunners were dug in and well protected against anti-personnel bombs. Worse, the radio signal Connor sent had blown his cover and left his men a sitting target for a nearby machine-gun nest. He recalled: 'The sound of the crack and thud all around still sticks in my mind. Our job was to go ahead of the battalion and locate the enemy to assist the commanding officer's battle plan. I was only doing what I had been trained for. Every man in 2 Para would have done the same.'

As the hail of bullets continued, Connor led his team away from the area. They hid in chest-deep water for half a day with the young lieutenant relaying intelligence messages back to base until his radio batteries faded. He added:

We were totally cut off and the only way out was to run for cover. We certainly didn't have time to be frightened – we were too busy. The atmosphere is hard to describe. It was ugly, but I was glad to have been there. I would have felt like a fireman who missed the fire brigade's biggest blaze had I not gone.

Everything was moving so quickly no one realised our casualties were high. When I heard 'H' had been hit I was so shocked I just couldn't believe it. Everyone was stunned. Then we heard the Mirage jets screaming towards us, dropping napalm. It was close . . . but somehow we got out alive.

Colin's Military Cross citation records that his 'outstanding bravery' in spotting the enemy saved many British soldiers in the battle for Goose Green.

A member of 2 Para on patrol in West Belfast.

9. Northern Ireland

The Longest Campaign

The Parachute Regiment was among the first units to arrive in Northern Ireland late in 1969, on an emergency tour of duty that was expected to last a few months as troops set out to defuse violence between Protestant and Catholic communities by creating a climate of security. Nobody could have predicted that it would develop into the British Army's longest active service campaign. Few would have thought that for the next ten years the regiment would either have a battalion in Ulster or be preparing to deploy another, or that from the early 1980s at least one battalion would be permanently based in the Province on a two-year tour and would often be joined by another battalion deployed on a roulement tour.

With the exception of the Ulster Defence Regiment, later renamed the Royal Irish Regiment, the Parachute Regiment has served in Ulster every year since 1969, accumulating more than a decade of operational service across the Province, during which their success against terrorism has instilled a fear among IRA units. Troops were first sent to reinforce the Ulster garrison and deploy on security duties after the Northern Ireland government called on the Labour Prime Minister, Harold Wilson, for military assistance. This followed months of sectarian violence between rival Catholic and Protestant communities in Londonderry which had exhausted the 3,200-strong Royal Ulster Constabulary.

Trouble had flared up throughout the 1960s as Protestant extremists hit back at nationalists following the failure of the IRA campaign. This took place between 1956 and 1962 and cost six members of the RUC and eleven B Specials their lives. The Ulster Volunteer Force shot dead a Catholic on 27 April 1966, then another victim was shot in June. A period of calm returned for several years, then, in 1968, there was more civil unrest when a Northern Ireland Civil Rights March, formed by Catholics from across the social sectors, marched into Londonderry on 5 October 1968. It had been banned by the Home Affairs Minister and when it went ahead police units moved in with batons, and seventy-five people were injured.

Throughout 1969 tension increased as the situation deteriorated. The Army's senior officer, Lieutenant-General Sir Ian Freeland, had just 2,500 troops already based in Ulster, and had made contingency plans to deploy them to guard Government buildings. By July the Wilson government had approved the use of CS gas by the Royal Ulster Constabulary and on 12 August it was used for the first time in the United Kingdom as riots flared in the Bogside area of Londonderry. On 13 August 300 troops from the Prince of Wales's Own Regiment of Yorkshire were sent to HMS *Eagle*, a naval shorebase in Londonderry, and a day later they were deployed to the Bogside after an exhausted RUC requested military assistance. In Belfast, on the night of 15 August, 10 civilians were killed, 145 were injured and 4 policemen wounded in gun battles.

More troops were committed to Ulster and on 12 October 1969 the 1st Battalion the Parachute Regiment arrived in Belfast on what was called Operation Banner. Its task was to protect the Catholic community from extremist Protestant attacks and the Paras were welcomed with smiling faces, clapping and offers of tea and cakes.

Within hours of arriving the battalion was on the streets as a baying mob of 500 Protestants rioted in the Shankhill Road. The Paras quickly took control of the situation and, working with the RUC, made sixty-nine arrests, seized arms, ammunition and a pirate radio station. A day after they arrived troops were ordered to fire back at snipers and bombers.

A corporal who deployed to Belfast in 1969 with 1 Para recalls:

When we arrived in Belfast there were no-go areas where the police and troops were not allowed in: I thought it was madness. We were protecting Catholics from Protestant gangs and they welcomed us,

Tea and cakes. In the early days of the conflict in 1969 members of the Parachute Regiment were welcomed with smiles and refreshments, but that was soon to change and within 12 months the regiment was facing bombs and bullets.

but trouble would always flare at the weekend when the pubs turned out and the Protestants started, but at first we could defuse it by talking to the ringleaders.

This was aimed at building confidence in the community and it seemed to work, but the next time I returned to the Province it had all turned sour; shootings and riots were commonplace and the republican community had turned on us, they hated us and seemed to have forgotten that we had been sent to protect them.

We had left that first tour with good strong links with the locals. I remember the CO saying we had won the hearts and minds of both communities. When we returned in 1970 and were deployed to assist in a riot at the bottom of the Shankhill Road, where we had been in 1969, a senior officer said take your helmets off and put your berets on.

He thought that the locals would remember who we were from 1969, and the violence would stop. Instead they threw more bricks; it was incredible: the area was a war zone. The violence was bad, burning vehicles and angry people, but what was worse was the fact that a year earlier we had stood laughing and joking with these people and we could not understand why they had changed so much.

Within twelve months of the first troops being sent in the friendly atmosphere had changed completely. Along with other units, the Paras found themselves under attack. Cakes and buns earlier handed out to the Red Berets by Catholic housewives as a thank you for protecting them were still passed round – but they now contained powdered glass and rat poison.

Para Bernie Winter says he remembers vividly the constant sniper shootings in Belfast during the early 1970s, which kept every soldier alert whenever he went out on patrol. He recalled:

The honeymoon period soon ended. There was a shooting almost every night and we often returned fire. Belfast was like Dodge city.

I can remember the 'hearts and minds' theme being drummed into us by our company commander, but while we could talk to the elder members of the community the youngsters just saw us as targets on which to vent their anger. When they attacked us we went in hard, made arrests and ended the problem as quickly as possible – if you didn't you could be standing around with a baton and shield with bricks being aimed at you all night.

One of the biggest problems in the early days was making sure you didn't open up [fire at] on another regiment when you were operating in Belfast. Our boundaries were obviously very close and there were several incidents in which various units fired at each other at night – thinking they had an IRA contact.

To be fair it was an easy mistake to make. If you had just been fired on, then saw a person with a gun you could mistake him for a gunmen and at the same time he was probably going through the same process in his mind. To add to the chaos and confusion communications were sometimes difficult in some areas of the city.

The soldiers of the Parachute Regiment, unlike those from other units, were easy to distinguish with their maroon berets and different smocks, while their high reputation as one of the British Army's most respected regiments meant that wherever they served in the Province they inevitably attracted attention. During riots it had almost become

A patrol of 1 Para, on the left, secures the street after a bomb explodes in Belfast during the 1970s.

accepted procedure for army units to simply stand behind their riot shields and defend themselves against the hail of bricks, bottles and petrol bombs, mounting the occasional snatch squad to arrest ringleaders. But the regiment adopted a more aggressive 'no nonsense' policy: instead of standing meekly behind riot shields they took the initiative, they went straight in and detained those throwing the petrol bombs, the aim being to defuse the situation and restore public order.

Quickly the IRA accused the Paras of excessive 'use of force' in a well-organised propaganda campaign intended to discredit the regiment and the British Army's presence in Ulster. During the 1970s the IRA mounted a number of 'stage-managed propaganda stunts' within nationalist housing estates to further discredit the Army.

In the early days a classic example of this involved an IRA officer pretending to be a loyalist and making a telephone call to tip off the security forces about weapons hidden in a house. The property, the home of an innocent nationalist family living on a Republican estate, who had nothing to do with the IRA, and no sympathy for their violence, would then be raided by the RUC and the Army. Convinced they were about to hit gold and find rifles or ammunition, the security forces would rip the property apart and find nothing, leaving only a distressed family whose experience influenced them to support the IRA. Later, the procedure for house searches was changed and more checks made prior to the search operation – but in many cases the damage had been done.

There were, of course, many mistakes made by the security forces in those early days, often resulting from an innocent enthusiasm to get results, and these added further fuel to the propaganda fire started by the IRA, which included exaggerated accounts of Army activity, claims that soldiers had adopted a 'shoot to kill' policy in nationalist areas and that the Army was only deployed in Catholic areas.

In early 1971 the 2nd Battalion, which had been in Londonderry, moved to Belfast to take over from the 3rd Battalion. The routine for the Paras in Belfast centred on dealing with barricades, bus hijacks, bomb scares and regular shootings. The Provisional IRA had now raised its head – a militant splinter group of the official IRA – and had mounted a campaign to attack RUC stations.

On 25 May 1971 the Parachute Regiment lost its first man when Sergeant Mick Willetts was killed by an IRA bomb at the Springfield Road police station. A suitcase containing the bomb was thrown in through the doorway and Willetts used his body as a protective shield to allow two adults and their children to escape, sacrificing his own life to save them. His bravery and courage in saving the lives of these young children did not raise one gesture of thanks from the nationalist community. Sergeant Willetts was posthumously awarded the George Cross and to this day, when young Paras undergo pre-Northern Ireland training they are always reminded of the incident. (The first British soldier to be killed was Gunner Robert Curtis. He was shot by an IRA gunman on 6 February 1971. By the end of the year forty-eight soldiers had been killed.)

In July the level of violence escalated further. The operation log report for the 2nd Battalion recorded twenty explosions, five shootings and twelve hoax bomb calls in

A member of 2 Para mans a vehicle checkpoint in West Belfast.

just one night. The bombing campaign increased and was used to attract the security forces to an area where IRA gunmen would be waiting, ready to shoot at the troops as they arrived to deal with the bomb blast. A soldier serving with the 2nd Battalion in Belfast in 1971 remembers the night a nail bomb was thrown at his patrol as it passed through a Republican housing estate in the Ballymurphy area.

The former private, who is now working in London with an insurance company, recalled:

There were six of us and it was late. We were heading back to our location after what had been a pretty uneventful evening.

We were on foot and the idea was to stop and search those we suspected, ask what people were doing, in the aim of building up some form of intelligence picture. As I crossed the road I remember seeing a flash in the window of the house to my front. I hadn't got a clue what it was, then almost straight away I felt a blast on my back and heard this huge bang.

It probably wasn't huge really, but it seemed it to me. I had been hit in the leg and still wasn't sure what had happened when my mate came over and told me not to move. A nail bomb had been chucked over a wall as we passed and three of the lads mounted a quick follow-up while two remained with me.

A mobile patrol seemed to be with us almost straight away: I had four nails in my leg. They looked fairly small to me, but what I couldn't see was that they had gone right into the leg. A fragment of metal had also opened up my calf and I was bleeding like the proverbial stuck pig. They put me in the back of the Land Rover and took me to Musgrave Park. [A military hospital in Belfast.]

I spent two weeks in Musgrave, then I was transferred to the Cambridge Military Hospital at Aldershot. Twenty-seven stitches that cost me. Two years later I was a hundred yards away from a car bomb when it went up. It cost me my hearing in one ear and my career. I suppose I was lucky to survive it.

By now mobs were out on the streets every night stoning soldiers, torching buildings, hijacking buses and generally destroying the infrastructure and economic fabric of Ulster. This high level of public disorder, combined with increased terrorist attacks against the security forces, resulted in the government introducing internment on 9 August 1971, during which suspects were arrested and detained.

On Monday 9 August 1971 battalions across Northern Ireland were given allocated areas in which they were to 'lift' suspects. The 2nd Battalion the Parachute Regiment was assigned the large area of Belfast which included the Ballymurphy, Turf Lodge, Whiterock, Beechmount, South Suffolk, Clonard and all of Andersonstown. The operation was codenamed 'Demetrius' and was launched across the Province in the early hours of that morning. To assist in the operation the battalion had under command 'C' company of 1st Battalion the Parachute Regiment, elements of the Parachute Squadron Royal Armoured Corps, 'B' Squadron the 15th/19th King's Royal Hussars and 54 Battery Royal Artillery.

Reaction to internment was fierce and crowds gathered to protest throughout the nationalist areas, barricades were erected and, as troops removed them, petrol bombs rained down. Support Company of 2nd Battalion engaged at least twelve snipers in the area of Moynard flats, and at least five IRA gunmen were killed in this operation.

Bloody Sunday. Members of the 1st Battalion round up suspects for questioning after the civil rights march which ended in thirteen deaths.

In January 1972 the 1st Battalion were moved from their base at Palace Barracks to Londonderry, having been ordered to provide support to the RUC at a mass civil rights march. This was scheduled to take place in the Creggan Estate and Rossville Flats area of the city on Sunday 30 January. The march, like all such demonstrations in Northern Ireland at the time, was illegal and intelligence reports had indicated that armed opposition was expected from the Provisional IRA. As a result 1 Para had been tasked by 8 Infantry Brigade to make arrests within a specified area beyond what was called the 'containment line'.

On Sunday 30 January 1972 more than 900 marchers set off from the Creggan Estate, and later the number is believed to have swelled to 3,000 plus. The exact details of what happened that afternoon remain the subject of much controversy.

By early afternoon the Royal Anglians, the resident battalion in the area, were facing an intense barrage of bricks and stones. The Paras who had been drafted in as the brigade reserve were ordered to go in and make arrests. At 1607 hours the first snatch squads stormed the barricades and moved into Rossville street to make arrests. In the following hour thirteen people were shot dead by the Army; the exact detail of each contact is not known but more than 100 rounds were fired by the battalion. The Paras later stated that they were fired on, while the Republican marchers claimed that no

The Parachute Regiment Officers' Mess – a soft target bombed by the IRA three weeks after Bloody Sunday. The attack killed seven people, none of them military staff.

shots were fired at the Army. In a built-up area such as this complex of flats it may have been very difficult to determine where a sniper shot had come from, and the Paras had to make split-second decisions. As far as they were concerned they were being attacked. Hundreds, possibly thousands of people, an atmosphere of high tension, people looking out of windows, silhouettes of people near the flats – it must have been a difficult job to try and identify who was shooting who. Whatever happened the outcome was tragic and gave the Provisional IRA a recruiting tool that they continue to use in the 1990s.

The Paras have always had a reputation for getting the job done and in Londonderry the military command had decided that they would use this march to set an example, and illegal marchers would be arrested. It was a particularly dirty job and left the Army in a definite 'no-win' situation. Witnesses alleged that the Paras fired wildly into the crowd but if their fire had been indiscriminate as the IRA claimed, it would be reasonable to expect that at least one woman or child in a crowd of 3,000 would have been hit. In fact all those shot were male and between the age of eighteen and twenty-six, and while the PIRA had a well-oiled publicity machine, the British Army public relations effort was very poor in contrast.

Subsequently nicknamed 'Bloody Sunday', the events of 30 January 1972 seem certain to remain the subject of controversy for years to come. The 1st Battalion was accused of murder but in a tribunal held under the Lord Chief Justice Widgery he found that the intention to use 1 Para as an arresting force was sincere and that the commanding officer of the battalion did not exceed his orders. The report further concluded that while all of the victims were unarmed the Paras were not guilty of murder or unlawful killing.

A captain who served in the 1st Battalion recalls events on 30 January 1972. He said:

Our mission that day was clear, make maximum arrests of the hooligan element within the crowd. These marches were illegal and there had been several since Christmas. This was the biggest and the command structure wanted action.

The problem was that while our aim was clear, it did not take account of what we should do if we found ourselves in the Bogside. The plan was to make arrests 300 metres over what we called the

A member of 2 Para prepares to lead a patrol out of a border police station during a tour of duty in 1997.

A Parachute Regiment QRF (Quick Reaction Force) awaits orders late in the evening near the Shankhill Road in Belfast during a disturbance in the mid-1970s.

containment line, but black and white plans never hold water once you are on the ground. We were given a task and we completed it, we were attacked and we reacted, we moved in, made arrests and held the ground to await orders – to withdraw.

We were in a no-win situation, it was a high risk operation and it was given to us. We do not stand around and let people shoot at us. I know they say there were no shots fired at us, but then that is easy to believe if you were not there and were not fired on.

I was saddened that innocent people may have died that day, but it should not be forgotten that hundreds of innocent people have died in Northern Ireland in tragic circumstances. What sickens me is the growing band of armchair experts who sit back and analyse what we did in 1972; perhaps if they had been under fire or looked a crowd of rioting yobs in the eye, then they would be qualified to judge – but the fact is they haven't and they're not.

Twenty-five years after the event the former commanding officer, Lieutenant-Colonel Derek Wilford, who now lives abroad, said in a television interview that his men had acted in a most professional manner, adding that had the battalion deliberately shot anyone, as had been suggested, then the Bogside area would have been full of body bags.

Just a month after Bloody Sunday, the IRA bombed the officers' mess of 16th Para Brigade at Aldershot in Hampshire, clearly aiming to murder officers of the regiment. For the IRA, however, it was a disaster: seven civilians were killed, among them five women, a gardener and a Catholic padre. One of the women was a Mrs Bosley, the mother of a Parachute Regiment corporal. In 1998 the Provisional IRA called, via political groups, for an official apology from Prime Minister Tony Blair and his Labour government in respect of Bloody Sunday, but to date have shown no remorse for the murders at the Aldershot mess – and have instead called for the Parachute Regiment to be withdrawn from Ulster.

By the middle of 1972 Catholic 'no go' areas had spread across West Belfast and Londonderry, and the violence had increased as gunmen sought refuge from the security forces in Nationalist estates: here they were free from capture. After Bloody Friday on 21 July 1972, when bombs shattered Belfast and left nine people dead, a plan was drawn up to clear the 'no go' areas and restore law and order in the Province.

Codenamed 'Motorman' the operation was the largest to be mounted by the British Army since Operation 'Musketeer', the air and sea assault into Suez. It involved 21,000 troops from 27 different units and included four Centurion tanks in the Armoured Vehicle Royal Engineers (AVRE) role, which were deployed from landing craft on the River Foyle and used to smash barricades in the estates of Londonderry. Hundreds of armoured vehicles supported the operation which began at 0400 hours on 31 July. The 2nd Battalion Parachute Regiment moved into an area that embraced the west side of the city. There was little resistance to this massive force, barricades were smashed down, weapons and ammunition were seized and the 'no go' enclaves opened up.

The Parachute Regiment's contribution to the defeat of terrorism in Northern Ireland has been immense. Perhaps more than any other regiment they have been the butt of much IRA vilification and propaganda, most of this arising from Bloody Sunday, and they continued to be a top target of the IRA throughout the 1970s.

Driving through Whiterock one evening, a mobile patrol of two Land Rovers from the Parachute Regiment foiled an elaborate IRA attempt to kill soldiers. It was common practice for military patrols to quickly 'follow up' a shooting or a bombing by either calling for reinforcements or investigating it themselves. The driver, who for security reasons cannot be named, saw what he thought was a discarded cigarette end flash over his windscreen but almost instantly realised it was a blast bomb. Both Land Rovers pulled over and, as the device exploded, the crews jumped out and took cover while the patrol commander radioed a 'contact' report of the incident to their base. As the Paras sat crouched in alleyways and alongside garden walls a taxi pulled up and a gunman with a Thompson sub-machine-gun jumped out and opened fire on them. A warning was given and in the exchange of fire the gunman was killed. The taxi driver was arrested. Such Wild West attacks by the IRA were commonplace in the 1970s and were often carried out by new recruits to the Provisionals as a form of initiation to prove their value to the terrorist group.

A van packed with beer kegs full of explosives erupts in Belfast.

A soldier of 2 Para pictured between the rival headlines of two newspaper hoardings in the border regions otherwise known as 'bandit country'.

In the late 1970s procedures for searching houses had been significantly reviewed but an incident reported in a Belfast newspaper sums up the propaganda battle that the regiment continued to face. Members of the 2nd Battalion had searched a house in west Belfast along with the RUC and left without causing offence, taking with them two items for further examination. The following day the Paras were headline news in the local paper. The woman who owned the house that had been searched claimed that the patrol had smashed her toilet and urinated on her son. When she arrived to collect the items taken the previous day the company commander drew her attention to the story and after agreeing that it was lies she commented cheerfully, 'Never mind, that's just our propaganda'.

In 1976 trouble flared in the border regions of south Armagh and Fermanagh when IRA patrols attacked security force bases at Forkhill, Crossmaglen and Newry. The 3rd Battalion moved into Bessbrook in early 1976 and mounted a vigorous campaign to win 'hearts and minds' while at the same time actively pursuing terrorists. Within minutes of taking over from the Royal Scots the battalion came under attack. A Wessex helicopter with members of 'A' Company aboard was hit at Crossmaglen by an RPG7 rocket and small-arms fire as it landed. They quickly returned fire and in the follow-up operation five men were arrested. Fortunately the helicopter sustained only minor damage. This incident on day one of the tour was to set the pace: scarcely a day passed without a shooting or bombing occurring in the unit's tactical area of operation, which covered 303

Members of 'B' Company, 2 Para, near Duncairn Gardens, pictured in the 1970s.

miles of border and 290 crossing places. In May 'C' Company discovered seven beer kegs containing 100 lb of home-made explosives in a shed close to the border.

A month later another patrol from 'C' Company was deployed on the road that runs from Meigh via Drumintee to Forkhill. They were ordered to carry out random vehicle checks at checkpoints late at night. A landmine had been buried in the verge and it was detonated as the last member of the patrol drew level with it. The landmine, later discovered to contain 200 lb of explosives, blew the patrol off their feet, although luckily no one was injured. As the patrol recovered from this a car pulled up and the section commander ordered the driver to turn his lights off. Suddenly a second car approached the scene and accelerated at speed past the stationary vehicle. One soldier fired a single warning shot at the car and other members of the patrol, who thought the the shot had come from the vehicle, also opened fire and killed the driver. It was later established that the driver was a young man from Warrenpoint, an innocent civilian, who had probably panicked when he saw armed men on the darkened road. He was killed in a tragic error made by men who had reacted in a split second, while still suffering from the effects of a huge explosion at close range.

Late in June 1976, as the United Kingdom baked in a heatwave, the men of the 3rd Battalion were operating across South Armagh, concentrating around the Cullyhanna area. A twelve-man patrol had been deployed to reconnoitre a landing site to help extract another patrol. Once the site had been cleared the rest of the patrol moved in to secure it. As the second section moved towards the site a huge explosion erupted injuring three men, one of them seriously. All were flown to Musgrave Park hospital in Belfast, with Private Snowdon, the most seriously injured man, being transferred to the Royal Victoria Hospital. He later died of his wounds. Investigations later showed that the device consisted of 40 lb of commercial explosives and was triggered by radio control, probably initiated by a terrorist concealed on the republican side of the border.

Three days later a patrol from 'B' Company spotted four armed and hooded men getting out of an estate car, with a fifth man remaining in the vehicle. A firefight took place and the Paras trapped the terrorists in a nearby bungalow and captured Joseph Quinn and Raymond McCreesh – the other three men remained at large. During the night elements of the company remained on the ground to search the area; this proved successful. Daniel McGuinness was captured and an armalite rifle seized.

Parts of South Armagh proved very difficult to regularly patrol and so the battalion built a permanent observation post (OP) on a feature overlooking the border village of Jonesborough. The OP consisted of twelve gun pits, some of which were manned by mannequin dummies, and numerous dug-in shelters for communications and sleeping. Codenamed 'Phoenix' the observation post consisted of two gunpits with GPMGs in the sustained fire (SF) role, both of which overlooked the terrain towards the border. To ensure that the locals were aware of the Paras' presence they erected a flagpole and flew the Union Jack, which generated numerous complaints from the community.

Three years later the regiment experienced its blackest day in Northern Ireland when

A car bomb in Belfast. A body lies in the road next to the car.

A mobile patrol of 2 Para pictured in West Belfast.

A soldier of the 2nd Battalion pictured in West Belfast during 1992.

Prince Charles, Colonel-in-Chief of the Parachute Regiment, chats to Paras stationed in Northern Ireland during a visit in the 1980s.

a patrol was attacked at Warrenpoint Castle in South Armagh. A road alongside a border river was regularly monitored by the Paras and other regiments, including the RUC, to prevent terrorists from planting bombs. But at some point the Provisionals had concealed a huge bomb alongside the road, possibly in milk churns. On 27 August 1979 a convoy consisting of a Land Rover and two 4-ton trucks carrying men of 'A' Company was travelling along the coastal road from Ballykinler en route for 'A' Company's base at Newry RUC station. The Provisionals had left their bomb in a hay trailer and as the convoy passed the Narrow Water Castle the 500 lb device was detonated by remote control. The rear truck had been destroyed and five members of 'A' Company were killed instantly. The front vehicles stopped and their occupants quickly deployed to assist the casualties, but as they did so they came under fire from across the lough. A Royal Marine detachment on patrol in Warrenpoint heard the explosion and radioed a contact report to 'A' Company's base in Newry.

'A' Company's commander, Major Peter Fursman, and two Land Rover mounted patrols from the machine-gun platoon headed for Warrenpoint, quickly followed by another two vehicles that had been patrolling Newry. Meanwhile, the Queen's Own Highlanders based at Bessbrook dispatched its airborne reaction force in two Wessex helicopters. One helicopter remained airborne while the second put down on the road to disembark medics who set about treating the wounded. A Gazelle helicopter landed and the commanding officer of the Queen's Own Highlanders jumped out and ran down the road to the gatehouse of the castle, where he could see Major Fursman and his two patrols who had arrived from Newry.

At this point the Wessex helicopter on the central reservation was loaded with injured members of 'A' Company and was about to take off. At the very moment it started to lift a second bomb, which was packed in the gateway where Major Fursman, the CO of the Highlanders and the two patrols had taken cover, was detonated. This massive 1,000 lb device killed twelve more men, including Major Fursman and Lieutenant- Colonel Blair, and seriously injured two others. In total eighteen soldiers, sixteen of them Paras, had been killed. Later that same day the IRA murdered Lord Mountbatten who was on a fishing holiday in Northern Ireland.

Throughout the 1980s the regiment's three battalions continued to deploy to the Province on two-year resident tours and six-month roulement tours; these covered the hunger strikes in 1981 and the widespread rioting which followed the death of hunger striker Bobby Sands. Nine more strikers died between 12 May and 20 August 1981.

In 1988 the IRA attempted to kill dozens of sleeping Paratroopers when they planted a device at the barracks of the 2nd Battalion in Ternhill. But, fortunately, an alert sentry cleared everyone from the building. By the end of the 1980s the Provisionals were hitting the mainland of the United Kingdom and the security forces, and in November 1989 a mobile patrol of the 3rd Battalion the Parachute Regiment was caught by a remote-controlled bomb hidden in a stone wall by the roadside near Newry. Three Paras were killed: Lance Corporal Stephen Paul Wilson, Private Donald MacAulay and Private Matthew Marshall. Just before the funeral of Private MacAulay in Liverpool, his mother Irene told the media: 'I want to smile at the cameras so those bastards in the IRA can see they aren't going to get me down.'

In 1992 the 3rd Battalion was on an emergency tour in East Tyrone when it was hit again. A foot patrol was caught in a booby-trap bomb while on duty in Coal Island and paratrooper Alistair Hodgson took the full blast of the explosion – he lost both legs. The Colonel-in-Chief Prince Charles wrote to him and sent him a special 'get well' bottle of whisky. Despite contracting meningitis while in hospital Alistair had made an initial good recovery within four months of the explosion. When the battalion returned from Ulster they arranged a special fund-raising day to help Alistair in the future. The event was intended to be a battalion day only but more than 2,000 men from across the airborne brigade turned out, including Lieutenant-General Hew Pike, and raised more than £20,000 for their colleague.

The Parachute Regiment remains in Ulster throughout the 'ceasefires' of the late 1990s, ready and waiting for a permanent peace to be agreed by the Labour government. However, in almost thirty years of trouble in Ulster, politicians from all parties have presented their solutions and theories to the Ulster's problems, but little has changed – and paratroopers are still serving in Northern Ireland today.

A Pathfinder comes into land in a perfect sunset.

10. *Utrinque Paratus –* 'Ready for Anything'

Britain's military emphasis in the late 1990s is focused on units specifically equipped for high-intensity conflict which are flexible and highly mobile, ready to react at speed to a broad spectrum of unpredictable crises involving UK interests anywhere in the world. It is a force, in fact, 'Ready for Anything'. Today's modern airborne brigade has two battle groups constantly at readiness to move, one by parachute insertion, the other air-landed. In a crisis these spearhead elements of the formation could seize an airfield or suitable landing strip for Hercules aircraft to fly in additional elements of the force, together with its light armour and logistics. The change in the UK's concept of operations followed the collapse of the Soviet Union, and its military threat to the West, where widespread economic instability quickly erupted into conflict as breakaway Russian states sought independence.

Now, in the late 1990s, growing political tension continues to threaten the so-called New World order and to meet Britain's requirement for a strategic intervention force, 5 Airborne Brigade was selected as a core component of the UK's Joint Rapid Deployment Force (JRDF), which was formed in August 1996 as an 'on-call' force at permanent readiness for operations anywhere in the world. The 4,000-strong brigade forms part of 3 (UK) Division and has a priority role to the Allied Rapid Reaction Corps in respect of combat and humanitarian missions in support of NATO, such as the deployment of peace-keeping troops to Bosnia, but it is the commitment to the JRDF and national contingency operations that have secured the brigade's future. In 1996, the entire force of 5 Airborne Brigade took part in a massive JRDF exercise in America to demonstrate its capability in mounting a strategic deployment. Called Purple Star, the exercise involved numerous airborne assaults and a night jump involving 5,100 British and US Paratroopers. It was the biggest parachute assault since the Second World War.

In 1998 new proposals to change the title of the JRDF to the Joint Rapid Reaction Force were drawn up and only the Lead Parachute Battle Group, as opposed to the entire brigade, will be assigned to the JRRF as a theatre entry force, with the retained capability to parachute into an operation. The Brigade's new role as a rapid reaction force has been assisted by the development of new techniques and procedures that have ensured that Britain's airborne force is a step ahead of its adversaries. In particular 5 Airborne Brigade is the only force in the world to adopt a revolutionary

TALO – Tactical Air Land Operations – are rehearsed by members of the Princess of Wales's Royal Regiment using Scimitars and Land Rovers to provide mobility and firepower support to their infantry soldiers.

new low-level parachute (LLP). The new canopy allows the leading battle group the capability to drop at only 250 ft, enabling RAF crews to evade enemy radar by flying at low level. To put that in perspective the low-level height is equivalent to jumping from the fifteenth floor of Canary Wharf Tower in London, which is 800 ft tall.

Such a drop at night significantly boosts the effectiveness of a modern parachute assault, putting soldiers on to a drop zone within nine seconds. This capability will be further enhanced when the RAF equip and train the whole Transport Support (TS) fleet with night-vision goggles (NVG), permitting true low-level night insertion and resupply. The new C-130J will enter service in the very near future and is fitted with a Defensive Aid Suite (DAS) which will markedly improve its ability to penetrate hostile airspace.

In September 1997, trials of the new parachute were carried out at a remote lake near Toulouse in France. Several Parachute Regiment officers, a trials team from Boscombe Down and Andy Cowley – the man who designed the LLP – carried out a series of jumps. The height was progressively reduced from 600 ft to 250 ft, although all the jumps were made into the lake, not on to land. It is now expected that a battalion will make a tactical drop at 250 or 300 ft within the next twelve months, although at present the canopy is being used at 800 and 1,200 ft. Lieutenant-Colonel Simon Barry, one of the most experienced parachutists in the Parachute Regiment, who helped form the brigade's Pathfinder platoon in 1985, said: 'Now the capability has been tested live we have a capability that is unique in the world.'

The core of the brigade's readiness is based on a Lead Parachute Battle Group (LPBG) and a Lead TALO Battle Group (LTBG) [TALO – Tactical Air Land Operations], ready to move at five days' notice. The balance of the brigade is at ten days' notice. These two types of airborne insertion provide the force with immense flexibility. When the Lead Parachute Battle Group deploys it requires up to twenty-five C-130 Hercules aircraft to airlift its paratroopers and equipment to the drop zone. These Hercules are escorted by fighters which fly ahead and 'sanitise' an air corridor of protection for the assault force to fly through.

Referred to as Composite Air Operations (COMAO), these operations utilise the full spectrum of RAF and alliance/coalition aircraft to punch a hole in an enemy's air defences in order to protect the stream of aircraft carrying the assault force, to and from the target.

The political benefit of airborne operations in the 1990s lies in the psychological impact of 'threatening intent', without necessarily dropping men into action. A Parachute Battle Group can be flown to a forward mounting base and held in isolation without the need to commit forces on the ground. A parachute deployment could well consist of a Leading Parachute Battle Group (LPBG) insertion, with a Follow Up Parachute Battle Group (FUPBG) coming shortly after. The LPBG is an all-arms

A Scimitar light armoured vehicle dropped by parachute is checked after a successful trial in the United States during Exercise Purple Star.

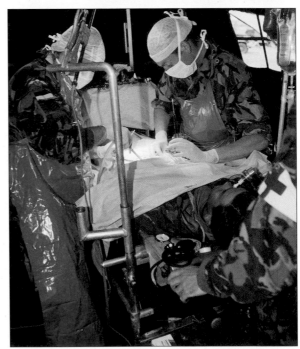

Above left: Brunei; above right: Belize; above: Egypt.

Airborne medics of 23 Parachute Field Ambulance are the brigade's medical specialists and can deploy a field surgical unit anywhere in the world.

Global operations. Troops from 5 Airborne Brigade often train in Jordan, Oman and North Africa to ensure they are ready to operate in any environment if required.

organisation from across the brigade, making it a self-contained fighting force capable of seizing and holding an objective, in readiness for the main force insertion.

The value of airborne forces in today's Army clearly seems to have been recognised, yet it was perhaps only as a result of the regiment's outstanding performance in the Falklands war. Prior to the conflict the only operational infantry brigade 'at readiness to move' was 3 Commando Brigade, Royal Marines. Earlier in the 1970s, the 16th Parachute Brigade had been disbanded and when the 3rd Battalion the Parachute Regiment sailed to the south Atlantic they did so as part of the Royal Marine brigade. After the conflict 5 Infantry Brigade, which had reinforced the initial troops, was renamed 5 Airborne Brigade and the airborne force was put to work. Returning to its wartime structure of parachute and air-landed troops, today's 5 Airborne Brigade is built on two Parachute Regiment battalions and two infantry battalions, who are assigned to the brigade in the TALO role.

During the Second World War the Airborne Brigade consisted of air-landed troops,

Mass drop of Paras using the new low-level parachute.

who arrived by glider, and parachute forces; both wore the red beret although only parachute-trained soldiers wore wings. After the war the glider role was made redundant and only the parachute capability retained.

Today, the modern brigade includes two parachute-trained battle groups but also has the air-landed concept to enhance its manoeuvre readiness. Parachute-trained personnel wear parachute wings as they did during the war, while air-landed personnel, who fly into battle aboard a C-130 Hercules, are entitled to wear the Pegasus emblem of the airborne brigade and in some cases the maroon beret.

At present two infantry battalions, currently drawn from the Gurkhas and the Princess of Wales's Royal Regiment, form the basis of the brigade's air-land force and they regularly train in Tactical Air Land Operations in which they are delivered into battle aboard C-130 Hercules aircraft. The flexible capability of the airborne brigade to deploy by parachute, TALO, aboard a fleet of support helicopters or more conventional means of transport; its ability to react to a broad spectrum of operations with rugged determination, as well as being able to sustain itself independently in difficult terrain, resulted in the brigade being selected as a core component of the UK's Joint Rapid Deployment Force.

The TALO procedure involves a rapid insertion by a C-130 Hercules on to an airfield during which a composite force of infantry and light armour can deploy out of it to carry out a raid, reinforce an operation or support an evacuation of British nationals. The concept involves the landing of up to four C-130 aircraft in a *coup de main* operation to seize a target – usually at night – a method used at Prague in 1968, Entebbe in 1978 and Kabul in 1979. The advantages of this form of assault are that the force arrives grouped and ready for action, and such an operation can achieve enormous surprise. TALO requires a single runway length of at least 1,500 m. If parallel taxi-ways or runways are available it may be possible to TALO on to these simultaneously. Surprise is achieved by making use of the capabilities of the C-130: a very low approach, a sudden steep descent, a rapid stop and deplaning of vehicles and infantry into assault formation.

As part of the JRDF, 5 Airborne Brigade maintains a number of all-arms components at readiness to deploy for operations, while alternating the commitment with its colleagues in 3 Commando Brigade, Royal Marines. It also maintains leading elements of the force as the spearhead group, on twenty-four hours' and seventy-two hours' notice to move.

THE BRIGADE

The Airborne Brigade is a complex formation of specialists and combat troops and includes Pathfinders, light armour, artillery, engineers, medics, signallers and logistic support – all of which can be parachute-dropped or air-landed as the operation requires. Both the battle groups include specialist troops drawn from these units, but the plan can be altered to give priority to medics or engineers depending on the

Paras take part in a live firing exercise in Brecon, Wales. These regular exercises make sure the units of the airborne brigade are constantly ready to deploy anywhere in the world.

The use of support helicopters is a key element of the brigade's airborne operations in the 1990s. Here RAF Puma helicopters prepare to airlift Paras during Exercise Pegasus Strike in Scotland in 1997.

Parachute gunners fire a battery of 105 mm light guns.

A paratrooper with fixed bayonet makes a chilling assault.

A section commander screams orders at his team during an exercise.

Satellite communications: vital equipment for a modern brigade such as 5 Airborne.

A Hercules deploys paratroopers using the new low-level parachute.

mission requirement and the brigade commander's plan. During the Falklands conflict and numerous other operations both artillery and engineer support proved vital. In fact any operation is limited without the support of such specialists.

The sequence of events once detailed planning has been finalised starts with the mobilisation of either the Lead Parachute Battalion Battle Group or the Lead Tactical Air-Land Battle Group, or both. Planning, control and command is directed by the brigade headquarters using secure communications and satcom, where required, being provided by 216 Parachute Squadron Royal Signals. The battle groups may then be moved to an isolation area, such as the Air Mounting Centre (AMC) at South Cerney, where they wait for further orders. This period often provides politicians with the chance to express their intent to another country, before making a final decision. If the requirement is for rapid intervention the force can be airlifted from RAF Lyneham in Wiltshire or Brize Norton in Oxfordshire where a dedicated RAF UK Movements team is on call to move the battlegroup anywhere in the world.

A parachute insertion requires advance forces to locate and secure a drop zone,

Airborne gunners take delivery of their 105 mm light gun which has been flown forward to their position by Chinook. The para-trained gunners deployed to Bosnia with these guns.

Communications are the life-blood of a modern force. Here a soldier of 2 Para uses a Clansman manpack radio.

Machine-gun team pictured in the dawn desert sun of North Africa.

A member of the Pathfinder Platoon free-falls out of a Hercules aircraft. These specialist troops are the advance force who must parachute in ahead of the main force to locate and secure a drop zone.

The Pathfinder Platoon prepares to jump from the ramp of a Hercules aircraft at night. Each man is carrying full equipment and weapons. The unit is a 'Purple' force in that it accepts potential recruits from all three services.

before the main force leaves the UK. This role is carried out by the Pathfinders, a small reconnaissance team which provides 'eyes and ears' surveillance for the commander of the brigade; they parachute in ahead of the formation to identify and mark the drop zone, establish communications and deny the enemy access to the landing force. All the Pathfinders are trained in military free fall, including High Altitude Low Opening (HALO) and High Altitude High Opening (HAHO), as well as demolition, long-range communications and other skills to assist their role. Formed in 1985, the Pathfinders recruit from across the British Forces, not just from within airborne forces. On the ground they will mark the drop zone with small lights at night or a series of coloured triangles during the day at a point known as the Alpha – at which the parachute jump instructors will start to deploy the first sticks of men.

The four fighting battalions of the brigade, two parachute and two air-land units, constantly train for potential operations. Training is mainly at night to make use of the element of surprise, and can involve up to an entire brigade jumping on to one objective, with vehicles and supporting weapons. In addition they are trained in helicopter assault operations; these can be used to mount raids or fly forward support weapons such as artillery guns and logistics supplies. The Chinook helicopter can also be used for the parachute insertion of small teams.

The fighting battalions of the brigade are supported by a dedicated airborne artillery unit, the 7th Parachute Regiment Royal Horse Artillery, which is equipped with 105 mm light guns which have a range of 17 kilometres. These can be dropped by parachute or flown forward by support helicopters. The gunners also provide an air defence capability for the brigade using Javelin low-level anti-aircraft missiles. Engineer skills are vital in identifying minefields and clearing obstacles as the force advances. The brigade is supported by its own parachute-trained squadron which is provided by 36 Engineer Regiment. The sappers of 9 Independent Parachute Squadron Royal Engineers are an integral part of the brigade and at least one troop is always on call as part of the Lead Parachute Battle Group.

The brigade also has a squadron of light armoured reconnaissance vehicles attached to it. The crews are parachute-trained and the vehicles can be dropped by air or delivered in the air-land role. A successful trial was carried out in 1996 during Exercise Purple Star when a Scimitar tank was parachuted into the exercise.

Directing air support is a vital asset and the brigade has two Tactical Air Control Parties who co-ordinate offensive air support and close air support from RAF and Royal Navy aircraft such as Harriers, Tornados and Jaguars.

5 Airborne Brigade has its own logistics support, called the Combat Service Support Battalion, which can provide everything from ammunition, fuel, food and a full range of technical support. It is this logistics supply chain which will directly influence the brigade's ability to achieve its objective.

Medical support is provided by 23 Parachute Field Ambulance, which includes a field surgical team. During the Gulf War 100 members of the unit were sent as reinforcements to 33 General Hospital.

OPERATIONS IN THE 1990s

In October 1996 the headquarters group of 5 Airborne Brigade was told to plan an operation to mount a parachute insertion into Zaire as part of a multi-national humanitarian operation to save thousands of starving refugees who had been displaced from their villages by armed tribesmen.

The mission, codenamed Operation 'Purposeful', was ordered by the then UK Defence Secretary, Michael Portillo MP, after the world's media had focused on starving refugees in the central African state. The refugees had fled into a remote area of the African jungle and difficult terrain prevented any immediate overland assistance by vehicle.

Speed was essential if lives were to be saved and at the Permanent Joint Head-quarters in Northwood, Middlesex, the Chiefs of Staff decided a parachute insertion was the quickest and most effective way in which Britain could assist the multinational operation. The Brigade's Leading Parachute Battle Group, which is always in a state of readiness to move at short notice, was directed to prepare for an operation in Africa.

At their base in Aldershot, Hampshire, Paratroopers spent several days quietly preparing for the jump; engineers, medics and signallers who served with the battle group packed specialist equipment and weighed it in preparation for the operation. A programme of inoculations was carried out and the brigade headquarters staff finalised the planning for Operation 'Purposeful'.

Security was tight and there were no leaks to the media. The brigade commander did not want to alert armed tribesmen or anyone else of his intent. In the Falklands the advance of the 2nd Battalion on Goose Green was compromised when the unit's 'assault plan' was broadcast to the world by the BBC – the incident has never been forgotten by the regiment. The Paras would be joined on the operation by their Royal Marine colleagues in the Joint Rapid Deployment Force and key staff from Arbroath-based 45 Commando travelled to Aldershot to assist in the planning process. The Marines would follow the 1st Battalion the Parachute Regiment, the Leading Parachute Battle Group, in a follow-on operation.

Brigadier Graeme Lamb, then Commander of 5 Airborne Brigade, was eager to see his brigade cut its teeth within the JRDF organisation, but the big problem identified by planning staff at Northwood was the fact that the refugees had disappeared into the bush and could not initially be located by satellite. At RAF Strike Command the plan for the airborne operation included more than twenty C-130 Hercules, twelve of which would carry the leading elements of the force into Zaire. Flying from the UK they would land in Cyprus at night and jump into Africa at first light the following day.

But just as soldiers prepared to say goodbye to their families news came in that the refugees had been located and within twenty-four hours the international aid agencies

A section of Paras prepares to go over the top during an exercise.

Paratroopers on exercise in Egypt board an RAF Chinook helicopter to be flown forward.

A parachute-trained engineer clears mines.

Pathfinders, their marker deployed on the DZ, wait for the main force as a lead aircraft passes overhead.

Members of 5 Airborne Brigade's Pathfinder Platoon prepare to jump from the ramp of a Hercules aircraft.

Pathfinders exit a Hercules aircraft en masse.

announced that there was no longer a requirement for a military intervention force. Like so many operations that were planned during the Second World War the parachute assault was cancelled, but it had been proved that in the 1990s the airborne forces are a valuable asset, particularly in humanitarian operations where refugees can be isolated in remote and inhospitable areas.

Since the JRDF was formed the brigade has been on standby for five operations, including the evacuation of British nationals from Albania in 1997 (Operation 'Helvin' and 'Alleviate') and the deployment of a battalion group to the Congo (Operation 'Determinant') in 1997, to prepare for the evacuation of British nationals. The brigade has also been deployed in support of numerous United Nations operations and prepared contingency plans for other situations. Since British troops first deployed to the former Yugoslavia soldiers from 5 Airborne Brigade have been in Bosnia both in a peace-keeping capacity and, where required, in a military role. Gunners from 7 Parachute Regiment Royal Horse Artillery deployed a battery to the region and when NATO forces carried out bombing raids, Tactical Air Control Parties from the brigade were among the Alliance troops who directed the aircraft missions. Then, in 1997, the gunners deployed to Bosnia again as part of a force called in to monitor the elections, along with troops from the brigade's Royal Gurkha Rifles and medics from 23 Parachute Field Ambulance.

In early 1998 Tactical Air Control parties from the Brigade were back in action in northern Iraq, directing and monitoring coalition aircraft and tasked to enforce the 'no fly zone' established after the Gulf War. Then, as tension mounted in the Gulf in February, the air control teams prepared to deploy into Kuwait.

THE FUTURE AIRBORNE BRIGADE

In the past decade Britain's airborne brigade has introduced fundamental changes to its concept of operations and tactical capability, ensuring that it is ready to deploy as a rapid reaction force anywhere in the world and face the military challenges of the twenty-first century. While formations across the British Army have all benefited from new equipment and weapons, the airborne brigade has focused on improvement in its own mobility with the introduction of the Low-Level Parachute (LLP), the development of air-landed operations and the extensive use of support helicopters.

The brigade's established pedigree in mounting successful parachute and tactical air-land assaults in the dead of night, to support military or humanitarian operations, as well as its growing work alongside French and American airborne forces, have placed it in a strong position for deployment as part of a multi-national force. In addition, the deployment of existing weapons systems to enhance firepower, the adoption of small all-terrain vehicles for use as equipment 'mules', and the planned procurement of new weapons, such as the automatic grenade launcher, has provided the platform to allow a commander to project a well-armed battle group into action at low level.

The introduction of twenty-four Milan systems to the Lead Battle Group (parachute and air-landed) as well as twelve heavy machine guns (HMG), was made in 1996 as a direct response to the increased military capability of potential adversaries. In parts of Africa and other 'hot spots' a lightly armed airborne force could be pitched against well-armed militia equipped with 30-mm calibre weapons, mounted on-off road vehicles called 'technicals'. However, the increased weapons systems, which are not particularly portable over any distance, could easily slow the pace of an assault force in its advance from the drop zone. As a result the brigade launched a trial in September 1996 in which Quad all-terrain vehicles (ATV) were employed to carry the weapons systems.

These trials were initially carried out by the 1st Battalion the Parachute Regiment with the ATVs being assigned to company groups, the Machine Gun and Anti-Tank Platoons. The trials were a great success and it was found that the small four-wheel Quads could access severe terrain over which Land Rovers could not operate. To further boost its firepower the brigade is seeking to procure a highly mobile all-terrain vehicle that can provide heavy-fire support and incorporate an accurate anti-tank system. The German Wiesel has been looked at and is already a key player in German air mobile operations, being deployed by support helicopters and the C-130 Hercules.

These enhancements have qualified the Brigade as a rapid intervention force – a role that has become the cornerstone of military operations in the late 1990s in response to the growing global instability caused by political and economic tensions which constantly threaten to erupt into conflict. The fall of the Berlin Wall in 1989 ushered in a new strategic era for the United Kingdom and other NATO partners. The Alliance's previous stance of preparing to defend against a full-scale attack from the old Warsaw Pact is no longer seen as either appropriate or necessary. In a fast-moving world the day of sailing to war with a ship full of tanks may have passed; in the late 1990s a fast response is required. Improved global communications have added to the demand for immediate information, which has added to regional instability combined with economic, social and political tensions; these now threaten security across the globe. The end of the Cold War has not resulted in a world free from the threat of conflict.

In the past ten years British armed forces have been deployed on more operations than ever previously recorded in peacetime. The former Yugoslavia, the Gulf War, numerous humanitarian missions and, of course, tours of duty in Northern Ireland, are just a few of the areas that have required a military response. In the next decade the British government may be faced with a number of potential scenarios which could include the evacuation of hundreds of British holiday makers from a war zone, deploying an intervention force to enforce a United Nations mandate, protecting starving refugees from armed militia or mounting a full scale 'Falklands-style' assault to recover sovereign land.

Any of these scenarios may require a response 'reaction force' – the ability to put military forces into a potentially hostile environment and achieve their mission quickly.

Black Hawk helicopters during the Panama invasion. These troop-carrying helicopters are widely used by the US 82nd Airborne and provide the US paratroopers with a heliborne capability.

11. THE AMERICAN AIRBORNE FORCES

British airborne forces have continued to maintain close links with their US airborne counterparts since the Second World War. In particular 5 Airborne Brigade is closely associated with the 82nd Airborne Division and maintains an officer exchange programme with the unit.

The paratroopers of the 82nd Airborne Division, known as 'America's Guard of Honor', serve in a division with a proud history and well-deserved reputation which dates back to the First World War. Originally formed as the 82nd Infantry Division on 25 August 1917, at Camp Gordon, Georgia, 82nd soldiers were nicknamed the 'All-Americans' when it was discovered that the division contained men from every state in the union. The nickname resulted in the famous 'AA' shoulder patch, which 82nd paratroopers still wear proudly today.

The division deployed to France in the spring of 1918. In nearly five months of combat, the 82nd fought in three major campaigns and helped break the fighting spirit of the Imperial German Army. Two 82nd soldiers earned the Medal of Honor, America's highest decoration for valour. Lieutenant-Colonel Emory J. Pike, division machine-gun officer, was conducting a front-line reconnaissance mission on 15 September 1918, near Vandieras, France, when heavy artillery shelling disrupted the advance of his division units. Pike reorganised the units and secured the position against enemy attack. He was severely wounded by shell fire when he went to the aid of a wounded soldier at an outpost. Corporal Alvin C. York, Company 'G', 328th Infantry, earned his Medal of Honor for bravery in action near Chatel-Chéhery, France, on 8 October 1918. York took command of his platoon after three non-commissioned officers had been wounded or killed. He fearlessly charged a machine-gun nest, capturing four German officers, 128 men and several weapons.

The 82nd was demobilised after the First World War. For more than twenty years, the 'All-Americans' would live only in the memories of men who served in its ranks during the conflict. With the outbreak of the Second World War, however, the 82nd was reactivated on 25 March 1942, at Camp Claiborne, Louisiana, under the command of Major General Omar N. Bradley. On 15 August of that year, the 82nd became the first airborne division in the US Army, redesignated as the 82nd Airborne Division.

On 15 August 1942, 82nd Airborne Division paratroopers set sail for North Africa under the command of Major-General Matthew B. Ridgway to puncture the soft underbelly of the Third Reich. The division's first two combat operations were parachute and glider assaults into Sicily and Salerno, Italy, on 9 July and 13 September 1943. While temporarily detached from the division, the 504th Parachute Infantry Regiment earned the nickname 'Devils in Baggy Pants' for their fighting prowess in the conflict at Anzio in January 1944. The remainder of the division had, meanwhile, pulled out of Italy in the autumn and moved on to England to prepare for the liberation of Europe.

With two combat jumps under its belt, the division was ready for the most ambitious operation of the war, Operation 'Overlord', the amphibious assault on the northern coast of Nazi-occupied France. The airborne segment of the operation, which the 82nd was going to take part in, was called Operation 'Neptune'. 'Neptune' was the largest airborne assault in history. To prepare for it the division was completely reorganised. Two new parachute infantry regiments, the 507th and the 508th, joined the division. Due to its depleted numbers following the fighting in Italy, the 504th Parachute Infantry Regiment did not take part in the invasion. On 5–6 June 1944, the 82nd's paratroopers and glidermen boarded hundreds of transport planes and gliders. Floating down out of the night sky, they were among the first soldiers to fight in Normandy.

By the time the 82nd was pulled back to England, it had seen thirty-three days of combat and had 5,245 paratroopers killed, wounded or missing. The Division's post-battle report read '. . . 33 days of action without relief, without replacements. Every mission accomplished. No ground gained was ever relinquished.' Following the Normandy invasion the 82nd became part of the newly organised XVIII Airborne Corps, which consisted of the US Army's 17th, 82nd and 101st Airborne Divisions. In September 1944, the 82nd began planning for Operation 'Market Garden' in Holland. This operation called for three airborne divisions to seize and hold key bridges and roads deep behind German lines. The 504th, now back at full strength, rejoined the 82nd, while the 507th went to the 17th Airborne Division.

On 17 September the 82nd Airborne Division conducted its fourth combat jump of the war into Holland. Fighting off ferocious German counter-attacks, the 82nd was then ordered back to France. Suddenly, on 16 December 1944 the Germans launched a surprise offensive through the Ardennes Forest which caught the Allies completely off guard. Two days later the 82nd joined in the fighting and General George Patton was so impressed with the 82nd's honour guard that he said, 'In all my years in the Army and all the honor guards I have ever seen, the 82nd's honor guard is undoubtedly the best.' Hence the 'All Americans' became known as 'America's Guard of Honor'.

The 82nd returned to the United States on 3 January 1946. Instead of being demobilised, the 82nd made its permanent base at Fort Bragg, North Carolina, and was designated a regular army division on 15 November 1948. Life in the 82nd during the 1950s and '60s consisted of intensive training exercises in all environments and locations, including Alaska, Panama, the Far East and the continental United States.

In April 1965 'America's Guard of Honor' were alerted for action in response to the civil war raging in the Dominican Republic. Spearheaded by the 3rd Brigade, the 82nd deployed to the Caribbean in Operation 'Power Pack'. Peace and stability was restored by 17 June when the rebel guns were silenced. Three years later the 82nd Airborne

Division was again called to action. During the Tet Offensive, which swept across the Republic of Vietnam in January 1968, the 3rd Brigade was alerted and within twenty-four hours was en route to Chu Lai. The 3rd Brigade performed combat duties in the Hue-Phu-Bai area of the sector. Later, the brigade was moved south to Saigon, and fought battles in the Mekong Delta, the Iron Triangle and along the Cambodian border. After serving nearly twenty-two months in Vietnam, the 3rd Brigade troopers returned to Fort Bragg on 12 December 1969.

During the 1970s division units were deployed to the Republic of Korea, Turkey and Greece for exercises in potential battlegrounds. The division was also alerted a further three times. War in the Middle East in the autumn of 1973 brought the 82nd to full alert. Then, in May 1978, the division was alerted for a possible drop into Zaire; again, in November 1979, the division was made ready for a possible operation to rescue American hostages in Iran.

On 26 and 27 October the 1st Battalion, 505th Infantry and the 1st Battalion, 508th Infantry, with their support units, deployed to Grenada. Military operations in Grenada ended in early November. This mission, codenamed Operation 'Urgent Fury', tested the division's ability to act as a rapid deployment force. The first aircraft-carrying division troopers touched down at Point Salinas seventeen hours after notification.

In March 1988 a brigade task force, made up of two battalions from the 504th Parachute Infantry Regiment, conducted a parachute insertion and air-land operation into the Honduras as part of Operation 'Golden Pheasant'. The deployment was billed as a joint training exercise but the paratroopers were ready to fight. The introduction of armed paratroopers into the Honduran countryside caused the Sandinistas to withdraw back to Nicaragua. 'Golden Pheasant' prepared the paratroopers for future combat in an increasingly unstable world. On 20 December 1989 America's Guard of Honor, as part of Operation 'Just Cause', conducted their first combat jump since the Second World War on to Torrijos International Airport, Panama. The paratroopers' goal was to oust a ruthless dictator and restore the duly elected government to power there. The paratroopers were joined on the ground by 3rd Battalion, 504th Parachute Infantry Regiment, who were already in Panama. After the night combat jump and seizure of the airport, the 82nd conducted follow-on combat air assault missions in Panama City and the surrounding areas. The victorious paratroopers returned to Fort Bragg on 12 January 1990.

Seven months later the paratroopers were again called to war. Six days after the Iraqi invasion of Kuwait on 2 August 1990, the 82nd became the vanguard of the largest movement of American troops since Vietnam. The first unit to reach Saudi Arabia was a task force including the division's 2nd Brigade. The rest of the division followed soon after. Intensive training then began in anticipation of fighting in the desert with the heavily armoured Iraqi Army.

On 16 January 1991 Operation 'Desert Storm' began when an armada of Allied war planes pounded Iraqi targets. The ground war got under way almost six weeks later. On 23 February the vehicle-mounted 82nd Airborne Division paratroopers protected

Paratroopers of the US 82nd Airborne as they prepare to board a helicopter during Operation 'Desert Storm', in the Gulf War.

British and US paratroopers wait to board C-141 Starlifter transport planes for a divisional night drop in the US. This jump, which took place during Exercise Purple Star in 1996, was the biggest peacetime drop since the Second World War.

A paratrooper of the US 82nd Airborne waits at the door of a C-141 Starlifter for the green light to jump. He is wearing the American T-10 parachute, which has a healthy safety record.

British paratroopers are presented with their American Para wings after completing the US jumps course. In 1996 joint exercises were carried out during which members of the US 82nd Airborne jumped with the new British Low-Level Parachute.

the XVIII Airborne Corps' flank as fast-moving armoured and mechanised units moved deep inside Iraq. A 2nd Brigade task force was attached to the 6th French Light Armoured Division, becoming the far left flank of the corps.

In the 100-hour ground war the vehicle-mounted 82nd Division drove deep into Iraq and captured thousands of Iraqi soldiers and tons of equipment, weapons and ammunition. After the liberation of Kuwait, the 82nd began its redeployment back to Fort Bragg, with most of the division returning by the end of April.

In August 1992 the division was alerted to send a task force to the hurricane-ravaged area of South Florida and provide humanitarian assistance following Hurricane Andrew. For more than thirty days, division troopers gave food, shelter and medical attention to a grateful Florida population.

To maintain its posture of readiness, conduct training and support, the 82nd employs a 'cycle' training system. One-third of the division is on 'mission cycle' and is ready to respond to any contingency mission around the world. Another third is on 'training cycle' during which paratroopers and units train to be prepared to accomplish any wartime mission. The remainder of the division is on 'support cycle'. Units on support cycle help other division units prepare their vehicles and equipment for deployment, and support other divisional and post activities. Having the support cycle frees the other two-thirds of the Division to concentrate on mission preparedness and intensified training.

Climate and terrain are major factors to consider for any military operation. These factors are especially important for the 82nd Airborne Division since it must be able to deploy at very short notice. To prepare for the wide range of environments to which the Division might be called, the 82nd Airborne Division conducts a comprehensive off-post training programme. Units routinely deploy to the National Training Center at Fort Irwin, California, to train with mechanised and armoured forces in high-intensity mock battles; the Joint Readiness Training Center at Fort Polk, Louisiana, to train with light infantry and mechanised forces in low to mid-intensity conflict; and to the Jungle Operations Training Center at Fort Clayton, Panama, to train as a lightly equipped force conducting low intensity military operations in a jungle environment.

At the 82nd Airborne Division's home base at Fort Bragg division units concentrate on reinforcing basic soldier skills such as marksmanship and physical fitness. Battalion-size units are periodically evaluated on how well they conduct more complicated missions, such as airborne assaults, airfield seizures, anti-armour defences, and air assault operations. The scenarios for these larger training events are based on possible or current threats to national security and are intended to provide realistic, stressful situations for paratroopers, right through from the brigade commanders to the riflemen. Using sophisticated night-vision devices, every division unit trains during the hours of darkness to maintain its night operations proficiency, vital to its success on today's battlefield.

Fort Bragg has more than seventy-five modern, well-maintained firing ranges and impact areas for improving the combat effectiveness of the division's paratroopers. A full-scale model town, as large as a city block, is used to hone the paratroopers' skills

Members of the US 82nd Airborne take part in a mass drop at Fort Bragg. The troops are using the T-10 parachute and their equipment containers can be seen swinging beneath them.

American paratroopers of the US 82nd Airborne drop from a C-141 Starlifter aircraft. On average US paratroopers make twelve jumps per man every year.

when fighting in urban areas. Overall, training is rugged, realistic and continuous. In a given year a paratrooper trains nearly 270 days, runs 700 miles, conducts a minimum of 12 parachute operations and participates in several day and night live-fire exercises.

Today, 82nd Division paratroopers are deployed across the globe and are on constant standby for future operations. A field artillery regiment, a division support command and an aviation brigade each support the infantry regiments. In addition, the division has engineer, signal, armour, military intelligence and air defence battalions, each consisting of more than 400 paratroopers. To support the infantry, the division's inventory also includes M-119 105 mm howitzers, the Avenger Air Defence weapon system, which fires the Stinger missile from an 8-missile pod mounted on a vehicle, the shoulder-fired Stinger missile and the Sheridan armoured reconnaissance vehicle. The 82nd Aviation Brigade has both the UH-60 Black Hawk and the OH-58D Kiowa Warrior helicopters. Separate battalions, such as the 307th Engineers, the 82nd Signal and the 313th Military Intelligence, each have their own high-technology equipment that can be employed to provide vital support to the division. Virtually all of the division's weapons and equipment can be delivered by parachute. Sophisticated night-vision equipment is used by 82nd paratroopers to gain command of the battlefield at night. The troops are able to perform their missions as quickly and efficiently under the cover of darkness as they can in broad daylight.

This deadly combination of intensive training, sophisticated weapons and cutting-edge technology make the 82nd Airborne Division one of the most awesome fighting forces in the world. This division continues to preserve the traditions established in its combat operations. As the contingency division that forms the core of the United States' strategic combat force, the 82nd is always ready to deploy anywhere in the world within eighteen hours. The 82nd Airborne Division is a force of professional soldiers who truly are 'America's Guard of Honor'.

The Colonel-in-Chief, HRH Prince Charles, with the Colonel Commandant Major-General Rupert Smith.

AIRBORNE FORCES ROLL OF HONOUR, 1944

This list of those who were killed or died of their wounds during the D-Day operation and Arnhem has been compiled from official records held at the Airborne Forces museum. Due to the sensitive nature of some operations casualties were not recorded and this list therefore pays tribute to the 'Unknown Soldier'.

NORMANDY

6th (AIRBORNE) ARMOURED REGIMENT RECONNAISSANCE CORPS RAC

06.06.44	BELCHER, R.C.	LT
	DONE, M.P.	TPR
	EARWICKER, P.T.	CPL
	LAMONT, G.W.	TPR
	WILSON, A.H.	TPR
15.06.44	FRIEND, A.J.	TPR
	MUSTAVE, J.E.	TPR
16.07.44	HARRINGTON, E.R.	L.CPL
10.08.44	ELSEY, A.J.W.	CPL
	HUNT, W.G.	TPR
20.08.44	DAVEY, F.H.	TPR
	MARTIN, A.C.	TPR
	TONKS, C.	TPR
26.08.44	GREENWOOD, R.	TPR
21.12.44	HENDERSON, J.S.	TPR

2nd AIR-LANDING ANTI-TANK BATTERY (RA)

10.06.44	BLOWER, J.W.H.	LT

3rd AIR-LANDING ANTI-TANK BATTERY (RA)

06.06.44	NEWHAM, F.E.	GNR
	STANLEY, D.	GNR
	WHITNEY, W.C.	BDR
07.06.44	SHERRATT, A.	GNR
08.06.44	HALL, W.	SGT
09.06.44	BRADLEY, W.	BDR
	WEST, W.S.L.	SGT
10.06.44	WALKER, M.W.R.	GNR
16.06.44	MILLWARD, C.	GNR
	PERKS, G.E.	GNR

07.08.44	HEWITT, H.C. G.N.R.	
19.08.44	SYKES, J.	GNR
20.08.44	DYCHE, A.	GNR
	DUBOVITCH, M.	GNR
	WOODWARD, C.	SGT

4th AIR-LANDING ANTI-TANK BATTERY

06.06.44	HILL, J.A.	BDR
	KILBEY, F.A.	CAPTAIN
	LANE, A.J.	BDR
	LAZAROFOULO, P.	GNR
	LYONS, S.A.	LT
	MACHIN, J.H.	GNR
	SIDNEY, W.	BDR
	TAYLOR, R.K.	GNR
	WOODCOCK, F.L.	L.SGT
07.06.44	BYARD, J.H.	SGT
	GUEST, A.	L SGT
	WAINWRIGHT, J.C.	L.BDR
	WILLIAMS, W.H.	GNR
	YATES, J.H.	BDR
13.06.44	CRADDOCK, R.C.	GNR
06.07.44	JAMES, W.	GNR
	PORTMAN, C.E.	L.SGT
07.08.44	RUSSELL, A.	GNR
	THOMAS, F.	GNR

2nd LIGHT ANTI-AIRCRAFT BATTERY RA

06.06.44	DAVENPORT, A.	GNR
	DIX, G.R.	GNR
	GRANT, W.	PTE
	NUTLAND, F.	GNR
	SIMMONS, D.	GNR
	SMITH, A.	GNR

53rd (THE WORCESTERSHIRE YEOMANRY) AIR-LANDING LIGHT REGIMENT

05.06.44	HALL, H.	BDR
06.06.44	DENNISON, R.T.	GNR
	RODWELL, K.S.	L.BDR
	RUSSELL, J.	GNR
10.06.44	BARRAS, A.M.	LT
12.06.44	WARD, H.W.	CAPTAIN
17.06.44	PATERSON, A.	SGT
30.06.44	STONE, C.E.	CAPTAIN
05.07.44	BOWERS, D.W.	GNR
07.07.44	THOMPSON, A.	GNR
12.06.44	BRYANT, C.H.	L.BDR
11.08.44	ANDERSON, D.J.T.	GNR
	FOSTER, W.R.	L.BDR
	McWILLIAMS, J.	GNR
	PEERS, F.L.	BDR
	SNOWDEN, B.	L.BDR
12.08.44	PIRKIS, S.H.B.	WO.1

3 PARACHUTE SQUADRON ROYAL ENGINEERS

06.06.44	MATHESON, J.A.	SPR
	ROBINSON, P.	SPR
07.06.44	JONES, G.L.	SGT
10.06.44	GILLOTT, L.E.V.	L.CPL
	WHYBROW, E.H.	SPR
11.06.44	PERRY, L.R.	L.CPL
13.06.44	GILL, W.R.	SPR
22.06.44	GREEN, A.F.	CPL
28.06.44	JUCKES, T.R.	CAPTAIN
29.07.44	ROWBOTHAM, H.	CPL
10.08.44	BENSON, J.	SPR
	CROSS, S.J.	SPR
	DIXON, G.A.	DVR
	KERRY, H.R.	PTE
14.08.44	HICKS, A.P.	SPR

591st PARACHUTE SQUADRON RE

06.06.44	AUSTIN, A.E.	SPR
	BRANSTON, K.W.	L.CPL
	EVANS, J.J.	SPR
	FRASER, T.A.	L.CPL
	KELLY, W.A.	CPL
	THOMPSON, G.	DVR
	WHEELER, D.H.	SPR
	WOLFE, F.	SPR
	YOUELL, J.	SPR
6/7.06.44	HANDLEY, A.	DVR
07.06.44	REARDON-PARKER, J.	L.CPL
09.06.44	HART, L.J.W.	SPR
	WHALE, F.T.	L.CPL
10.06.44	KERRY, G.E.	SPR
	PALIN, G.I.	DVR
11.06.44	COYLE, P.	SPR
17.06.44	WHARTON, G.	LT
24.07.44	SHAND, L.P.	LT
21.08.44	McCRIRICK, P.R.H.	LT

249th (AIRBORNE) FIELD COMPANY RE

09.06.44	GILES, F.	SPR
	McCULLOUGH, C.J.	SPR
10.06.44	ALEXANDER, A.W.	SPR
	ISAAC, R.	WO.II(CSM)

26.12.44	PREECE, D.G.	SPR
	SHOREY, F.G.	SPR

286th (AIRBORNE) FIELD PARK COMPANY RE

06.06.44	REID, N.W.	LT
07.06.44	GIBBONS, E.J.	DVR
	POWELL, R.	SPR
20.06.44	ALDOUS, W.T.	DVR
	CUTTING, C.T.	DVR
21.06.44	McDONALD, K.A.G.	CPL
02.09.44	GARNER, L.	SPR

22nd INDEPENDENT PARACHUTE COMPANY (THE PATHFINDERS)

06.06.44	HOWARTH, L.	L.CPL
	LENNOX-BOYD, F.G.	MAJOR
	O'SULLIVAN, E.D.	L.CPL
07.06.44	GLEN, E.	L.CPL
09.06.44	GILLUM, K.S.	PTE
	SCOGING, F.	SGT
	TAIT, I.A.	CAPTAIN
20.06.44	DE LAUTOUR, R.E.V.	CAPTAIN
21.06.44	ALLOCK, H.	PTE
26.08.44	HARRIS, C.T.G.	CPL

6th AIRBORNE DIVISION SIGNALS COMPANY

06.06.44	BICKERTON, R.H.	CPL
	COLQUHOUN, D.	SIGMN
	DAVIS, D.I.	SIGMN
	FREEMAN, B.G.	SIGMN
	MACKIE, W.S.	SGT
	MILNE, D.	SIGMN
07.06.44	FONE, R.J.	SIGMN
08.06.44	HURST, A.	DVR
	WALKLEY, W.S.	SIGMN
09.06.44	CONNOLLY, B.C.	SIGMN
	MOORE, J.F.P.	CPL
	SPARKS, J.	SIGMN
10.06.44	BOON, F.	SIGMN
13.06.44	COURTNEY, S.	SIGMN
15.06.44	STAFFORD, W.A.	SIGMN
16.06.44	JAMES, J.W.C.	SIGMN
25.06.44	HILL, D.H.	DVR
06.07.44	SKIDMORE, F.	SIGMN
22.06.44	SMALLMAN-TEW, D.	LT.COL
23.07.44	THOMPSON.	SIGMN
02.08.44	ALVARADO, P.M.	SIGMN
12.08.44	HEEKS, B.A.	SIGMN
19.08.44	BOND, F.C.	SIGMN
	LEATHERBARROW, R.E.	SVR
	PITT, H.W.	SPL
07.10.44	KNIGHT, K.J.S.	SGT
01.11.44	CAMBLE R.	SGT
	GILRY, A.E.S.	SPL

224th PARACHUTE FIELD AMBULANCE (RAMC) (UNDER COMMAND OF 3rd PARACHUTE BRIGADE)

06.06.44	HUTTON, P.	PTE
	LEACH, J.E.	PTE
	LEWIS, J.	PTE
	SARGENT, W.P.	PTE
	TINGLE, L.A.	PTE

04.07.44	GARRATT, C.W.	PTE
07.07.44	MC LAUGHLIN, W.J.	PTE
10.08.44	AYERS, M.T.	DVR
18.08.44	BASS, A.D.	PTE

225th PARACHUTE FIELD AMBULANCE (RAMC) (UNDER COMMAND OF 5th PARACHUTE BRIGADE)

06.06.44	CLEMENTS, J.	PTE
	LEGGETT, R.	PTE
07.06.44	LONGDON, W.R.	PTE
	RIDOUT, R.S.	PTE
	RUSSELL, R.F.	L.CPL
13.06.44	EMMETT, R.C.	DVR
16.06.44	HARVEY, T.	PTE
07.08.44	CARTER, H.O.	SGT
	EARL, G.	PTE

284th PARACHUTE FIELD AMBULANCE (RAMC)

25.08.44	FERRY, O.	PTE

195th AIR-LANDING FIELD AMBULANCE RAMC (UNDER COMMAND OF 6th AIR-LANDING BRIGADE)

06.06.44	HEARNE, P.	PTE
	WORGAN, L.	PTE
09.06.44	KARSTON, F.J.	L.CPL
	SCOTT, P.W.	PTE
08.08.44	MORRIS, D.J.	PTE
25.08.44	KAITS, H.	PTE

(THE FOLLOWING SERVICEMEN ARE RECORDED AS RAMC ATTACHED TO THE AIRBORNE FORCES)

06.06.44	HARRIS, G.	SGT
07.06.44	MAITLAND, R.R.	MAJOR
	VENTHAM, T.C.J.	PTE
19.08.44	HOLTAN, R.S.	CAPTAIN

ROYAL ARMY ORDNANCE CORPS (RAOC)

30.06.44	ALLEN, R.G.	PTE

ROYAL ARMY SERVICE CORPS 6th AIRBORNE DIVISION

07.06.44	CANE, W.T.	SGT
	PIPER, W.P.	PTE
12.06.44	REDDALL, A.L.	PTE
19.06.44	WADE, B.	CPL
23.06.44	NAYLOR, R.S.	CPL

63rd (AIRBORNE) DIVISIONAL COMPOSITE COMPANY RASC

6/7.06.44	STANNARD, A.	CPL
07.06.44	BUTCHER, A.L.	CPL
	CORDELL, A.	DVR
	DALBY, J.A.	DVR
	McNALLY, P.	DVR
	O' LOUGHNANE, B.T.	DVR
	ROE, D.E.	DVR
	SMITH, D.J.	DVR

	TURNER, R.	DVR
	WILLIAMS, A.G.O.	L.CPL
	WOOLLARD, S.	CPL

398th (AIRBORNE) COMPOSITE COMPANY RASC

06.06.44	PARKER, F.W.	DVR
	SMUTHWAITE, W.T.I.	DVR
07.06.44	EDDINGTON, B.H.	DVR
13.06.44	APPLETON, R.J.	DVR
	MASON, J.C.	DVR
	ORTON, J.W.	DVR
	SPROSON, J.	DVR
	VAUGHAN, W.H.T.	DVR
	WELLS, J.	DVR

716th (AIRBORNE) LIGHT COMPOSITE COMPANY RASC

06.06.44	CANNING, W.	DVR
	FIELDER, R.E.	PTE
	HARPER, I.R.	DVR
	HOSEGOOD, B.S.	DVR
	LUNN, J.W.	DVR
	RIPO, F.	DVR
	SILVERT, P.	LT
07.06.44	CRAWFORD, F.J.	DPL
	McKEE, J.E.	DVR
08.06.44	COATES, D.W.S.	DVR
10.06.44	CURTIS, S.	DVR
	DOCHERTY, C.	DVR
22.06.44	BLAND, F.J.	DVR
	SPARK, R.L.L.	CPL
23.06.44	FITZPATRICK, L.L.	CPL
	McGRATH, J.L.	CPL
0 6.07.44	MARTIN, G.F.	DVR
	SMITH, F.	DVR
07.06.44	WILSON, J.S.	CPL

ROYAL ELECTRICAL & MECHANICAL ENGINEERS 6th AIRBORNE DIVISION WORKSHOPS REME

06.06.44	JACOBS, A.G.	CFN
10.06.44	THOUMINE, T.A.	CFN
10.06.44	STASULFVICH, G.E.	CFN
20.06.44	HALL, H.C.	CPL
12.08.44	COCHRANE, R.V.	L.CPL

10th AIR-LANDING LAD REME

25.06.44	BARNARD, J.R.	CFN

12th AIR-LANDING LAD REME

12.08.44	HALLIDAY, A.R.	CFN
	SLAUGHTER, T.D.F.	CFN

CORPS OF ROYAL MILITARY POLICE 6th AIRBORNE DIVISIONAL PROVOST COMPANY

06.06.44	NIMMO, T.B.	L.CPL
07.06.44	DAVIES, S.A.	L.CPL
08.06.44	SCOTT, A.R.	SGT
09.06.44	BUNTING, C.G.	L.CPL
20.07.44	DRUMMOND, A.	L.CPL

**245th HQ PROVOST COMPANY
(ATTACHED TO 6th AIRBORNE DIVISION)**

07.06.44	HENDERSON, T.J.	CPL

**SERVICEMEN OF DIFFERENT UNITS
(UNDER COMMAND OF OR ATTACHED TO 6th
AIRBORNE DIVISION)**

06.06.44	BICHNELL, A.	GNR
	POPE, A.A.	MAJOR
10.06.44	SCHOLES, F.C.	CAPTAIN

**(ATTACHED TO HQ ROYAL ENGINEERS, 6th
AIRBORNE DIVISION)**

06.06.44	GUARD.P.	SPR

**(SERVICEMEN RECORDED TO BE OF OR
ATTACHED TO 6th AIRBORNE DIVISION)**

18.06.44	McBRYDE, J.R.	CAPTAIN

**(SERVICEMEN OF OR ATTACHED TO
ARMY AIR CORPS (AAC))**

12.06.44	BREWER, B.M.	LT
19.06.44	CLINTON, R.A.	PTE

**325th (AIRBORNE FIELD SECURITY
SECTION INTELLIGENCE CORPS)**

03.10.44	JAGO, H.T.	SGT

**THE PARACHUTE REGIMENT
ARMY AIR CORPS, VARIOUS UNITS.**

06.06.44	MAX, J.H.	CAPTAIN
07.06.44	GREENWOOD, C.E.	CAPTAIN
19.08.44	FITZGERALD, P.E.	LT
21.08.44	CRAMP, C.A.	MAJOR

3rd BN THE PARACHUTE REGIMENT AAC

06.06.44	DELAHUNT, D.	PTE
	JOHNSON, G.	PTE
08.06.44	WILKINSON, A.T.	CAPTAIN
10.06.44	CALVER, F.R.	PTE

5th BN THE PARACHUTE REGIMENT AAC

19.06.44	DIMMICK, W.	PTE
07.07.44	TROTTER, J.W.	PTE

1st BN THE BORDER REGIMENT

6/7.06.44	BULL, E.	PTE
17.06.44	OLIVER, B.	LT

**THE GLIDER PILOT REGIMENT
ARMY AIR CORPS**

06.06.44	BEVERIDGE, H.	SGT
	BRABHAM, J.P.	SGT
	BROMLEY, J.L.	LT
	CHADWICK, R.	SGT

	CODDINGTON, J.F.S.	SGT
	FUELL, J.H.	SGT
	GIBBONS, J.R.M.	SGT
	GOODCHILD, F.J.	SGT
	HAINES, V.	SGT
	HOPGOOD, C.H.	S.SGT
	HOWE, W.R.	S.SGT
	LIGHTOWLER, E.	SGT
	LUFF, R.S.	SGT
06.06.44	MARFLEET, W.K.	S.SGT
	MARTIN, E.	LT
	OCKWELL, H.V.	S.SGT
	NASH, J.H.	SGT
	NEW, R.G.	S.SGT
	PERRY, S.W.	SGT
	PHILLIPS, D.F.	SGT
	PHILLPOT, G.E.	S.SGT
	POWELL, B.	SGT
	RIGG, A.	SGT
	ROBINSON, C.B.	S.SGT
	SAUNDERS, V.C.	S.SGT
	STANLEY, E.	SGT
	SEPHTON, A.H.	SGT
	STEAR, A.T.	S.SGT
	STONEBANKS, W.H.	SGT
	TAYLOR, E.M.	SGT
	TURVEY, P.P.	S.SGT
	WRIGHT, D.P.	S.SGT
07.06.44	RIDINGS, L.	S.SGT
09.06.44	FLETCHER, S.	S.SGT
09.06.44	HIBBERD, L.R.	SGT
18/19.06.44	FOSTER, P.	SGT.F.SQN
04.07.44	SIMPSON, F.W.	S.SGT
10.07.44	ANSELL, H.J.	SGT
	DOWDS, H.M.	S.SGT

**3rd PARACHUTE BRIGADE 8th
(MIDLAND COUNTIES) PARACHUTE BN**

06.06.44	BILLINGTON, T.W.	PTE
	BOYLE, J.P.	L.CPL
	CANTIN, R.F.	PTE
	CARTER, H.M.	PTE
	COOPER, C.A.P.	PTE
	COX, S.G.	PTE
	DAVIES, J.	SJ
	DOCKERILL, A.	SGT
	FEWINGS, S.R.	CPL
	FRYER, A.	PTE
	HINDS, D.W.	PTE
	HIPKISS, E.G.	SGT
	HOLLIS, C.F.	PTE
	HOPKINS, T.J.	PTE
	HORNER, J.	SGT
	HUMPHRIES, A.	PTE
	ILIFFE, J.A.	SGT
	ISAACS, J.	CQMS
	JOHNSON, D.	PTE
	JONES, E.	PTE
	KENT, R.P.	PTE
	KUTTNER, A.R.	PTE
	LANGDON, R.W.	CPL
	LIVERSUCH, A.F.	PTE
	LONGMAN, T.R.H.	CPL
	MEIKLEJOHN, M.	PTE
	MILLS, J.A.	PTE
	MOIR, J.A.	AJT

	PIGGOTT, W.	PTE
	PLATT, A.	PTE
	RICHARDSON, W.	PTE
	ROBINSON, J.	PTE
	ROGERS, J.M.	CPL
	RUSSON, D.	PTE
	SCOTT, R.T.	PTE
	SMITH, L.F.	CPL
	THORPE, W.H.R.	PTE
	WALTON, S.S.	PTE
	WARNER, A.H.	PTE
	WATKINS, J.H.	PTE
07.06.44	DOCHERTY, W.H.	PTE
	EVANS, J.W.	L.SGT
	KAY, G.A.	REVD
	LUKE, D.R.	PTE
09.06.44	HARVEY, J.T.	L.CPL
10.06.44	RUFF, F.C.	PTE
11.06.44	TISDALE, M.A.	SGT
	WOODHOUSE, J.	PTE
13.06.44	KEIGHTLEY, G.W.	CPL
	PYE, G.R.	PTE
16.06.44	BONHAM, C.E.	PTE
	CHARTERS, J.	PTE
	COWAN, D.	CPL
	DAVIES, J.W.	PTE
	DUNCAN, A.H.	PTE
	KELLY, A.P.	L.CPL
	MOUNCE, E.R.	SGT(INSTR)
	NEIL, G.	PTE
	RUSHTON, D.V.	PTE
	SCOTT, J.	SGT
	SIMMONS, G.P.	PTE
	VINE, N.A.	PTE
17.06.44	HEYDEN, R.V.	PTE
	McINAW, J.	PTE
18.06.44	NOTLEY, A.W.	PTE
27.06.44	IMPEY, H.R.	CPL
28.06.44	MILLER, L.C.	PTE
30.06.44	CHURCHILL, M.C.	PTE
	TAYLOR, G.H.	PTE
01.07.44	FREEMAN, G.A.	PTE
02.07.44	CASSON, T.	PTE
	HODDINOTT, J.H.	PTE
19.06.44	RAYNER, J.	PTE
28.07.44	PANNELL, J.F.	L.CPL
31.07.44	SMITHIES, J.	PTE
02.08.44	LLEWELLYN, A.	PTE
05.08.44	BATES, F.J.	PTE
09.08.44	CARTWRIGHT, F.E.F.	L.CPL
17.08.44	COLLINS, M.	PTE
	PORTER, E.	L.CPL
	SKEGGS, A.E.	PTE
18.06.44	FALCONER, J.M.	PTE
	ROBERTS, W.S.	SGT
19.06.44	BROWNSWORD, S.A.	PTE
20.06.44	KNIGHT, R.G.	PTE
	RATTICAN, J.	SGT
	RUDDICK, J.G.	LT
21.08.44	BAXTER, N.H.	PTE
	BROGAN, J.	PTE
	CHAMBERLAIN, C.A.H.	PTE
	COX, C.E.A.	PTE
	DAW, C.	PTE
	EVANS, H.J.C.	PTE
21.08.44	GILBERT, H.	PTE
	HILL, E.	PTE

	HORTON	2/LT
	JORDAN, S.	PTE
	KILBRIDE, P.	CPL
	LANCASTER, R.S.	PTE
	SHRIMPTON, J.D.	PTE
25.08.44	BOX, R.	PTE
	CALDICOTT, J.K.	PTE
	CLAYTON, S.	PTE
	COOPER, S.	PTE
	DEVONSHIRE, G.W.	PTE
	GLOVER, A.	CPL
	HAMILTON, J.	PTE
	HOARE, E.L.	PTE
	JONES, E.W.J.	PTE
	JONES, T.E.	PTE
	LITTLEWOOD, W.E.M.	SGT
	THOMPSON, R.J.	PTE
	WARDLE, E.	PTE
	WILLIAMS, H.B.	PTE
25/26.08.44	McILHARRGEY, C.R.	L.SGT
26.08.44	CLARKE, J.F.	LT
10.09.44	BROWN, N.	PTE

9th (HOME COUNTIES) PARACHUTE BN

06.06.44	ADSETT, G.D.	PTE
	ARMSTRONG, A.J.	PTE
	CATLIN, D.S.	LT
	CLARKE, E.J.	L.CPL
	CORP, B.N.	PTE
	CORTEI, E.S.	PTE
	DAVIES, A.E.	CQMS
	DAVIES, A.M.	PTE
	DOWLING, M.J.	LT
	DURNEY, L.W.	PTE
	ERCKET, S.G.T.	L.CPL
	HALL, R.R.	SGT
	HANNEN, T.L.	PTE
	HARDING, S.F.	PTE
	HARNESS, D.V.	PTE
	HULL, E.T.	L.CPL
	HUGHES, A.	LT
	LITTLE, K.R.	PTE
	McGUIRK, M.J.	CPL
	McKEE, R.	PTE
	MANDER, J.	PTE
	NICHOLLS, A.	PTE
	PAINE, H.	PTE
	PARRIS, M.W.	CPL
	PECK, N.	PTE
06.06.44	PERRY, R.D.	CPL
	PETERS, G.F.	LT
	PHILPOTT, N.R.	PTE
	PLEDGER, R.	CPL
	PLESTEAD, S J.	L/CPL
	ROBINSON, P.G.	L/CPL
	SHARPLES, P.J.	PTE
	SHEATH, F.J.	PTE
	SMITH, T.W.	CPL
	WALTER, P.F.	PTE
	WHITE, G.V.	PTE
	WILSON, J.T.	PTE
	WISE, D.W.H.	PTE
	YORK, G.E.	PTE
	YOUNG, J.	PTE
	YOUNGER, J.	PTE
07.06.44	BEDFORD, G.A.	PTE

The airborne cemetery at Oosterbeek, which is maintained by the Commonwealth War Graves Commission.

Date	Name	Rank	Date	Name	Rank
	DUNK, H.	PTE		FINCH, P.S.	PTE
	HALLIBURTON, T.C.	LT		FISHER, C.W.	L.CPL
	HURLEY, D.R.	PTE		FRANCIS, R.A.E.	PTE
	ROLLINGSON, J.T.	L/CPL		FROST, V.P.C.	PTE
	TAYLOR, B.E.	PTE		GARNETT, F.	PTE
08.06.44	ROSE, J.E .	SGT		GASCOIGNE, J.	L.CPL
	WILLIAMS, F.J.	PTE		GEMMELL, W.	PTE
	TOWNSEND, W.V.	PTE		HAYWARD, S.D.	L.CPL
09.06.44	CHARLTON, E.G.	MAJOR		HARDING, J.P.	CPL
	PARFITT, G.S.	LT		HEK, W.	PTE
	ROCHE, T.M.	PTE		HILL, M.R.	LT
10.06.44	RAYNER, E.M.	PTE		HOUNSLOW, E.S.	SGT
	SPENCER, W.	PTE		HOPGOOD, W.G.A.	PTE
11.06.44	BLUCK, H.	PTE		HUGHES, P.	PTE
12.06.44	CHRISTIE, M.W.	LT		HUNT, G.W.	CFM
	JEPP, R.S.	PTE		HUTCHINGS, J.E.P.	WOII (CSM)
	McSORLEY, G.F.	PTE		JACKSON, F.	L.CPL
	SANDERSON, P.	PTE		JARVIS, E.W.	SGT
	TOPHAN, W.	PTE		HUISH, W.L.	PTE
	WILSON, P.	PTE		KEARNS, J.P.	PTE
	WINGROVE, F.W.	PTE		KEMP, A.R.	CPL
17.06.44	CUNNINGHAM, W.J.	RSM		KERR, D.	PTE
	GIBSON, H.F.	PTE		KINGSLEY, R.	PTE
	TARRANT, R.T.	SGT		LEAMER, G.H.	CPL
21.06.44	PENSTONE, D.G.	PTE		LEARY, T.C.	PTE
02.07.44	TAYLOR, K.M.	L/CPL		LOTHIAN, A.	PTE
05.07.44	MUNRO, G.	PTE		McARA, J.	PTE
15.07.44	LAING, J.	PTE		McGEE, M.J.	PTE
19.07.44	EDE, C.	PTE		MILLS, R.H.	PTE
23.07.44	ECOTT, A.D.	SGT		MITCHELL, R.L.	L.CPL
	TOWNES, L.V.	PTE		MORTIMORE, J.H.	PTE
24.07.44	SEBIRE, C.J.H.	PTE		PANTON, D.	CPL
25.07.44	FOWLER, R.S.N.	SGT		PARRY, G.E.M.	RVD
27.07. 44	PEDLER, C.E.C.	PTE		PADLEY, A.	PTE
	REVELL, F.J.T.	PTE		PHILLIPS, L.H.	PTE
08.08.44	YARWOOD, W.S.	PTE		RENNIE, J.R.	PTE
15.08.44	SHERMAN, W.K.	PTE		RILEY, L.	PTE
17.08.44	BECKWITH, W.G.	CSM		SAUNDERS, A.	PTE
	SHEPPARD, W.	PTE		SCHWARTZ, D.R.	PTE
19.08.44	CLARK, T.	PTE		SCOTT, W.	PTE
	FRITH, J.H.	PTE		SHUTT, D.	PTE
	HAMMOND, J.F.	PTE		SMITH, F.	PTE
	JONES, G.	PTE		SMITH, J.W.	PTE
	MAYHEW, W.C.	CPL		STOBBART, R.W.	PTE
	PARSONS, R.G.	PTE		STRINGER, C.K.	PTE
	SPENN, C.F.	PTE		STUBBINS, C.C.	PTE
	STEWART, A.H.	PTE		SURMAN, C.J.	PTE
	WARD, A.	L.CPL		SUTTON, C.F.	PTE
	WATTAM, A.	PTE		THOMPSON, S.C.	PTE
20.08.44	BOLINGBROKE, S.	PTE		TRUEMAN, M.J.	PTE
22.08.44	WRIGHT, L.V.	PTE		TWIST, R.	L.CPL
25.08.44	BANKS, M.R.	OTE		VAN RYNEN, A.	CPL
				WALKER, J.	PTE
				WEY, L.C.	PTE

5th PARACHUTE BRIGADE

Date	Name	Rank	Date	Name	Rank
				WHITTINGHAM	L.CPL
06.06.44	BARRATT, P.	PTE		WHITTY, A.W.	PTE
	BEARD, A.H.J.	L.CPL	07.06.44	TAPLIN, H.F.	PTE
	BEECH, A.J.	SGT		VILLIS, F.R.	SGT
	BOWIER, W.	CAPTAIN		VINCENT, K.	PTE
	BURGESS, K.I.H.	PTE	7/8.06.44	BOWLER, J.A.	LT
	BROOKMAN, H.E.R.	PTE	09.06.44	BALDING, L.G.	SGT
	CAVEY, J.	PTE	10.06.44	BRANSON, W.	PTE
	CHAPPELL, A.E.	L.SGT		GRATHAN, A.R.	PTE
	COPSON, G.	PTE		JOHNSTON, J.B.	PTE
	DENHAM, H.	CPL		McCANN, T.K.	PTE
	ELLMER, A.A.	PTE		METCALFE, C.E.	CPL
	FIDDLER, J.E.	SGT		REED, C.W.	PTE

Date	Name	Rank	Date	Name	Rank
10/11.06.44	SHELDON, C.H.	CPL		HOWE, R.	PTE
11.06.44	ROBERTS, G.S.	PTE		JONES, W.	CPL
13.06.44	MUNDY, E.H.	PTE		JOYCE, D.	PTE
14.06.44	SAVILL, S.C.	CQMS		LOCKETT, P.J.	PTE
16.06.44	DAVIES, E.G.	PTE		LONSDALE, T.G.	PTE
	LEADBETTER, R.	PTE		MASLIN, R.E.	PTE
	TEMPLE, W.A.B.	LT		MILBURN, F.	SGT
17.06.44	JONES, B.	PTE		NELSON, G.E.	SGT
18.06.44	DURBIN, F.E.	WO.II (CSM)		O'SULLIVAN, D.	PTE
	FINDLAY, J.M.	PTE		ROBSON, R.	SGT
	HAND, G.	PTE		SKELLETT, T.A.	PTE
	SWAN, J.F.M.	PTE		TAYLOR, R.	PTE
	TROTMAN, H.C.	PTE		TURNBULL, G.	CAPTAIN
19.06.44	McCULLOCH, J.A.	CPL		VICARY, H.J.	PTE
20.06.44	BLACKSHAW, E.E.	L.CPL	07.06.44	BLACKBURN, E.	PTE
	PEGG, W.F.	PTE		DRAGE, R.T.	PTE
	RAWLINGS, E.J.C.	PTE		JOHNSON, L.	PTE
	WOODGATE, D.A.	PTE		WILFORD, P.L.	PTE
21.06.44	COOLING, H.Q.	PTE	09.06.44	BEDWELL, W.J.	L.CPL
	LIDDELL, D.S.	PTE		BOWERMAN, R.G.	PTE
23.06.44	ROAST, A.E.	PTE		CAIRNS, D.	SGT
25.06.44	BENNETT, R.D.	PTE		DERRY, W.A.A.	CPL
	GWILLIAM, S.F.	PTE		FIRTH, W.	PTE
29.06.44	MacDONALD, I.G.	LT		HOLT, L.	PTE
07.07.44	ATKINSON, R.N.	LT		McGOWAN, S.	CPL
	HODGES, G.F.	PTE		McKENNA, S.E.	CPL
	REID, G.	PTE		PARR, N.	CPL
	TRAFFORD, R.H.	PTE		PHILBURN, H.	PTE
10.07.44	COULTHARD, A.J.	L.CPL		POOLEY, P.H.D.	PTE
	PRICE, S.A.	L.CPL		STEVENSON, G.H.	CAPTAIN
	VARNEY, A.T.	PTE		TAYLOR, H.R.	PTE
	WILLIAMS, D.R.B.	PTE		WALSH, M.K.	CPL
25.07.44	HINDLEY, E.	L.CPL		WHITE, A.F.	PTE
10.08.44	BURDEN, A.L.	PTE	10.06.44	HULL, D.F.	PTE
	ELY, P.O.W.	PTE		McKILLOP, A.	PTE
	WEBSTER, J.D.	PTE		MAYERS, G.H.E.	PTE
19.08.44	BALDWIN, J.	PTE		WINDER, E.	L.CPL
	FAY, V.C.	SGT	12.06.44	ARMSTRONG, A.	L.SGT
	KEMPSTER, F.G.	SGT		BOWYER, K.J.	SGT
20.08.44	WILSON, W.G.	CPL		CARTLIDGE, H.	L.SGT
22.08.44	BALL, F.W.	CPL		COLWELL, W.L.	PTE
	DOWNES, W.E.	PTE		DUNN, G.	PTE
	THOMPSON, B.B.	L.CPL		ELLIOTT, W.L.	PTE
23.08.44	BLAKEWAY, A.V.S.	SGT		FISHER, E.C.	PTE
	O'BRIEN, J.R.	PTE		FRYER, F.W.	PTE
26.08.44	BUSHELL, H.R.	CPL		GORDON, R.A.	PTE
	EVANS, S.H.	PTE		GRAKAUSKAS, J.	L.CPL
	KING, M.H.	PTE		HACKETT, T.H.	PTE
	HOLDROYD, D.W.	PTE		HARCOURT, C.W.	SGT
				JOHNSON, A.P.	LT-COL
				KIRBY, A.W.	SGT

12th PARACHUTE BN
(10th BN THE GREEN HOWARDS)

Date	Name	Rank	Date	Name	Rank
				MARWOOD, J.T.	WO.II (CSM)
				MASTERS, C.J.B.	PTE
06.06.44	AUSTIN, A.T.W.	LT		PRITCHETT, A.	PTE
	BALDWIN, G.	PTE		ROGERS, H.D.	MAJOR
	BELL, F.	SGT		SPEAKMAN, W.	PTE
	BERRY, E.W.	L.CPL		STONES, W.	PTE
	BLACK, W.J.	L.SGT		SUTTON, R.A.	PTE
	BRANDON, S.A.	CPL		TANNER, J.W.	L.SGT
	BROADWELL, C.	PTE		THOMAS, I.	CPL
	BURGESS, E.J.	CPL		THOMSON, R.	CPL
	CYSTER, F.N.	PTE		TOWERS, J.A.	PTE
	DOBSON, W.A.	PTE	12.06.44	TRAYLEN, F.I.	PTE
	DRAPER, P.W.	PTE		WHITE, A.R.	PTE
	HATELAY, R.L.	L.CPL		WILLIAMS, G.	SGT
	HIGGINS, S.	SGT	13.06.44	AUTY, F.	PTE
	HOWARD, T.	PTE		CAMPBELL, J.R.D.	LT

Date	Name	Rank	Date	Name	Rank
	SAUQUILLO, L.	PTE	14.06.44	COX, A.E.	PTE
14.06.44	HEYWOOD, E.F.	PTE		RAINE, J.T.	PTE
16.06.44	WALKER, K.G.	PTE	16.06.44	GREEN, H.A.	CPL
17.06.44	KIPLING, H.	PTE		MELBOURNE, A.	PTE
04.07.44	STEER, W.H.E.	SGT		STANYON, R.A.	PTE
07.07.44	FRIEDLANDER, G.E.	PTE	23.06.44	OSBORNE, S.	SGT
08.07.44	THOMPSON, W.J.	CPL	25.06.44	LIGHTFOOT, V.A.	L.CPL
10.07.44	ALLAN, W.	PTE		PREW, E.R.G.	PTE
	BLISS, C.L.	CAPTAIN		SMITH, C.	PTE
	BOYD, W.	L.CPL		WARE, S.L.	L.CPL
	BULL, J.W.	PTE	28.06.44	BARKER, L.	PTE
	GILLON, E.	PTE	05.07.44	RICHARDS, R.D.	PTE
	RICHARDSON, T.G.	PTE	07.07.44	ARMITAGE, J.N.	PTE
19.08.44	BENNETT, G.G.	PTE	10.07.44	DIXON, G.H.	SGT
	McCOMBE, R.H.	PTE		LORD, D.A.	PTE
	WINFIELD, F.H.	PTE	12.07.44	BRITLAND, H.F.	PTE
	WISE, W.H.	S.SGT		O'BRIEN-HITCHING, G.H.	LT
20.08.44	WALKER, E.	SGT		SMITH, G.	PTE
22.08.44	ADAMS-ACTON, M.	PTE	15.07.44	DONNELY, T.J.	L.SGT
	BERCOT, J.M.	LT	18.07.44	LYSAGHT, J.J.	CPL
	CAMPBELL, J.H.	PTE	23.07.44	JOHNS, R.E.	PTE
	DAVIES, F.C.	L.SGT	07.08.44	MEARES, T.	PTE
	EVANS, P.T.	PTE	08.08.44	CRATES, J.E.	PTE
	FRANCE, H.	PTE	19.08.44	ASHFORD, H.	L.CPL
	GILBERT, W.J.	PTE		ATTRIDGE, G.A.	PTE
	HAYES, J.J.	L.CPL		BARTON, F.D.	CPL
	LANE, H.C.	PTE		BOTT, F.	CPL
	LATHAM, A.	PTE		BRASSINGTON, R.	CPL
	McINNES, W.	PTE		CRUTCHLEY, T.H.	PTE
	McKINLAY, J.	PTE		DUGGAN, F.	PTE
	McLEAN, J.	SGT		FUNNELL, E.W.	PTE
	RABBITS, A.T.	PTE		GLOVER, C.E.	PTE
	WATTS, K.B.	PTE		HELLIER, A.V.	PTE
	WILSON, F.E.	PTE		HEWITT, W.G.	PTE
01.12.44	GILLARD, L.R.	L.CPL		HUNTER, W.A.	CPL
				JENKINSON, S.	PTE

13th PARACHUTE BN
(2/4th BN THE SOUTH LANCASHIRE REGIMENT)

Date	Name	Rank	Date	Name	Rank
				KELLY, G.	SGT
				KNOWLES, C.W.	L.CPL
				LYONS, A.	CPL
06.06.44	ALDRED, J.	PTE		McCRUDDEN, W.P.	PTE
	DAISLEY, S.	CAPTAIN		McNALLY, W.	PTE
	DAY, J.	L.SGT	19.08.44	MOLLOY, T.W.	PTE
	FARMER, R.K.	PTE		MORRIS, R.	PTE
	HALLAS, J.	CPL		PHILLIPS, J.	L.CPL
06.06.44	HARDGREAVES, A.	PTE		PROWSE, A.	PTE
	JOHNSON, T.H.	PTE		PYATT, A.W.	PTE
	MACKENZIE, D.J.	PTE		RENYARD, R.G.	PTE
	MIDDLETON, G.R.	PTE		RODWELL, B.V.	PTE
	PIDDLESDEN, R.R.	CPL		RUSDALE, C.R.	PTE
	POTTER, E.E.	PTE		SANDS, H.	PTE
	SHEPHERD, C.R.	PTE		SEDDON, H.	PTE
	SUCKLEY, H.L.	PTE		TONGUE, H.	PTE
	WAIN, R.S.	PTE	21.08.44	FREUDE, W.M.	L.CPL
07.06.44	DARBY, C.V.	PTE	22.08.44	BEST, J.P.	PTE
	PARKER, J.W.	CPL		BIBBY, E.M.	LT
08.06.44	ELLISON, F.A.N.	CAPTAIN		GREGORY, A.F.	PTE
	HARBET, S.	PTE		TURNER, H.F.	PTE
09.06.44	CLOUSTON, W.	PTE	23.08.44	BINNS, F.	PTE
	SWINDLE, R.E.	PTE		ECKERT, C.A.J.	CPL
10.06.44	BANKS, J.M.	PTE		HINGHCLIFFE, G.	PTE
	BROWN, A.	L.CPL		HUGHES, E.	SGT
	BULL, K.F.	PTE		LOWTHER, J.	L.CPL
	CLYNE, F.	PTE		McKIRBY, D.	SGT
	COLLIER, W.C.	SGT		MEDLICOTT, T.W.	L.CPL
	ORRELL, A.	PTE		MISSING, J.E.S.	PTE
12.06.44	PRINCE, W.	PTE	26.08.44	WOOLHOUSE, W.T.	PTE
	WHITEHEAD, F.	PTE	28.08.44	TARRANT, R.M.	MAJOR

HQ 5th PARACHUTE BRIGADE
DEFENCE PLATOON

23.08.44	WHITEHEAD, R.	PTE

6th AIR-LANDING BRIGADE 12th (AIRBORNE) BN
THE DEVONSHIRE REGIMENT

06.06.44	DUNPHY, J.J.	CQMS
	NICHOLLS, J.D.	PTE
	PALMER, W.J.	PTE
07.06.44	BICKLE, G.H.	PTE
	CHUBB, L.H.	L.CPL
	FARLEY, W.J.	PTE
08.06.44	MORRISON, J.M.	PTE
09.06.44	LEIGH, C.W.	PTE
	SMITH, R.B.	PTE
10.06.44	CORBETT, P.J.	PTE
	GRIFFIN, C.	PTE
	KOSTER, J.R.	PTE
	LAVENDER, A.G.	PTE
11.06.44	GERMAIN, A.E.	LT
	SALISBURY, J.	PTE
	SAYER, D.C.	CPL
12.06.44	BAILEY, F.B.	L.CPL
	BAMPFYADE, J.A.F.W.	MAJOR
	BARRATT, L.A.	PTE
	FRY, I.L.	PTE
	GILMOUR, R.I.	PTE
	HOOPER, L.J.	PTE
	HYNAM, F.	PTE
	KITTOW, J.B.F.	LT
	MINTER, M.D.	PTE
	MULLINS, E.C.	PTE
	TAYLOR, C.A.	L.SGT
	WALTERS, H.J.	SGT
13.06.44	RUSSELL, R.A.	PTE
16.06.44	BENNING, L.A.	PTE
	CLARKE, A .	PTE
	FOWLER, W.H.	PTE
	PARROTT, G.H.A.	PTE
	VIANT, J.	PTE
21.06.44	JEANPIERRE, R.J.	PTE
22.06.44	TANNER, A.E.	PTE
23.06.44	THORNE, R.C.	PTE
28.06.44	JONES, G.A.	PTE
02.07.44	HARRIS, F.J.W.	CPL
	LEWIS, D.E.	LT
03.07.44	GREENSLADE, R.R.	L.CPL
05.07.44	PUTTICK, R.H.	PTE
11.07.44	COBDEN, A.F.	L.SGT
03.08.44	BERRY, E.J.	PTE
	CHIVERS, M.W.H.	PTE
	LEACH, W.C.	PTE
	YEOMAN, T.H.	L.CPL
06.08.44	GRANGE, D.C.I.	LT
08.08.44	TUCKER, R.L.	LT
13.08.44	WEIGHT, M.F.W.	PTE
17.08.44	ARMES, A.	L.CPL
	FOSTER, K.S.	CPL
19.08.44	HAMMOND, J.A.	PTE
	PARSONS, R.H.	PTE
20.08.44	LOCKETT, I.H.	PTE
21.08.44	TOVEY, F.S.	PTE
	WOODCOCK, E.A.S.	CPL
24.08.44	DAVIES, L.E.	PTE
	WEBB, L.V.	PTE

25.08.44	AMIS, K.A.	PTE
	MONTAGUE, T.	L.CPL
	SMITH, L.	CPL
26.08.44	PLUMRIDGE, C.R.	PTE
	RUSSELL, F.A.	PTE
28.08.44	BOYCOTT, J.H.	CPL
29.08.44	LOCKYER, E.L.	PTE

2nd (AIRBORNE) BN THE OXFORDSHIRE AND
BUCKINGHAMSHIRE LIGHT INFANTRY

05.06.44	DEACON, T.	LT
06.06.44	BROTHERIDGE, H.D.	LT
	KNOX, H.	CPL
	MILTON, C.	PTE
07.06.44	BARWICK, C.C.	SGT
	BOWDEN, P.W.	PTE
	ECKLE, F.J.	PTE
	EVERETT, E.J.	PTE
07.06.44	GREENHALGH, F.	L.CPL
	HIGGINS, L.C.	PTE
	HEDGES, W.P.	PTE
	KELLY, E.D.	PTE
	MORROW, T.	PTE
	NEWELL, E.G.	PTE
	PARK, J.	PTE
	REEVE, G.E.	L.CPL
	ROBERTS, C.L.	PTE
	SEFTON, F.J.D.	PTE
	SUMMERSBY, A.A.L.	PTE
	WHITE, A.D.	L.SGT
	WILKINS, W.S.	PTE
	WILKS, V.	PTE
	WILLCOCKS, C.E.	PTE
08.06.44	CHICKEN, G.C.	LT
	JOHNSON, K.F.	CPL
09.06.44	FROST, S.	L.CPL
	HIGGINS, C.H.	PTE
	MINNS, F.L.	L.CPL
	SILVESTER, W.J.	PTE
	STARR, J.F.	PTE
	SYMONDS, W.C.R.	PTE
	WILLIAMS, E.E.	WOII. (CSM)
10.06.44	BROOKS, B.	PTE
	COTTLE, D.T.	PTE
	MARRIOTT, J.	CAPTAIN
	MILLS, D.N.	PTE
11.06.44	LANGOHR, J.	L.SGT
13.06.44	TRESIDDER, W.E.P.	PTE
	VAN KLAVEREN, G.V.	LT
	WALKER, F.W.	PTE
	WREN, L.M.	CPL
	YOUNG, H.G.	PTE
14.06.44	CANTWELL, H.E.	L.CPL
	DREW, A.C.	PTE
	PANKHURST, J.A.	LT
15.06.44	ROBERTS, L.H.	PTE
	WILRYCX, D.A.	PTE
16.06.44	BLAIR, R.G.	PTE
	FLEXEN, R.	WOII. (CSM)
	MORLEY.G.	PTE
19.06.44	BRABNER, M.J.	CAPTAIN
	CREW, J.W.	WOII.(CSM)
	DANIELLS, R.C.	PTE
	FAVELL, E.V.M.	MAJOR
	HIBBARD, J.A.	PTE
	JAMES, J.	LT.(QM)

Date	Name	Rank
	PONTIN, D.A.	CPL
20.06.44	FULLER, C.H.	L.CPL
	PARSONS, W.C.	PTE
25.06.44	GEORGE, E.T.	PTE
	NICHOLLS, J.D.	PTE
	PHILLIPS, C.	PTE
	REYNOLDS, W.	CPL
27.06.44	LANGBRIDGE, E.H.	PTE
30.06.44	PEER, T.G.	PTE
02.07.44	EARL, C.E.	L.SGT
04.07.44	RUSSELL, P.J.N.	PTE
05.07.44	GILMORE, T.A.	PTE
15.07.44	PEPPERALL, D.	PTE
19.07.44	SMYTH, P.B.	PTE
23.07.44	REVNELL, G.I.	LT
25.07.44	YOUNG, K.E.	PTE
29.07.44	WHITE, H.W.	PTE
07.08.44	DRAGE, C.E.	PTE
10.08.44	CLARIDGE, R.A.	PTE
13.08.44	READER, C.A.	PTE
17.08.44	DREW, J.R.A.	CPL
22.08.44	CLIFFE, W.J.	PTE
	STACEY, J.	PTE
25.08.44	BANNATYNE, G.	PTE
26.08.44	BULFORD, P.G.	LT
27.08.44	CLAPTON, M.C.	PTE
07.12.44	REEVES, J.W.C.	PTE

1st (AIRBORNE) THE ROYAL ULSTER RIFLES

Date	Name	Rank
06.06.44	WOODBURN, J.	RFN
07.06.44	BARRY, P.E.	L.CPL
	BOUSTEAD, J.D.A.	LT
	COYLE, J.	SGT
	GLASS, S.	RFN
	GODSAVE, P.A.	RFN
	HALVEY, J.P.	RFN
	HANKEY, T.	RFN
	JEFFERSON, N.	CPL
	JOHNS, W.H.	RFN
	LOWE, L.	RFN
	McCAYNA, G.	CPL
	McFARLAND, N.	RFN
	McQUILLAN, R.N.	RFN
	MAGUIRE, P.	RFN
	MERRELL, W.R.	RFN
	MOORE, W.J.	L.CPL
	MORGAN, R.N.	CAPTAIN
	NELSON, J.H.	RFN
	O'BRIEN, C.	L.CPL
	O'CONNOR, P.J.	L.CPL
	OLIVER, J.C.	RFN
	O'REILLY, M.	RFN
	REILLY, J.J.V.	RFN
	SHAKESPEARE, A.	RFN
	STEVENSON, R.J.	RFN
	TESTRO, L.G.	RFN
	TURNER, W.	RFN
	WINFIELD, W.	L.CPL
	WRAY, T.	L.CPL
08.06.44	CHARLES, A.	L.SGT
	GREER, H.	L.CPL
	MULLINS, P.J.	RFN
	PAYNE, E.D.	RFN
	RAYNHAM, S.R.	CPL
	STARR, A.L.	RFN
09.06.44	McILROY, J.	RFN
	MEARNS, H.	RFN

Date	Name	Rank
	PROSSER, R.H.J.	RFN
	WILLIS, N.	RFN
10.06.44	GREER, J.	RFN
	STOGDALE, J.	CPL
11.06.44	MAGILL, N.M.	RFN
12.06.44	SAWER, A.C.J.	RFN
13.06.44	CHAMBERS, T.	L.CPL
13.06.44	COUSINS, C.J.H.	RFN
	HEGAN, W.J.	RFN
	McCARTHY, T.	CPL
	TURRELL, H.G.	RFN
14.06.44	CRAWFORD, W.	RFN
16.06.44	GUALDI, R.	L.CPL
	QUINN, R.	LT
19.06.44	JOHNSTON, W.	RFN
	KEOGH, P.F.B.	RFN
	McGUIRE, N.	RFN
	O'CONNOR, T.	RFN
	RILEY, R.	CPL
20.06.44	SMITH, W.H.	RFN
23.06.44	PARROT, T.A.	CPL
25.06.44	ARCHDALE, M.M.L.	LT
06.07.44	O'FLANAGAN, P.	RFN
07.07.44	DEMPSTER, E.	CPL
09.07.44	McBURNEY, W.A.	RFN
10.07.44	BLYTHE, J.	RFN
	CRANSTON, A.S.	LT
	GRAHAM, T.G.	RFN
12.07.44	EDMONDS, G.	RFN
13.07.44	MOFFETT, J.C.	RFN
18.07.44	MAGINNIS, G.A.	LT
06.08.44	DILLON, E.C.	RFN
17.08.44	TOPPING, S.	RFN
18.08.44	GARMAIN, R.E.	RFN
	TAYLOR, D.	PTE
20.08.44	WALKER, G.J.	RFN
22.08.44	JOHNSTON, E.F.	MAJOR
23.08.44	SCANLON, B.J.	RFN
	SOUTHAM, E.	CPL
24.08.44	FEENEY, C.	RFN
25.08.44	SMYTH, J.T.	RFN
11.09.44	McCONNELL, C.	RFN
13.09.44	EDMONDS, D.P.	LT
04.10.44	MacFANNEN, J.T.N.	LT
11.11.44	DWYER, S.	RFN
26.12.44	GILBERT, W.E.	RFN

ARNHEM

SERVICEMEN OF OR ATTACHED TO HQ 1st AIRBORNE DIVISION

Date	Name	Rank
18.09.44	GIBSON, V.	PTE
	GOULD, K.G.	DVR
20.09.44	JONES, L.D.	DVR
21.09.44	MADDEN, D.J.	MAJOR
22.09.44	CHEESEMAN, D.H.	DVR
	SMITH, B.B.	L.CPL
23.09.44	DEVONSHIRE, W.G.	PTE
	SANKEY, C.E.P.	LT
24.09.44	CHAPMAN, A.	CPL
25/26.09.44	BROWN, R.D.	S.SGT
02.10.44	KEESEY, J.H.	CAPTAIN

1st AIR-LANDING SQUADRON RECONNAISSANCE CORPS RAC

Date	Name	Rank
17.09.44	BRUMWELL, R.	TPR
	BUCKNALL, P.L.	LT

	EDMOND, W.M.	TPR
	GORRINGE, E.J.	TPR
	GOULDING, L.P.	TPR
	McGREGOR, T.	L.SGT
	STACEY, W.C.	L.SGT
18.09.44	BAKER, A.C.	L.CPL
	CHILTON, F.W.	TRP
19.00.44	BRAWN, F.	TRP
	McSKIMMINGS, R.	TRP
	PEARSON, H.E.	LT
	SALMON, J.G.	TRP
	WEAVER, J.M.J.	TRP
20.09.44	CHRISTIE, J.A.	LT
	MASON, D.H.K.	CPL
22.09.44	IRALA, J.M.	TRP
23.09.44	PLATT, H.A.	CAPTAIN
24.09.44	ODD, A.H.	TRP
	PARK, J.R.C.R.	CAPTAIN
	PASCAL, A.F.	LT
	WALKER, T.A.W.	TRP
25.09.44	GILES, D.	TRP
	HOLDERNESS, G.E.	SQMS
25/26.09.44	CAIRNS, L.	CPL
	TICKLE, S.	TRP
27.09.44	McNABB, T.V.P.	LT
13.11.44	POTTS, R.	L.CPL

ROYAL REGIMENT OF ARTILLERY
1 AIR-LANDING ANTI-TANK BATTERY

17.09.44	BOOTH, H.	GNR
18.09.44	RAMS, M.	SGT
19.09.44	BRADLEY, W.H.	BDR
	WEATHERELL, H.B.	GNR
19/20.09.44	HAMMOND, R.	GNR
20.09.44	COOK, L.R.	BDR
	MITCHELL, J.	GNR
	RYDEN, L.G.H.	L.BDR
	SLATER, E.C.	GNR
	WHITTAKER, H.	LT
20/21.09.44	DOIG, H.E.	SGT
	LOCK, A.F.	GNR
21.09.44	FORDER, F.G.	GNR
21.09.44	LARKIN, L.G.	GNR
	UNDERWOOD, L.C.	GNR
	WYATT, J.H.	SGT
	BAXTER, B.	GNR
23.09.44	WARWICK, T.S.	GNR
25.09.44	RICHARDSON, A.C.	GNR
26.09.44	McCULLOCK, J.J.	BDR
	MARTIN, P.D.	L.BDR
	OGDEN, R.	GNR
	ROBSON, G.	GNR
	THOMAS, G.E.	SGT

2 AIR-LANDING ANTI-TANK BATTERY

18.09.44	CRAWFORD, R.J.	SGT
	McLAREN, R.I.	LT
19.09.44	EDWARDS, L.E.	GNR
	FLYNN, F.S.	L.SGT
	GLOVER, R.D.	LT
	PALMER, C.	LT
20.09.44	BAXTER, H.J.	WOII. (BSM)
	McCRACKEN, R.	GNR
	SENDALL, D.E.	GNR
21.09.44	GRAHAM, A.	BDR
	HOWARD, W.N.	GNR

	LOVELL, S.	GNR
	STEELE, F.G.	GNR
22.09.44	MacHENRY, J.	L.SGT
23.09.44	BURGESS, D.H.	GNR
24.09.44	McCULLOCH, J.J.	BDR
25.09.44	BULLOCK, L.	GNR
	SWEETINGHAM, L.R.	GNR
25/26.09.44	BETHELL, T.	L.BDR
26.09.44	BARRON, P.R.M.	CAPTAIN
	CALLEN, A.I.	GNR
	JONES, S.	GNR
	McFARLANE, W.	SGT
	MOORE, E.	GNR
01.10.44	PECK, E.W.	GNR

1st AIR-LANDING LIGHT REGIMENT

17.09.44	BROWN, F.V.	GNR
	HEMPTON, R.W.	BDR
	STUBBS, E.	GNR
	TUSTIN, H.T.	GNR
18.09.44	HALL, J.K.	GNR
	MORGAN, T.G.	L.BDR
19.09.44	BINGHAM, H.	GNR
	PITT, A.	GNR
19/20.09.44	LAWSON, D.	WOII, (BSM)
20.09.44	GRAY, G.	GNR
21.09.44	LAKIN, G.R.	GNR
	MEIKLE, I.O.	LT
22.09.44	NORMAN-WALKER, A.F.	MJR
22.09.44	PATCHETT, H.J.	GNR
	SIMF, T.	GNR
23.09.44	GREEN, G.R.	L.BDR
	HALLIDAY, K.C.	LT
	MUIR, J.	GNR
	PEARSON, H.C.	L.BDR
24.09.44	ADAMS, O.J.	GNR
	BAISDEN, A.V.	GNR
	LEITCH, C.S.	LT
	TAYLOR, F.H.	GNR
	TAYLOR, P.A.	CAPTAIN
24/25.09.44	DOVE, W.S.	BDR
25.09.44	KEELING, M.A.	GNR
26.09.44	KNIGHT, M.J.	BDR
	MARRIOT, H.	SGT
	PLUMMER, D.E.	GNR
	WOODS, J.H.	LT
25/26.09.44	JONES, K.B.	GNR
26.09.44	ALDRED, P.N.	GNR
09.10.44	CHARD, P.	CAPTAIN
18.10.44	HOLDEN, B.	L.BDR
31.10.44	HARDY, S.E.	SGT
08.12.44	TATTON, S.R.	L.BDR

1 (AIR-LANDING) FORWARD OBSERVATION UNIT

19.09.44	ACTON, E.	GNR
	BOWERMAN, D.C.O.	CAPTAIN
	BUCHANAN, H.S.	CAPTAIN
	GOW, R.G.A.	CAPTAIN
21.09.44	HIGGINSON, H.	GNR
22.09.44	MAHY, W.J.	BDR
24.09.44	STEVENS, R.H.	CAPTAIN
21.09.44	ROBERTSON, R.A.	LT

1 PARACHUTE SQUADRON RE

17.09.44	MADDEN, W.	SPR
18.09.44	GUERAN, S.F.	SPR

	MORRISON, W.	DVR		19.09.44	CLOSE, J.H.	SPR
19.09.44	GILLHAM, H.E.	SPR			ROGERS, W.J.R.	SPR
	GRAY, D.	SPR		19/20.09.44	TROUSE, R.G.W.	SPR
	HEMMING, S.K.	SPR		20.09.44	PINK, H.A.	CPL
	HICKS, T.G.	SPR		21.09.44	GWILLIAM, G.R.J.	DVR
20.09.44	BRETHERTON, J.	SPR			MORRIS, T.O.	SPR
	HAZLEWOOD, W.V.	CPL		23.09.44	KELLY, J.M.	SPR
	HOATH, F.J.	SGT			RYDER, J.G.	L.SGT
	NEVILLE, D.	L.CPL		24.09.44	BINYON, R.B.	CAPTAIN
	SHERWOOD, H.M.	SPR			LAWSON, A.	SPR
	SIMPSON, W.L.G.	CPL			SNOW, H.E.	S.SGT
21.09.44	BROOKS, T.	SPR		25.09.44	ASHWORTH, N.B.	CPL
	TAYLOR, G.	SPR			CLARKE, K.	SPR
22.09.44	CAMPBELL, J.	SPR			EVANS, R.F.E.	CPL
25.09.44	ADAMS, W.B.	PR		25/26.09.44	MAY, G.H.	SPR
28.09.44	KILL, W.C.	L.CPL			SHELLEY, L.F.	SPR
22.12.44	WAKE, A.V.	SPR		29.11.44	EVERITT, J.	SPR

4 PARACHUTE SQUADRON RE

261 (AIRBORNE) FIELD PARK COMPANY RE

18.09.44	COOPER, J.B.	CPL		20.09.44	SKINNER, W.H.	LT
	TAYLOR, R.F.	CPL		25.09.44	ANDERSON, L.T.	SPR
	WALKER, R.	DVR				
19.09.44	EPPS, P.S.	SPR		**ROYAL MECHANICAL & ELECTRICAL ENGINEERS**		
20.09.44	ACKLAND, L.J.	L.CPL		**1st (AIRBORNE) DIVISION WORKSHOP**		
	ADDERLEY, R.L.	SPR				
	MORRISON, G.F.W.	SPR		18.09.44	WARE, C.W.	CFN
	SALMON, C.E.	L.CPL		20.09.44	GIBB, A.	CFN
	THOMAS, N.B.	CAPTAIN		21.09.44	HARVEY, V.J.	CFN
	YATES, F.	SPR		25//26.09.44	MURPHY, J.W.	CPN
21.09.44	EDEN, M.C.	LT				
	WILLIAMS, R.J.	SPR		**THE GLIDER PILOT REGIMENT ARMY AIR CORPS**		
22.09.44	WILLERS, R.	SPR				
23.09.44	HIGGINS, B.	SPR		17.09.44	BAXTER, G.S.	S.SGT
	RAWLINGS, L.D.	SPR			BRACKSTONE, C.T.	SGT
24.09.44	CUNNINGHAM, T.	SPR			COOK, L.A.L.	SGT
26.09.44	SEABROOK, D.	DVR			FRASER, R.A.	SGT
29.09.44	BALL, W.	L.CPL			GARDNER, L.J.	S.SGT
					JOYCE, T.A.	SGT
9 (AIRBORNE) FIELD COMPANY RE					LAWSON, E.	SGT
					MALTBY, R.A.	LT
17.09.44	ALLEN, R.H.	L.SGT			ROWLAND, R.R.	SGT
	BEALE, J.C.	SPR			TARRANT, H.A.P.	S.SGT
	BURROWS, W.H.	L.CPL			THOMSON, J.W.R.	SGT
	CALVERT, C.W.	SPR			WHITE, D.A.	S.SGT
	CARNEY, R.	SPR			WINKWORTH, C.W.	SGT
17.09.44	CLAMPETT, A.L.	CPL		17/25.09.44	WORTHINGTON, B.G.	SGT
	CUTHBERTSON, A.	SPR		18.09.44	ADAMS, N.V.M.	LT
	DAVIS, F.A.S.	SPR			ADAMS, R.A.	SGT
	EVANS, J.	SPR			BASHFORTH, A.L.	S.SGT
	FERNYHOUGH, J.	SPR			BOORMAN, N.J.	SGT
	GODFREY, E.J.	SPR			BOSLEY, J.	S.SGT
	HALL, A.	SPR			BRALEE, S.	SGT
	HOLTHAM, D.E.	SPR			CARTLIDGE, D.	S.SGT
	OAKEY, A.F.	SPR			CHANDLER, F.J.	SGT
	PICKBURN, E.V.	L.CPL		18.09.44	CLARK, A.A.	S.SGT
	SHEPPARD, E.E.	SPR			CROFT, R.M.	SGT
	STREET, A.R.	SPR			DUNN, H.	S.SGT
	TURNER, C.	SPR			EVANS, J.	SGT
	WATT, A.G.	SPR			GELL, C.	SGT
	WESTFIELD, J.	SPR			HARRIS, J.W.R.	S.SGT
	WILLIAMSON, J.S.	SPR			HOLLOWAY, E.J.	S.SGT
	HOLDSTOCK, R.F.	SPR		18.09.44	HUMPHREYS, C.H.	S.SGT
	TIMMINS, R.E.J.W.	LT			HUXLEY, B.	SGT
17/25.09.44	COTTLE, A.A.	SPR			JONES, L.V.	SGT
18.09.44	GREIG, P.	SPR			JONES, P.R.	S.SGT
	RUSSELL, R.V.	SPR			LAWRENCE, A.C.	S.SGT
	TAKLE, W.T.N.	L.CPL			LAWSON, G.	SGT

Date	Name	Rank		Date	Name	Rank
	LEE, J.B.	WOII. (CSM)			CULVERWELL, S.M.	LT
	LYON, M.	SGT			CUMMINS, B.A.	S. SGT
	McCARTHY, A.F.	SGT			DOWNING, M.W.	LT
	MAYES, T.W.	S.SGT			EVANS, W.E.	S. SGT
	PALMER, J.	S.SGT			FIRTH, E.H.	S. SGT
	PHILLIPS, E.	S.SGT			FRANKS, R.	SGT
	RICKWOOD, G.A.	S.SGT			IRVINE, R.	LT
	SMITH, T.M.	SGT			JONES, A.L.	SGT
	SPENCER, H.H.	SGT			KERR, D.F.	S. SGT
	WATSON, L.F.	S.SGT			MARKWICK, E.J.	LT
	WHITE, R.E.	S.SGT			RICHARDSON, W.K.	SGT
	WILLIAMS, L.E.	SGT			RUBENSTEIN, T.A.	SGT
	WISEBAD, J.	SGT			SHARROCK, J.J.	SGT
18/25.09.44	FREW, E.	S.SGT			SMITH, H.W	SGT
	SNUSHALL, J.A.W.	SGT			TAYLOR, JD.	SGT
	WOOD, H.	SGT			THOMAS, J.D.	SGT
19.09.44	BANKS, R.	S.SGT		23.09.44	BOYD, J.F.	S. SGT
	DANIELS, D.D.	S.SGT			BRIGGS, G.R.	S. SGT
	DERBVSHIRE, F.A.	LT			FOWKES, T.	SGT
	DODD, W.	S.SGT			McMANUS, V.D.	S. SGT
	GREEN, K.W.	SGT			MANN, J.R.	SGT
	HANNAM, I.C.	SGT			MILLS, K.S.	LT
	HEBBLETHWAITE, B.	SGT			MOON, E.B.	SGT
	JOHNSON, P.D.	SGT			NEWMAN, D.H.	SGT
	LEVISON, J.O.	SGT			SHARP, H.	SGT
	LIVINGSTON, D.M.	SGT			SHUTTLEWORTH, D.H.	CAPTAIN
	McCLAREN, W.C.	S.SGT			SMELLIE, J.F.	CAPTAIN
	MURPHY, T.	SGT			STEWART, T.W.	S. SGT
	NEILSON, R.C.	SGT		23/24.09.44	BRAZIER, P.J.	LT
	OSBORNE, R.F	S.SGT			GOULD, R.P.	S. SGT
	PATTINSON, L.R.	SGT		24.09.44	BAKER, E.J.	S. SGT
	WHITEHOUSE, N.K.	SGT			BONSEY, R.A.	SGT
	WOODROW, E.W.	S.SGT			FORRESTER, R.	SGT
	WRIGHT, J.	S.SGT			GOODWIN, W.	S. SGT
	YATES, A.G.	SGT			KIFF, L.T.	SGT
19/20.09.44	BONHAM, J.F.	SGT			NAYLOR, C.	SGT
	WEST, J.	SGT			PIDDUCK, D.F.	SGT
20.09.44	BELL, A.	S.SGT			PLOWMAN, T.A.	CAPTAIN
	FISHER, C.	S.SGT		24.09.44	RANGER, N.J.	SGT
	GAULT, B.T.	SGT			REDDING, F.G.	SGT
	GRAHAM, J.F.	SGT			SMALLWOOD, W.A.	S. SGT
	HARDIE, N.G.	CAPTAIN			WALLACE, D.B.	S. SGT
	HOWELL, H.G.	S.SGT			WRIGHT, J.R.	S. SGT
	HOWES, L.H.	SGT		24/25.09.44	ALLISON, G.S.	SGT
	LEYSHON, L.	S.SGT			MIDGLEY, G.	SGT
	MACKENZIE, B.W.	SGT			RICHARDS, A.E.	S. SGT
	McGOWAN, D.	SGT			YEATMAN, F.J.	S. SGT
	PARKINSON	SGT		24/26.09.44	BROWN, H.V.	S. SGT
	ROYLE, J.P.	MAJOR			NADEN, J.E.P.	S. SGT
	SIMION, E.	SGT		25.09.44	ANDERSON, D.G.	LT
20.09.44	SMITH, S.R.	LT			BINNINGTON, G.L.	S.SJT
	TAYLOR, C.C.	LT			BROWN, J.W.	SJT
	THOMPSON, D.	SGT			BRUCE, R.C.	SJT
	WADSWORTH	S.SGT			BURRIDGE, G.H.	SJT
	WHYBORN	SGT			CASTLE, V.E.	S. SGT
20/22.09.44	GREEN, J.C.	SGT			CURLEY, J.	S. SGT
21.09.44	ANDREWS, D.	SGT			DAVIES, D.G.	S. SGT
	CHITTLEBURGH, K.T.	LT			DAVEY, T.E.	SGT
	COLE, H.C.L.	LT			DOBBINGS, W.D.	SGT
	DALLIMORE, A.J.	SGT			DRUREY, B.	S. SGT
	HOGG, G.H.	SGT			ELLIN, J.B.C.	S. SGT
	MARRIOTT, C.	SGT			GOOLD, D.S.	S. SGT
	RAGGETT, D.B.F.	SGT			GREENHILL, F.W.	SGT
	WEST, E.L.	SGT			HARRIS, H.S.	S. SGT
	WITHINGTON, T.	SGT			HIGHAM, R.B.	SGT
	WYATT, D.	SGT			HILL, P.B.	S. SGT
22.09.44	BRIGGS, G.A.	SGT			HOLDREN, C.R.	S. SGT
	CLARKE, E.E.	S. SGT			HUNTER, J.S.	SGT

	JEAVONS, WT	SGT
	JOHNSON, J	SGT
	MATHEWS, SF	S. SGT
	McMILLAN, AC	S. SGT
	MOORCOCK, D.E.	S. SGT
	MUIR, I.C.	CAPTAIN
	NEWARK, M.C.	PTE
	NEWMAN, R.F.	SGT
	PHILLIPS, A.	SGT
	PICTON, R.K.	S. SGT
	POWELL, H.E.	S. SGT
	RICHARDSON, C.D.	S. SGT
	SHIPP, D.H.	SGT
	TAYLOR, H.C.	S. SGT
	TOMLINSON, E.B.E.	SGT
	TURL, J.	SGT
	WALTERS, J.	SGT
	WILKINSON, S.A.	S. SGT
	WILLIAMS, N.D.	SGT
	WOODS, R.O.	S. SGT
25/26.09.44	BURGE, J.G.	SGT
	GITTINGS, J.H.	SGT
	MANBY, H.M.	S. SGT
	PAINTER, G.	SGT
	SMITH, J.C.	SGT
	TAYLOR, F.W.	SGT
	WHITE, A.	S. SGT
25/27.09.44	WILTON, D.C.	SGT
26.09.44	COWAN, E.A.	SGT
	DITCH, R.R.	S. SGT
	NEALE, F.J.T.	CAPTAIN
26.09.44	OGILVIE, J.G.	CAPTAIN
	SAUNDERS, R.H.	S. SGT
	TOSELAND, P.	S. SGT
27.09.44	PICKFORD, E.	S. SGT
28.09.44	MILLS, G.T.	CAPTAIN
29.09.44	WALKER, H.	SGT
02.10.44	BARRIE, W.N.	CAPTAIN
04.10.44	FENDWICK, H.	S. SGT
	GWINN, M.A.	SGT
	HUARD, J.F.	SGT
	WATERHOUSE, A.	SGT
06.10.44	HOLLINGSWORTH, T.	SGT
06.10.44	WEST, R.W.	S. SGT
08.10.44	OXENFORD, A.R.	CAPTAIN
16.11.44	HARRIS, A.A.	S. SGT
07.12.44	BEWLEY, J.M.	LT
09.12.44	WINSPER, L.	S. SGT
23.12.44	FOLLINGTON	SGT

ROYAL CORPS OF SIGNALS
1st AIRBORNE DIVISION SIGNALS

18.09.44	DUNNING, G.C.	SGN
	WATERSTON, G.M.	PTE
	WILES, R.C.	SGN
19.09.44	HARRIS, R.L.W.	SGN
	NORBURY, D.J.	SGN
	WESTALL, L.	L. SGT
20.09.44	BLATCH, S.L.	CAPTAIN
	SOUTHWARD, E.	SGN
	SPIRES, C.D.	DVR
21.09.44	PETERS, J.A.L.	SGN
	THOMPSON, J.D.	L. CPL
	THOMSON, A.	SGN
	WATKINS, J.	L. CPL
	WOLFE, D.J.V.	SGN
	DEAN, J.	SGN

	BLOOMFIELD, J.E.	SGN
23.09.44	FREW, A.B.M.	DVR
24.9.44	MIDDLING, H.	SGN
	SHAW, W.T.P.	SGN
	STEWART, D.W.	SGN
25.09.44	DAY, P.E.	CPL
	SMITH, C.E.	SGN
	THOMPSON, A.W.	SGN
25/26.09.44	HIBBITT, R.H.	DVR
26.09.44	ELLAM, T.	SGN
	GREGG, R.A.	LT
	OXENHAM, L.J.	SGN
02.10.44	GAULT, J.D.A.	SGN

HQ AIRBORNE TROOPS SIGNAL SECTION

17.09.44	GEE, F.G.	LT
	SELLERS, F.A.	CPL
06.10.44	DOLPHIN, J.K.	SGN

1st (AIRBORNE) DIVISIONAL ORDNANCE FIELD PARK ROYAL ARMY ORDNANCE CORPS

25.09.44	GRANTHAM, F.W.	CPL
25/26.09.44	ANDREWS, K.C.W.	CPL

ROYAL ARMY MEDICAL CORPS 16 PARACHUTE FIELD AMBULANCE

17.09.44	HAGGART, J.R.	PTE
17/25.09.44	HOPE, A.S.	PTE
19.09.44	MACDONALD, T.J.	PTE
21.09.44	SHAW, R.K.	PTE
27.11.44	WEBSTER, S.	PTE

133 PARACHUTE FIELD AMBULANCE

18.09.44	COOKSLEY, S.	L. CPL
	JAMES, J.H.	DVR
	PARKER, J.	DVR
	THOMPSON, T.	PTE
19.09.44	PILEBEAM, A.W.	SGT
24.09.44	LOUIS, P.	CAPTAIN
25.09.44	LEECH, J.	PTE

181 AIR-LANDING FIELD AMBULANCE

21.09.44	DOYLE, J.T.	CAPTAIN
22/23.09.44	DADSWELL, D.	L. CPL
25.09.44	BIGGS, S.D.	PTE
27.09.44	DUKE, W.A.	PTE
	FINDLAY, W.	PTE

ROYAL MILITARY POLICE 1st (AIRBORNE) DIVISIONAL PROVOST COMPANY

18.09.44	HOOKWAY, E.J.	L.CPL
19/21.09.44	CALLAWAY, H.L.	SGT
22/23.09.44	ROBERTS, A.	SGT
26.09.44	FALCK, R.J.	LT
	NEWBY, J.T.F.	L.CPL
26/27.09.44	JONES, P.W.	CPL
29.09.44	GRAY, W.B.	CAPTAIN

89 PARACHUTE SECURITY SECTION INTELLIGENCE CORPS

17.09.44	MAYBURY, A.	CPL
27.09.44	SCARR, P.D.	CPL

250 (AIRBORNE) LIGHT COMPOSITE COMPANY
ROYAL ARMY SERVICE CORPS

17.09.44	BONDY, R.C.	DVR
18.09.44	BENNETT, W.	DVR
	KENNELL, J.J.	DVR
	PLANT, L.	L.CPL
	THOMAS, R.J.	DVR
18/25.09.44	BUTTEN, J.S.	DVR
	WHITTET, H.G.	CPL
19.09.44	FIELD, M.J.	DVR
	GEERE, K.J.	DVR
	KAVANAGH, D.T.	CAPTAIN
	McKINNON, J.G.	DVR
	WIGGINS, A.	CPL
21.09.44	BURNS, J.D.	DVR
	HILL, F.W.	DVR
	PEACOCK, L.	DVR
	SNELLING, R.J.	S.SJT
22.09.44	MORTON, J.	PTE
	DAVIES, H.C.	L.CPL
23.09.44	DOCHERTY, A.F.	L.CPL
24.09.44	DOUBLEDAY, R.	CPL
	HATTON, D.	DVR
25.09.44	LAW, A.	DVR
	WALSH, J.	SGT
25/26.09.44	SHARP, W.R	CPL
01.10.44	PRESTON, W.R.	DVR
02.10.44	BELL, R.F.	L.CPL
15.10.44	JUDD, T.J.G.	CPL

SERVICEMEN OF 1st BRITISH AIRBORNE DIVISION
BUT SPECIFIC UNIT NOT KNOWN

19.09.44	KIRKHAM, H.L.	PTE
	WALFORD, J.A.	DVR
22.09.44	MADDOCKS, S.	PTE

2nd (AIRBORNE) BATTALION, THE OXORDSHIRE &
LIGHT INFANTRY
1ST AIRBORNE DIVISION DEFENCE PLATOON

21.09.44	BASS, R.J.	PTE
22.09.44	TOES, J.A.	PTE
24.09.44	BARTON, L.J.	PTE
25.09.44	MATTIEU, F.G.	PTE
25/26.09.44	SMITH, W.G.J.	PTE

21st INDEPENDENT COMPANY
THE PARACHUTE REGIMENT AAC

17.09.44	JONES, J.A.	CPL
20.09.44	LANDON, W.	PTE
	MARTIN, D.B.	SGT
21.09.44	MAY, M.L.	PTE
21/23.09.44	PHILPOT, A.E.	PTE
22.09.44	FIELY, J.V.	PTE
23.09.44	AVALLONE, J.P.	PTE
	DUNBAR, T.M.	L.CPL
	ROSENFIELD, H.	CPL
	THOMPSON, E.V.	SGT
23/25.09.44	MITCHELL, G.	L.CPL
25.09.44	BLEICHROEDER, T.A.	PTE
	HART, J.E.	PTE
26.09.44	CAMERON, J.	PTE
	GYLLENSHIP, W.J.	L.CPL
27.09.44	HORSLEY, J.	LT
29.09.44	ROBERTS, K.	PTE

20.10.44	HILLIER, F.J.	PTE
05.11.44	MORRIS, J.	PTE
13.12.44	SWALLOW, B.C.	SGT

1st PARACHUTE BRIGADE
1st BATTALION PARACHUTE REGIMENT AAC

17.09.44	BUNE, J.C.	MAJOR
	COOPER, N.	PTE
	DOUGAN, R.A.	PTE
	GORDON, O.	PTE
	GRIFFITHS, J.	PTE
	LEWIS, W.G.	L.CPL
	MOORE, W.G.	PTE
	NASH, L.A.	CPL
	NICHOLLS, C.C.	PTE
	TOWHEY, J.	PT
	WHITMORE, W.T.H.	PTE
17/18.09.44	GREEN, P.J.	PTE
18.09.44	BAILEY, T.	PTE
	BAKER, A.E.	PTE
	BOLAND, A.H.A.	PTE
	BUCHANAN, R.	CPL
	CARTMAN, J.T.	PTE
	CAST, H.	PTE
	COGHLANE, E.	PTE
	CURTIS, R.H.	PTE
	DEAN, R.L.A.	PTE
	DYER, L.W.	PTE
	ELLIS, S.	PTE
	FAIRWEATHER, J.	PTE
	GOULDEN, J.R.	PTE
	HARWOOD, A.	CPL
	JOHNSON, E.J.	PTE
	KATIFF, J.B.	PTE
	KNAPPER, J.	PTE
	PHILLIPS, G.W.	PTE
	PROUD, B.	PTE
	SMITH, C.E.	PTE
	SUMMERS, H.E.	PTE
	TIMBRELL, E.W.	PTE
18/19.09.44	REYNOLDS, A.	CPL
19.09.44	BERMINGHAM, J.	SGT
	CORT, A.R.	PTE
	CUPPLES, A.R.	PTE
	DALZELL, R.A.	PTE
	DAVIES, C.G.	PTE
	DOBROZYSKI, F.P.	PTE
	GEDNEY, V.	L.CPL
	KILMARTIN, M.G.	LT
	MORRIS, F.	SGT
19.09.44	TAYLOR, G.A.	PTE
20.09.44	BLUNDELL, G.M.	CAPTAIN
	BOOSEY, J.R.	L.CPL
	CLARKE, E.	PTE
	CURTIS, L.A.	2ND.LT
20.09.44	CLARKE, E.	PTE
	CURTIS, L.A.	2ND.LT
	DEVLIN, W.J.P.	PTE
	McCARTHY, G.	PTE
	McKENZIE, A.	PTE
	MACKIE, A.	PTE
	McKNIGHT, J.B.	SGT
	TOMLINSON, C.	PTE
21.09.44	GOULD, R.D.	PTE
	HART, G.	PTE
	LENTON, A.V.	L.CPL
	MURRAY, G.S.	L.CPL

	OSBORNE, A.	CPL		SCOTT, W.W.	WOII, (CSM)
	WARREN, B.G.	PTE	22.09.44	BARNETT, F.	CPL
22.09.44	CLARKSON, A.D.	LT		McAUSLAN, A.H.	PTE
	DONALSON, R.D.	PTE		McDERMOT, A.J.	LT
	McGHIE, D.P.	L.CPL		THOMSON, J.	SGT
24.09.44	CLARKE, A.L.	CPL	23.09.44	MAY, G.E.	PTE
	GORDON, J.G.	PTE		ALLEN, S.	PTE
	PREEN, W.A.	PTE		McCRACKEN, G.E.	PTE
25.09.44	BEST, G.	PTE		PAGE, W.J.	PTE
	BROWN, L.H.	L.CPL	25.09.44	ALLMAN, F.	PTE
	DACEY, T.	PTE		SADLER, L.D.	PTE
	MATSON, G.E.	CPL		THOMPSON, B.E.	SGT
	REID, H.G.D.	SGT	14.10.44	WOODS, R.B.	LT
	STRACHAN, F.A.	PTE	16.10.44	FITTOCK, C.M.	PTE
	WARBURTON, H.	PTE	20.10.44	STOKES, R.W.	PTE
26.09.44	LLOYD, A.B.	CPL	27.10.44	KALIKOFF, M.	SGT
28.09.44	BEST, C.F.	PTE			
01.10.44	COLEWELL, T.W.	PTE	**3rd BATTALON THE PARACHUTE REGIMENT AAC**		
	WHITING, F.J.	CPL			
04.10.44	DANN, A.V.	PTE	17.09.44	BAMSEY, W.E.	LCPL
05.10.44	BAINBRIDGE, D.	PTE		BENSTEAD, J.W.	PTE
07.10.44	WATERWORTH, G.W.	L.CPL		CHENNELL, S.A.	PTE
05.11.44	PHEASANT, C.	PTE		COPE, B.H.	CPL
				GRAHAM, T.E.	SGT
2nd BATTALION THE PARACHUTE REGIMENT AAC				HILDYARD-TODD, T.E.	SGT
				MATTHEWS, G.	PTE
17.09.44	CANE, P.H.	LT		WARD, W.	PTE
	GIBSON, T.A.	PTE		WILSON, D.F.	SGT
	GRONERT, C.	PTE	18.09.44	AYRES, G.	PTE
	GRONERT, T.	PTE		BALL, L.P.	PTE
	LONEY, W.	L.CPL		DECKER, A.W.	PTE
	PARKER, W.L.	PTE		DOWNS, L.	PTE
	PRATT, T.A.	PTE		EVANS, A.C.	SGT
	ROGERS, E.H.	CPL		FERN, W.	PTE
	SHIPLEY, N.W.	PTE		HAMPTON, J.	CPL
18.09.44	BURNS, W.	SGT		HIBBURT, P.L.	LT
	CREW, W.F.	PTE		HILL, G.T.	LT
	DAVIES, G.	PTE		HOEFLING, H.E.W.	PTE
	MEADS, D.	PTE		HOPWOOD, F.W.	PTE
	ORBELL, E.	L.CPL		KEARNS, B.P.	PTE
	PRINCE, J.	PTE		RHODES, H.	PTE
	SMITH, J.R.	PTE		SHARP, H.R.	PTE
	WALLIS, D.W.	MAJOR		TATNALL, A.W.	PTE
18/19.09.44	MURRAY, P.M.	PTE		WADDY, A.P.H.	MAJOR
18/25.09.44	COLE, E.H.	PTE	18/25.09.55	COLLINS, K.	PTE
	REEVE, W.H.	PTE		YATES, W.H.	PTE
19.09.44	COCKBURN, A.	PTE	19.04.44	ALLEN, R.	.CSM
	BLISS, B.	PTE		ATKINSON, W.	PTE
	HIGGINS, J.	PTE		BOWLER, G.F.	PTE
	McCREATH, W.	SJT		BRYNING, W.T.M.	CPL
	ROUGHSEDGE, W.	PTE		CHAMPION, E.	PTE
	RUSSELL, W.J.G.	PTE		GREEN, J.	PTE
	WADDILOVE, C.R.	L.CPL		HASLAM, J.	PTE
20.09.44	BOITEUX-BUCHANAN	LT		LUCENA, M.R.	PTE
	FRASER, D.	PTE		PALMER, D.J.J.	PTE
	GRAYBURN, J.H.	CAPTAIN		PETTIT, B.	PTE
	MOON, R.W.A.	PTE		SMITH, W.	PTE
	PURNELL, R.S.	PTE		STOTT, H.	PTE
	RATTRAY, A.A.	CPL		WELSH, P.W.	PTE
	SIMPSON, J.	PTE	19/23.09.44	FITCH, J.A.C.	LT. COL
21.09.44	BATTRICK, H.J.	PTE	19/25.09.44	PERRYMAN, D.W.R.	SGT
	DODDS, F.W.	CPL	20.09.44	BURROWS, C.	PTE
	ELLINGFORD, G.E.	PTE		FRASER, W.A.	LT
	NICHOLLS, F.S.	CPL		HOPE, J.W.	PTE
	RUDDY, J.	CPL		HOUSTON, J.I.	MAJOR
	TATE, F.R.	MAJOR		RICHE, E.M.	PTE
21/25.09.44	POWER, S.	SGT	20.09.44	RUSSELL, G.W.	PTE

	SMITH, R.T.	PTE		OLIVER, J.W.	PTE
	STANLEY, W.H.	LCPL		PROBERT, M.G.	PTE
	SUMMERFIELD, R.H.	CPL		QUERIPEL, L.E.	CAPTAIN
	WHITE, M.	SGT		RADCLIFFE, H.C.N.	LT
21.09.44	DAVIES, D.J.	SGT		ROSE, W.F.	PTE
	DORRIEN-SMITH, G.R.	CAPTAIN		WALTER, A.D.	PTE
	SMITH, G.L.	SGT		WINTERS, F.	PTE
22.09.44	BLAKELEY, I.	SGT		WOOD, R.F.	L.CPL
24.09.44	HITCHEN, A.L.	PTE		YOUELL, G.A.	PTE
	WHITEHEAD, H.J.	CPL	19/20.09.44	EVANS, A.B.	PTE
25.09.44	FELTON, A.	PTE		NOYE, G.S.	PTE
	HOLDING, D.	PTE	20.09.44	ALLISON, E.N.	PTE
	NEWMAN, A.H.	PTE		BARHAM, W.S.	PTE
26.09.44	BECKETT, T.L.	PTE		BROCKELSBY, C.D.	PTE
	WRIGHT, G.J.G.	PTE		CLIFFORD, E.N.	SGT
	HODGSON, W.K.	CAPTAIN		DODD, R.G.W.	LT
10.10.44	BUSSELL, R.M.	LT		EMANUEL, G.A.	PTE
20.11.44	McDOUGALL, J.	PTE		HORSFALL, C.M.	CAPTAIN
				MCKENZIE, D.	PTE

SERVICEMEN OF OR ATTACHED TO HQ 1st PARACHUTE BRIGADE

			20.09.44	MORRIS, J.	PTE
				PROUDFOOT, G.	PTE
18.09.44	ROBERTS, R.T.	PTE		SECRETT, W.R.M.	L. CPL
	STEPHENSON, R.	PTE	21.09.44	BEARDMORE, C.M.	L. CPL
20.09.44	DUNBAR, W.T.	PTE		BURGESS, W.D.A.	LT
	O'ROURKE, J.E.	PTE		DAVIES, J.A.	L. CPL
	SHUTTLEWOOD, R.H.	PTE		DUNKERLEY, W.	L. CPL
				KIAER, L.H.S.	LT
				LEWIS, V.J.	L. SGT

4th PARACHUTE BRIGADE
10TH BATTALION PARACHUTE REGIMENT AAC

				MOSS, E.B.	PTE
				PARKINSON, H.	PTE
				RICHARDSON, E.H.	L. CPL
18.09.44	ALLEN, W.J.	PTE		TALBOT, G.J.	PTE
	BENNETT, F.W.C.	SGT	21/22.09.44	ASHWORTH, C.F.	MAJOR
	BURKE, J.	PTE		GARIBALDI, W.	L. CPL
	COLLIE, J.	SGT	22.09.44	BINKS, J.E.	PTE
	CROTHALL, S.A.	PTE		McDONALD, L.	CPL
	HOWS, D.F.	PTE		SAUNDERS, P.A.	LT
	LEE, R.E.	PTE	23.09.44	FARRAGE, T.O.	PTE
	MUIR, M.	PTE		ORMEROD, A.	PTE
	PARTINGTON, W.J.	SGT		WAITE, L.H.	CPL
	MACKEY, P.W.A.	LT		WHITE, F.J.	L. CPL
	PENWILL, A.W.	PTE	24.09.44	BENSON, G.G.	PTE
	POUPARD, P.M.	PTE	25.09.44	KELLY, V.	PTE
	RODERICK, H.C.J.	LT		SELBY, O.	PTE
	WRIGHT, A.E.	CPL		WEAVER, N.O.	PTE
	VERHOEFF, A.W.	PTE		WILLINGHAM, A.	PTE
18/20.09.44	PARTINGTON, G.E.	CPL		WOODCOCK, J.A.	PTE
18/25.09.44	FRANCIS, A.R.	SGT	29.09.44	ANSON, P.A.R.	MAJOR
	GOODHEART, V.H.	PTE	02.10.44	NEEDHAM, C.P.L.	PTE
	GLAZIER, J.C.J.	SGT	09.10.44	GREENHOW, S.	PTE
19.09.44	CARTER, L.F.	SGT	20.10.44	HOWARD, J.	CAPTAIN
	CHESSON, F.H.	SGT		McCLEAN, J.O.	PTE
	DRAYSON, G.F.H.	CAPTAIN	26.10.44	SMYTH, K.B.I.	LT. COL
	ENGLAND, D.J.	PTE	01.11.44	LOWMAN, C.F.	SGT
	FIFIELD, W.	PTE			
	FROST, J.	PTE			

11th BATTALION THE PARACHUTE REGIMENT ARMY AIR CORPS

	GARNETT, T.	PTE			
	GEE, A.	PTE			
	HENRY, J.M.	CAPTAIN	18.09.44	BARLOW, J.W.	PTE
	HIGNETT, G.	PTE		BELL, G.	PTE
	HILL, R.	PTE		BORLAND, M.	PTE
	HOLLAND, J.	PTE		HOUSHAM, F.	SGT
	HUNT, F.L.	L.SGT		JAMES, E.L.	PTE
	KEEN, D.M.	PTE		MORRIS, G.E.	PTE
	KINCAID, P.	SGT		PAGE, C.F.A.	PTE
	LAKEY, W.F.	PTE		ASHWORTH, A.	SGT
	LISHMAN, A.	PTE		BARTON, J.A.	PTE

Date	Name	Rank
	BEDFORD, T.	CPL
	BEST, P.	PTE
	GENT, N.	PTE
	HANSON, J.R.	PTE
	KENNEDY, L.	PTE
	KNOWLES, E.	CPL
	METCALFE, K.J.	L.SGT
	UNDERHILL, F.R.A.	PTE
18/25.09.44	SMITH, J.F.	PTE
19.09.44	BARTHOLOMEW, B.W.	SGT
	BOWERS, G.A.	L. SGT
	CHILD, H.	PTE
	COOKE, E.A.	CPL
	ELLIOTT, M.J.	SGT
	GOLDSWORTHY, M.W.B.	PTE
	HUGHES, T.J.	PTE
	JENKIN, H.W.	PTE
	PENNINGTON, E.H.	SGT
	PETTITT, E.	PTE
	THOMPSON, R.W.	SGT
20.09.44	ASHDOWN, G.W.	WOII. (CSM)
20.09.44	BENTLEY, R.	PTE
	BOOTH, K.E.	PTE
	DE LEUR, H.B.	SGT
	HARRINGTON, P.	L. CPL
	JOSLAND, A.J.	PTE
	LYONS, R.J.	CPL
	NIXON, H.	PTE
	ROGERS, T.P.W.	CAPTAIN
20/21.09.44	ODELL, J.E.	PTE
20/25.09.44	IRWIN, H.J.	REV
21.09.44	AIREY, B.B.	PTE
	BAKER, J.R.	SGT
	DOUGLAS, J.S.	CAPTAIN
	FOULIS, G.S.	PTE
	HARDY, G.S.	PTE
	MATTHEWS, C.E.	L. SGT
	RHYMES, K.	PTE
	ROBERTS, R.	S.SGT
	SPEKE, W.H.	2ND.LT
	SULLIVAN, P.	PTE
	THOMAS, R.	LT
22.09.44	CLARK, F.C.	PTE
	CRAWFORD, F.	LT
	HARDMAN, H.	PTE
	HEMPSTEAD, R.A.	PTE
	LEE, E.	PTE
	McCARTHY, P.	SGT
	McCULLAGH, J.J.	PTE
	McKENNA, J.L.	LT
	PEELE, R.D.C.	2ND. LT
23.09.44	BLACKLIDGE, G.L.	MAJOR
	BURKE, J.	PTE
	COCHRANE, E.	PTE
	KNOWLES, R.	PTE
	O'NEILL, J.	L. CPL
	SULLIVAN, J.T.	L. SGT
	WOOD, R.W.	LT
24.09.44	BOOTH, J.E.	PTE
	COWLEY, A.F.	PTE
	McCLUNE, J.	L. CPL
	RONSON, R.	PTE
	TOLLITH, H.	PTE
	WARDLAW, F.	CPL
24/25.09.44	ROGERSON, J.F.	LT
25.09.44	ANDERSON, G.	PTE
	BRENNAN, T.	DVR

Date	Name	Rank
	CARTER, C.H.	PTE
	COX, A.H.	PTE
	KNIGHT, S.B.R.	SGT
	GODWIN, H.	PTE
	REHILL, B.	PTE
25/26.09.44	GRIFFIN, R.	L. CPL
26.09.44	LOMAS, G.	PTE
	MAIDENS, J.A.	SGT
	WRIGHT, W.	L. CPL
29.09.44	GRUMOLI, I.	PTE
	ROGERS, J.E.	PTE
01.10.44	GATHARD, P.	PTE
01.11.44	ALLEN, F.F.	L.CPL
13.11.44	BEHAN, D.	SGT
22.11.44	STONE, W.D.	SGT
16.12.44	CRABB, F.C.	PTE
	MORRIS, R.	PTE
31.12.44	PYE, C.R.	PTE

156th BATTALION THE PARACHUTE REGIMENT ARMY AIR CORPS

Date	Name	Rank
18.09.44	BROWNLOW, G.T.	PTE
	BUTLER, A.	PTE
	CLAYTON, H.	PTE
	CLAYTON, J.F.	PTE
	FULLER, R.	PTE
	GEORGE, D.L.	PTE
	GILLIVER, G.H.	PTE
	HOPWOOD, H.	PTE
	JOHNS, E.E.	PTE
	KILLINGSWORTH, R.	PTE
	KINSLEY-SMITH, J.C.	SGT
	LILLY, O.	CPL
	PHILPOTTS, H.J.	PTE
	STANYER, H.	PTE
	STEVENS, T.	PTE
	TAYLOR, P.	PTE
	TUTTON, G.	PTE
	WILSON, J.	PTE
	BADGER, R.G.	WOII. (CSM)
	BIRD, J.A.	PTE
	BOYD, J.	PTE
	DAVISON, J.	LT
	DRAKE, G.M.W.	PTE
	GRAYSTON, R.C.	PTE
	HOSKINS, S.	PTE
	PARKER, E.D.	SGT
	PARKIN, F.	PTE
	PURTON, H.	PTE
	SLACK, L.	PTE
	THORP, D.G.	PTE
	IRONS, S.	PTE
18/19.09.44	TRUEMAN, A.D.	PTE
	WHITE, B.	SGT
18/24.09.44	WASLEY, W.	SGT
18/25.09.44	COBB, J.T.	PTE
	FROST, R.	L. CPL
	HUTCHINSON, R.F.	L. CPL
	LEACH, W.	CPL
18/25.09.44	McKINNON, N.	WOII. (CSM)
19.09.44	BARRETT, D.	PTE
	COWIE, S.	PTE
	DELACOUR, L.D.	LT
	DUNCAN, W.P.	PTE
	EVANS, A.W.	PTE
	LAYTON, G.W.	PTE

	MARRIOTT, S.K.	PTE		**1st AIR-LANDING BRIGADE**		
	MUNRO, A.	PTE		**1st (AIRBORNE) BATTALION THE BORDER REGIMENT**		
	POLLOCK, W.	PTE				
	SAUNDERS, G.A.	PTE	17.09.44	JOHNSON, J.	PTE	
	WALLACE, J.	PTE		RAYMOND, G.	PTE	
	WATLING, S.E.	LT	18.09.44	BURR, H.	SGT	
19/20.09.44	HUGHES, K.B.	SGT		CERVI, L.	L. CPL	
19/25.09.44	GILMOUR, C.V.	SGT		GRAY, W.F.	PTE	
20.09.44	BRUCE, G.F.J.	SGT		GALLACHER, N.	PTE	
	DES VOEUX SIR W.R. De B.	LT.COL		HUNTER, A.	SGT	
	FLETCHER, H.E.	PTE		SEARS, S.W.C.	SGT	
	HAGGERTY, D.	PTE		SMITH, E.	PTE	
	GIBBONS, J.M.	SGT		WALKER, J.	PTE	
	LANG, D.	PTE		WHITFIELD, F.G.	PTE	
	PAGE, M.S.	MAJOR		YAPP, F.	PTE	
	RITSON, E.V.	MAJOR	19.09.44	EDGE, C.	PTE	
	SMITH, W.H.	PTE		SMITH, L.	PTE	
	SNEDDON, J.	PTE		SMITHEN, J.	PTE	
	WAGENMAKERS, L.	PTE	20.09.44	AYRES, W.	PTE	
	WESBURY, F.V.	L. CPL		BORDERS, E.	PTE	
	WEST, R.J.	CPL		BRAGG, H.	PTE	
20/22.09.44	DOWSETT, W.H.	PTE		CAIN, V.L.	PTE	
21.09.44	CARNEY, M.H.	PTE		CHAPMAN, J.	L/CPL	
	DONALDSON, W.S.	LT		COATES, T.	CPL	
	GEORGE, J.	PTE		CRIMMEL, J.H.	PTE	
	HAMILTON, J.M.	PTE		HARTLEY, E.	SGT	
	HUNTER, D.H.	PTE	20.09.44.	MELLING, E.	CPL	
	LEWINGTON, H.W.	PTE		HUNTER, J.	SGT	
	STEAD, C.	L. CPL		PEAT, J.	CPL	
	TAPPIN, R.A.	PTE		PIPER, T.	L/CPL	
22.09.44	FISHER, J.L.S.	PTE		SYKES, L.	PTE	
25.09.44	BENNETT, C.E.	PTE		THOMAS, A R.	LT	
	BUDIBENT, J.W.	PTE		WELLS, J.	PTE	
	COOPER, E.	PTE		WILLIAMS, G.	L/CPL	
	CREASY, C.H.	PTE	21.09.44	ASTON, F.J.	PTE	
	EARDLEY, A.	PTE		BARNES, R.	PTE	
	FORD, D.E.	PTE		BARNES, W.C.	PTE	
	HAIKIN, B.	PTE		BRYSON, T.J.W.	L/CPL	
	LYNAS, E.	L. CPL		BUCKLEY, F.	PTE	
	MANNING, J.	PTE		CAVEN, J.	PTE	
	STIRLING, A.T.G.	L. CPL		DURBER, T.	PTE	
	TANSLEY, G.	PTE		ELLERY, R.	PTE	
	WALKER, A.O.	SGT		FOGGO, E.E.	L/CPL	
25/26.09.44	GREENWOOD, W.J.	PTE		FOSTER, A.	PTE	
26.09.44	GOLLEDGE, W.G.	PTE		FROUD, G.	CPL	
	MALCOLM, D.	PTE		HANSON, R.	SGT	
	SMITH, L.	PTE		HOLT, P.S.	LT	
28.09.44	WILSON, J.M.	PTE		SEED, F.	PTE	
01.10.44	COLEMAN, F.R.	PTE		WALL, H.	PTE	
10.10.44	CAMBIER, H.M.A.	LT		WATSON, T.	SGT	
31.12.44	CARTER, J.R.	PTE	21/22.09.44	MANCHESTER, N.	PTE	
18.09.44	HACART, Y.W.	LT		THOMPSON, W.N.	PTE	
				WILSON, G.	PTE	
SERVICEMEN OF OR ATTACHED			22.09.44	ALLEN, J.	SGT	
TO HQ 4th PARACHUTE BRIGADE				BELL, A.	PTE	
				CRANSWICK, A.H.	PTE	
20.09.44	DAWSON, C.N.B.	MAJOR		EDEN, W.	L. CPL	
	DOLAGHAN, F.G.	PTE		EVERINGTON, G.C.H.	PTE	
	DONNELLY, P.J.	PTE		FOWLER, R.B.	PTE	
	GOULD, A.J.	L. CPL		HURLEY, P.	PTE	
	GUTHRIE, A.	PTE		LANGHORN, T.	CPL	
	JAMES, E.D.	CAPTAIN		McGLADDERY, A.	WOII. (CSM)	
	McGLONE, J.	PTE		MIDGLEY, F.	PTE	
	SUTTON, E.	PTE		PEARSON, J.	PTE	
	WRIGHT, W.H.	L. CPL		POPE, A.	WOII.(CSM)	
25/26.09.44	WATTAM, C.	PTE		PRICE, F.W.	SGT	
	WHYTE, G.R.	DVR		SMITH, V.	PTE	

	STANLEY, T.E.	PTE		LIDDLE, J.W.C.	PTE
	TATE, J.	LT		MACFARLANE, P.	L. CPL
	WARREN, W.S.	PTE		McKAY, A.	PTE
22/25.09.44	JONES, T.D.	PTE		MOOR, W.	PTE
23.09.44	BROWN, G.E.T.	LT		MURRAY, A.D.M.	LT
	COULSTON, R.H.	LT		NOBLE, R.	CPL
	FIDDLER, T.	PTE		NORLEDGE	PTE
	GIBSON, J.H.	PTE		STEWART, J.	PTE
	HIRD, E.E.	PTE	18/25.09.44	ELCOCK, R.	PTE
	HOLDSWORTH, H.A.	L.CPL		ROBERTSON, E.J.	PTE
	HOLME, W.M.	PTE	19.09.44	BROWN, E.G.	PTE
	ISHERWOOD, W.	PTE		CORRY, J.	SGT
	NICHOLSON, E.	PTE		OLDS, A.	PTE
	SKELTON, N.	PTE		PEPPERELL, A.	L. CPL
	VASEY, H.	PTE	19.09.44	PLUMMER, L.	L. CPL
24.09.44	ADAMS, W.	CPL		STRANG, J.H.	LT
	AGER, E.	PTE		VERNON, J.	PTE
	ASHURST, T.	PTE	19/20.09.44	CHANDLER, C.F.	PTE
	BECK, W.	PTE		GRANT, A.	L. CPL
	CLAY, G.	PTE	20.09.44	CARRIGAN, T.J.	PTE
	EDGAR, T.	CPL		COCHRAN, A.V.	MAJOR
	FLETCHER, W.D.	CPL		CRIGHTON, A.K.	LT
	HALLIDAY, R.	L. CPL		DOVASTON, D.	PTE
	HOWE, G.W.	L. CPL		FISHER, J.	PTE
	JARVIS, F.E.	PTE		HILL, R.W.	PTE
	LONG, G.E.H.	L. CPL		HUNTER, A.R.	PTE
	LOWERY, D.	PTE		McDADE, W.	CPL
	McDONALD, T.	PTE		SAUNBY, G.	PTE
	OWEN, A.	SGT		URE, J.	PTE
	PECK, J.	PTE		WAYTE, A.E.F.	LT
	SMART, A.H.	PTE	20/21.09.44	FERGUSON, R.	SGT
24/25.09.44	MELLING, W.	PTE	20/24.09.44	CARLTON, G.	CPL
	SLOAN, W.	PTE	21.09.44	CASSIDY, S.	PTE
25.09.44	ATKINSON, B.S.	CPL		CROSS, S.P.	L. CPL
	CARR, J.	CPL		FENTON, A.	PTE
	COWIN, L.	CPL		GIBSON, W.	PTE
	ELLICOCK, G.H.	PTE		GRAHAM, A.	SGT
	ELVIN, W.L.	PTE		HART, R.	PTE
	FITZPATRICK, F.	PTE		HUNTER, J.M.	LT
	MARSLAND, W.	L. CPL		LEWIS, A.	PTE
	SMITH, F.A.	PTE		McLAUCHLAN, J.	PTE
	THOMPSON, E.M.	PTE		McLELLAN, D.	PTE
	WELLBELOVE, J.A.	LT		MASON, A.L.	PTE
	WIGHTMAN, J.	PTE		MEAKIN, H.	PTE
	STEPHENSON, F.	PTE		MIDDLEWEEK, W.F.	PTE
26.09.44	HARDY, S.R.	PTE		MURDOCH, D.	PTE
	McMULLEN, D.	PTE		PRINGLE, J.	L. CPL
27.09.44	DALTON, C.W.	PTE		RAE, T.B.	SGT
28.09.44	BARFOOT, J.	L. CPL		SHARPLES, A.D.L.	LT
	PILLING, E.	PTE		STEVENSON, E.K.	PTE
29.09.44	FORD, J.P.	PTE		TIMPSON, E.A.	L. CPL
03.10.44	HULSE, P.A.	PTE	21/23.09.44	GIRGAN, J.T.	PTE
23.10.44	JACKSON, R.	PTE	22.09.44	FAIRHALL, A.R.	PTE
25.10.44	LAYCOCK, N.	PTE		FLETCHER, J.G.L.	PTE
	SMITH, J.	WOII. (CSM)	22.09.44	NEAL, N.	PTE
29.10.44	HOOD, F.	L. CPL		TELFORD, W.	PTE
21.11.44	MONTGOMERY, T.E.	MAJOR		TYSON, J.	PTE
				WATSON, T.	PTE

7th (AIRBORNE) BATTALION THE KING'S OWN SCOTTISH BORDERERS

				WOODCOCK, J.O.	PTE
			23.09.44	BAILIFF, K.	PTE
				HENDRICK, M.	PTE
18.09.44	ALLWOOD, E.	PTE		HUNTER, J.K.	PTE
	CAMPBELL, J.	PTE		LOGAN, R.	PTE
	HAZLEWOOD, J.	PTE		LOW, R.	PTE
	HENDERSON, T.J.	PTE		McCLOY, J.A.	PTE
	HILL, H.R.	MAJOR		McKAY, H.E.	PTE
18.09.44	KIPPING, A.E.	LT		McLINTOCK, J.	CPL
	LEISER, J.	PTE		MURRAY, A.	PTE

Veterans of the Border Regiment visit the airborne cemetery at Oosterbeek in 1994, the fiftieth anniversary of Arnhem.

	PHILLIPS, A.T.	PTE			EGAN, R.D.	CPL
	TORLEY, M.	L. CPL			GATER, S.E.	PTE
	WILSON, C.	SGT			HULETT, H.R.	L.CPL
23/24.09.44	HUNTER, J.	L. CPL			MESSER, E.	PTE
	SCOTT, E.E.	L. CPL			SMITH, H.	PTE
24.09.44	BROWN, R.	PTE			WOOD, E.	PTE
	HANNAH, S.	PTE			WYSS, E.M.	CAPTAIN
	LAMOND, J.	PTE		21.09.44	BOYNTON, R.G.	PTE
	MEREDITH, E.D.	PTE			HODGKINSON, W.J.	PTE
	MITCHELL, W.H.	PTE			KNAPP, B.D.	L.CPL
	POLLARD, S.C.	PTE			RICHARDSON, G.M.	PTE
	ROGERSON, A.	PTE			ROGERS, C.J.	PTE
24/25.09.44	SIMPSON, S.	PTE			SMITH, L.J.	L.CPL
	TAYLOR, R.J.	PTE		21/25.09.44	ASH, C.	PTE
25.09.44	DENHOLM, T.	CPL		22.09.44	DEAN, H.	PTE
	DUNDAS, J.S.	CAPTAIN			FAIRBROTHER, A.	PTE
	HORSPOOL, G.H.	PTE			HOPWOOD, B.	PTE
	MARTIN, J.	CPL			MUSKETT, B.	PTE
	PENDRIGH, S.	L. SGT			PUSHMAN, P.	CPL
	ROGERSON, T.	PTE			ROWBERRY, I.	PTE
	STEELE, J.	PTE		23.09.44	FINCHETT, E.	PTE
	SWEETMAN, R.G.	CPL			JOHNSON, A.E.	PTE
	WEEMS, R.H.	PTE			WOODROW, J.	PTE
	WITHERSPOON, J.	PTE		24.09.44	AUSTIN, G.N.	LT
25/26.09.44	GRAHAM, D.W.	PTE			BROWNSCOMBE, B.	CAPTAIN
	HENDERSON, W.	PTE			HARRISON, D.W.	PTE
	MARSHALL, J.	PTE			HOLLOWAY, J.W.	PTE
	WILSON, R.	CPL			LEE, H.	PTE
26.09.44	HYAMS, E.	PTE			NOAKES, A.C.	PTE
	THOMSON, J.	CPL			PEARCE, F.H.	PTE
28.09.44	PERE, J.	PTE		24/25.09.44	BROOME, R.	PTE
29.09.44	KERR, R.L.	PTE		24/26.09.44	OWEN, W.	PTE
03.10.44	FORD, F.J.	PTE		25.09.44	BIRD, A.	SGT
11.10.44	PURVES, G.S.	PTE			CHILLINGSWORTH, V.	L.CPL
19.10.44	SWEENEY, J.M.	PTE			COBB, E.W.	PTE
02.11.44	COX, A.	PTE			EATON, H.	L.CPL
18.11.44	COKE, J.S.A.	MAJOR			PEGG, J.C.D.	CPL
	SMITH, J.	PTE			PHILLIPS, G.	CPL
					SALFORD, B.H.	L.CPL
					SIMONDS, J.M.	MAJOR
					WILLIS, J.J.	SGT
				25/26.09.44	CULLEN, R.G.	PTE
17.09.44	GREWCOCK, W.R.	PTE			DUTTON, S.	PTE
	HIGGINS, N.	PTE			HOLDEN, R.T.G.	PTE
18.09.44	BOOTT, R.	PTE			LANSDOWNE, R.A.F.	PTE
	HUNT, E.P.	L. CPL			SMITH, D.J.	L.CPL
	NETTLETON, T.	SGT		26.09.44	GOULD, J.	PTE
	NUNN, W.	L. CPL			HOOPER, F.H.	CPL
	YOUNG, L.	PTE			LE-LIEVRE, S.	L.CPL
19.09.44	BADGER, J.	LT			MITCHELL, T.	PTE
	BATES, F.	PTE			SPOONER, H.	L.CPL
	BILNEY, D.C.	CPL		28.09.44	ELLIS, A.B.	SGT
	CHALMERS, A.	PTE			GODFREY, D.A.	WO11. (C.S.M.)
	COLLETT, P.W.	PTE			NICHOLSON, F.W.	PTE
	DAVIS, E.P.	PTE		05.10.44	BROUGH, E.	L.CPL
	FELLOWS, J.G.	PTE		30.10.44	PERRY, R.	PTE
	HALE, J.H.	PTE		19.09.44	WRIGHT, P.R.T.	MAJOR
	HARMES, H.	PTE				
	HINGSTON, B.H.W.	CAPTAIN				
	LEWIN, A.J.	PTE				
	PARKES, G.T.	PTE				
	ROEBUCK, E.	LT		19.09.44	BARLOW, H.N.	COLONEL
19.09.44	TARLING, K.	PTE			SINGER, R.	L.CPL
	WHITE, F.C.	PTE		20.09.44	BURNS, W.R.	CAPTAIN
	WILLIAMS, E.	L.CPL			MOY-THOMAS E, A.	CAPTAIN
	WINNAL, R.E.	PTE		21.09.44	TOMS, W.H.	CPL
	WOODHOUSE, J.C.	PTE		24.09.44	MORGAN, L	WO11 (C.S.M)
20.09.44	ANDERSON, C.L.	PTE		27.09.44	BENSON, B J	REVEREND
	BASKEYFIELD, J.D.	SGT				

2nd (AIRBORNE) BATTALION THE SOUTH STAFFORDSHIRE REGIMENT

SERVICEMEN OF OR ATTACHED TO HQ 1ST AIR-LANDING BRIGADE

THE VICTORIA CROSS
AWARDED TO AIRBORNE FORCES

Lance-Sergeant John Baskeyfield – 1944
In the battle of Arnhem, Lance Sergeant Baskeyfield was in charge of a gun crew serving with the Airborne Brigade. He was badly injured and his crew killed. Despite his injuries he manned his gun and continued firing until it was put out of action. He then crawled to another 6-pounder and single-handedly engaged the enemy, destroying a self-propelled gun before he was killed himself.

Captain Lionel Queripel – 1944
Arnhem hero Captain Queripel was commanding a company which became pinned down by heavy enemy fire. He was injured in the face but carried a wounded NCO to safety, destroyed two enemy machine-guns and captured an anti-tank weapon. He ordered his men to withdraw while he stayed on firing his pistol and throwing grenades.

Lieutenant John Grayburn – 1944
During the battle for Arnhem Bridge Lieutenant Grayburn led his men in a heroic three-day stand and although twice wounded he refused to be evacuated. His citation stated that had it not been for his inspiring leadership and personal bravery the bridge could not have been held for as long as it was. The courageous officer was killed on the last night of his epic action.

Flight Lieutenant David Lord – 1944
Pilot David Lord was serving with Airborne Forces and dropping supplies at Arnhem when his Dakota was hit by anti-aircraft fire and set alight. He stayed at the controls to give his crew the chance to escape but before they could get out the Dakota exploded in flames. The plane's starboard wing collapsed and the aircraft plunged to the ground, killing him and all but one of his crew.

Major David Cain – 1944
Major Cain destroyed a German Tiger tank on his own at Arnhem. Then, armed only with a light anti-tank weapon, he went on to drive off three more tanks the following morning. Although wounded his courage and 'superb' leadership later held off a three-hour attack on his position, forcing the demoralised Germans to withdraw in disorder.

Corporal Fred Topham – 1945
As a medical orderly with 6th Airborne Division, Corporal Topham was constantly exposed to attack during the Rhine Crossing in 1945. After tending injured troops and suffering severe wounds himself he then rescued soldiers from a troop carrier which had suffered a direct hit. He dragged three men to safety over open ground as shells continued to explode all around him.

Lieutenant-Colonel Herbert Jones – 1982
Lieutenant-Colonel 'H' Jones, the commanding officer of the 2nd Battalion Parachute Regiment, was killed leading an attack in the Falklands battle for Darwin and Goose Green. He moved forward under heavy enemy fire then, with complete disregard for his own safety, charged the Argentine machine-guns. He was hit several times but continued his assault and fell just a few feet from the enemy position.

Sergeant Ian McKay – 1982
Sergeant McKay, of the 3rd Battalion the Parachute Regiment, made a heroic decision to break cover and charge the enemy after his platoon commander was shot and wounded during the 1982 Falklands campaign. Defying a hail of gunfire, which killed one man and injured another two, he pressed home his attack with grenades. His assault allowed the platoon to overrun the position where his body was found.

The Colonel-in-Chief, HRH Prince Charles, meets veterans of the Parachute Regiment Airborne Forces who fought in the Second World War.

CHRONOLOGY OF AIRBORNE FORCES

22 June 1940   British arborne forces officially created after Prime Minister Winston Churchill calls for a corps of at least 5,000 parachute soldiers to be raised. A base at Ringway, near Manchester, is selected, and Squadron Leader Louis Strange is put in command of training.

8 July 1940   Ground training officially starts at the Central Landing Establishment, RAF Ringway near Manchester. Instructors are drawn from the RAF and the Army's physical training instructors.

13 July 1940   First recorded parachute descents at Ringway by men of No. 2 Commando. The first course began on 21 July, then just five days later on 25 July 1940 Private Evans was killed when his parachute failed to open.

10 February 1941   First airborne raid is mounted on the Tragino aqueduct in Italy. Headed by Major Pritchard, 38 men took part in the raid, dropping from Whitley bombers which took off from Malta.

26 April 1941   Churchill views a parachute and glider demonstration at Ringway. But only 800 men have been trained for parachuting as opposed to the 5,000 called for by the Prime Minister. He later calls on his Chiefs of Staff to expedite training to achieve the 5,000-strong force. At this point the first balloon arrives at Ringway.

15 September 1941   The Central Landing Establishment at Ringway renamed the Airborne Forces Establishment. Formation of the 1st Parachute Brigade under Brigadier Gale. Later in November the 1st Airborne Division is formed.

21 December 1941   Formation of the Army Air Corps and Glider Pilot Regiment. When formed, the Parachute Regiment would operate as part of the Army Air Corps.

15 January 1942   The formation of the RAF's No. 38 group.

27 February 1942   Bruneval raid – first battle honour. 'C' Company of 2nd Battalion the Parachute Regiment drop into Bruneval and seize radar equipment which they recover to the UK for inspection and analysis by scientists. By May 1942 the maroon beret had been selected as the distinctive hallmark of British airborne forces.

1 August 1942   The Parachute Regiment is officially formed. The entire force wears the maroon beret but soldiers continue to wear the cap badge of their old units until 1943 when the regiment is issued with its own cap badge.

12 November 1942   First battalion-strong drop takes place at None airfield in North Africa when 3 Para mount a parachute assault and seize it. Paras fight across North Africa along with glider-borne troops. Here the Paras dropped from American Dakota aircraft and were nicknamed 'Red Devils' by the German Afrika Korps.

17 November 1942   Airborne raid into Norway to destroy a heavy water plant at Vermok (Operation 'Freshman') fails after aircraft crash in bad weather. After the war it is revealed that those who survived were captured and executed – some were tortured.

3 May 1943   6th Airborne Division is formed and training starts at Netheravon. This is the start of preparations for D-Day in June 1944.

9 July 1943   1st Air-Landing Brigade capture Ponte Grande bridge, Sicily, and on 13 July the 1st Parachute Brigade mount a parachute assault to capture Primosole bridge.

6 June 1944   Operation 'Overlord' – Allied invasion of Europe. 6th Airborne Division secure the left flank of the Allied amphibious landings: 6,000 men drop by parachute, 3,000 land by glider. 821 are killed and 2,709 injured.

12 July 1944   12th Battalion the Parachute Regiment captures Breville and prevents the beachhead being attacked.

15 August 1944   Independent Parachute Brigade sees action in southern France.

17 September 1944   1st Airborne Division drops into Holland. 2nd Battalion the Parachute Regiment are ordered to seize the bridge at Arnhem, but are cut off by the enemy – they hold out for several days before running out of ammunition. 10,095 personnel parachuted or landed by glider, fewer than 3,000 return across the river during the evacuation. Many are injured or taken prisoner and at the Arnhem-Oosterbeek War Cemetery 3,328 Allied airborne soldiers are buried after the battle.

12 October 1944   Operation 'Manna' – 2nd Independent Parachute Brigade seize Megara airfield for operations in Greece.

24 December 1944   6th Airborne Division deployed to the Ardennes.

3 January 1945   13th Battalion Parachute Regiment captures Bures in Ardennes.

24 March 1945   Operation 'Varsity' – Rhine crossing. 6th Airborne Division mount a massive parachute operation in conjunction with the US 17th Airborne Division. This is the final major airborne drop of the Second World War. 1,696 aircraft and 1,348 gliders ferry 21,680 troops into action.

21 September 1945   6th Airborne fly into Palestine to take part in internal security operations as violence flares up between Arab and Jewish communities.

15 November 1945   1st Airborne Division disbanded.

12 June 1948   2nd Parachute Brigade re-forms in Germany as the 16th Parachute Brigade – taking its title from the 1st and 6th Airborne Divisions. Later in August the 6th Airborne Division is disbanded.

19 July 1950   King George VI presents the first colours to all three battalions of the Parachute Regiment.

12 January 1956   3rd Battalion the Parachute Regiment deploy to Cyprus on internal security duties as EOKA terrorists attempt to free island of British rule.

5 November 1956   3rd Battalion the Parachute Regiment drop into El Gamil and seize the airfield at Suez. This is the regiment's first operational battalion drop since the end of the Second World War. It is an outstanding success from a military perspective, but a political disaster.

1 September 1957   Glider Pilot Regiment renamed Army Air Corps.

June 1958   16th Parachute Brigade fly into Jordan after civil war breaks out in Lebanon. Brigade arrives in Amman and remains in the country for three months as a deterrent force.

June 1961   2nd Battalion Parachute Regiment deployed to the border of Kuwait after Iraq threatens to invade. Paras are joined by Royal Marines as deterrent force and eventually pull out after three months.

May 1963   3rd Battalion Parachute Regiment deploy to Radfan following conflict in the Yemen.

May 1964   2nd Battalion Parachute Regiment on operations in Borneo.

December 1964   Paras deploy to Cyprus on United Nations duties.

October 1965   3rd Battalion the Parachute Regiment fly to British Guiana on internal security duty after unrest occurred in the weeks prior to the colony being given independence from the UK.

29 November 1967 1 Para cover the withdrawal from Aden and are the last British Army unit to leave.

6 June 1968   Browning Barracks, named after Major General F.A.M. Browning, becomes new depot of Parachute Regiment and is opened by Daphne du Maurier, widow of the late General Browning.

12 October 1969   1st Battalion the Parachute Regiment arrive in Belfast on emergency tour, Operation 'Banner'. The troops were greeted by smiling faces and cheers in Republican areas where they moved in to protect Catholic families. Tea and cakes were offered to the troops – but this attitude was to be short-lived. In November a battalion is deployed to Anguila on IS duty, and remains there for three months.

17 June 1970   Paras serving in Ulster as further violence erupts.

1 May, 1971   All three battalions in Northern Ireland.

25 May 1971   First member of the Parachute Regiment to be killed in Northern Ireland. Sergeant Mick Willetts of 3rd Battalion uses his body to shield children from an IRA bomb. He is awarded a posthumous George Cross.

30 January 1972   1st Battalion the Parachute Regiment are sent into Londonderry to monitor an illegal civil rights march. They are tasked by the Brigade Commander to make arrests, which they do, but the situation turns ugly. Thirteen people are shot dead. In the aftermath the IRA claim that not a shot was fired at the Army, the Paras claim 'on oath' at the Widgery Inquiry that shots were fired.

22 February 1972 The Officers' Mess 16th Parachute Brigade is bombed by IRA and seven civilians killed.

31 July 1972 During Operation 'Motorman', Northern Ireland, both the 1st and 2nd Battalion the Parachute Regiment are sent in to clear Republican 'No Go' areas. It is a massive operation involving more than 20,000 troops.

27 July 1973   Parachute Battalion on active service in Ulster.

15 July 1974   All three regular battalions including the 4th (Volunteer) receive second set of colours at Aldershot. Paras remain on operations in Ulster.

21 September 1975   Paras remain on operations in Northern Ireland.

31 May 1976   Paras remain on duty in Ulster. 3rd Battalion score major success against terrorists in South Armagh.

31 March 1977   Early in the month the indications are that the defence review will demand a cut in the parachuting role. At the end of March 16th Parachute Brigade is disbanded and replaced with 6th Field Force. The parachuting role is retained by an 'in-role' battalion. The perception of the defence staff is that an airborne brigade is no longer required. In June 1977 2 Para resident in Berlin.

4 May 1978   Parachute Regiment remain on operations in Ulster.

27 August 1979   16 members of Parachute Regiment killed at Warrenpoint after IRA planted a double bomb. After the first explosion a second blast is detonated as casualties are being evacuated.

30 March 1980   Members of Parachute Regiment on duty in Ulster.

15 October 1981   Members of Parachute Regiment on duty in Ulster.

2 April 1982   Parachute Regiment prepares to send two battalions to the South Atlantic. Both 2nd and 3rd Battalion deploy on Operation 'Corporate' and see fighting at Goose Green, Wireless Ridge and Mount Longdon. 1st Battalion is also deployed on operations in Northern Ireland.

1 November 1983   After the Falklands war defence chiefs renew parachute capability within the British Army and 5 Infantry Brigade is renamed 5 Airborne Brigade – with supporting logistics, medical and artillery units joining the airborne formation once again.

3 January 1985   Members of the Parachute Regiment on operations in Ulster.

3 April 1985   The Pathfinder platoon, the forward reconnaissance troop of the brigade, is formed. This specialist unit undergoes training in HALO procedures and is officially established in 1997 as a permanent wing of the brigade.

The balloon jump – not a popular form of descent. The first jump wasn't too bad because nobody knew what to expect. It was the second and subsequent jumps that caused concern, after the individual had experienced the feeling of falling 200 ft before the canopy opened. Many commented that it was like committing suicide as you experienced the speed of dropping and could do nothing about it, except hope that your parachute opened. First introduced during the Second World War the balloon jump was a regular part of the parachute training course until it was withdrawn in the early 1990s. At Brize Norton's No. 1 Parachute Training School, where the course is currently held, students would be ferried to Weston-on-the-Green in Oxford where the balloon jump took place. Four trainees at a time accompanied a Parachute Jump Instructor in the balloon cage and waited until the balloon reached 800 ft, then one by one they jumped out.

17 June 1986   Members of the Parachute Regiment on operations in Ulster.

9 September 1987   Members of the Parachute Regiment on operations in Ulster.

18 November 1989   Three members of 3 Para killed in landmine ambush.

22 June 1990   Prince of Wales, Colonel-in-Chief of the Parachute Regiment, heads a parade of 3,500 Paras in London marking the golden jubilee of airborne forces.

17 August 1990   Elements of 5 Airborne Brigade are put on standby for operations in the Gulf after Iraq invades Kuwait. A few selected members of the brigade on exchange duty with the 82nd Airborne deploy to Gulf with US forces.

20 January 1991   Parachute Battalion on operations in Northern Ireland.

1 August 1992   50th anniversary of formation of the Parachute Regiment. Battalion serving in Ulster. 5 Airborne Brigade is put on standby for several 'out of area' operations during the year – all are cancelled.

21 June 1993   The Parachute Regiment depot is closed as part of 'Options for Change' defence cuts. 580 Platoon is the last to undergo training at Aldershot. 'P' Company is transferred to Catterick and training rescheduled within the policy of the new Army Training Regiment system. Throughout the year a battalion is on operations in Northern Ireland.

15 May 1994   Members of the Parachute Regiment on duty in Ulster.

15 June 1995   Gorazde, Bosnia. British troops working for the United Nations are trapped under Serbian fire. 5 Airborne Brigade is tasked to prepare to mount a heliborne assault to airlift out UK troops. The heliborne assault is cancelled. Two British soldiers are injured, one of them, Fergus Rennie, a former paratrooper, dies from his wounds. Throughout 1995 a parachute battalion remains on operations in Ulster. Specialists from the brigade's tactical Air Control Parties and artillery battery are deployed to Bosnia in support of the United Nations.

1 August 1996   5 Airborne Brigade is selected to be a core component of the newly formed Joint Rapid Deployment Force along with 3 Commando Brigade. Earlier in the year the two brigades took part in exercises in USA. Throughout the year a parachute battalion remained on operations in Northern Ireland. Specialists from the brigade including an artillery battery, medical teams and Tactical Air Control parties deployed in Bosnia.

30 October 1996   5 Airborne Brigade is put on standby to mount a parachute assault into Zaire as part of a multinational humanitarian relief operation to assist thousands of starving refugees displaced by tribal violence. The brigade's Lead Parachute Battle Group prepares to head the assault with 45 Commando Royal Marines under command of HQ 5 Airborne Brigade. At the last minute the operation is cancelled.

1 April 1997   Pathfinder Platoon finally becomes an 'official' part of the Brigade Order of Battle, having existed as a phantom unit for thirteen years.

22 October 1997   'B' Company of 2nd Battalion the Parachute Regiment drop into Egypt to mark the 200th anniversary of the first parachute drop by André Jacques Garnerin in Paris. A parachute battalion remains on operations in Ulster.

9 February 1998   5 Airborne Brigade carry out trials to increase the effective firepower of the brigade. Quad All Terrain Vehicles introduced as a weapons platform. A parachute battalion remains on operations in Ulster. Tactical Air Control teams deploy to the Middle East to support operations in northern Iraq and Kuwait.

Parachute training. Trainees head towards their aircraft at Ringway, Manchester, as their course prepares to make a descent at Tatton Park. These men were volunteers from units across the British Army who came to Ringway and were the pioneers of today's Parachute Regiment. They came from Scottish regiments, country units such as the Borderers, the Welch Fusiliers and the Ulster Rifles. They all wore their own cap badges and berets until the red beret was issued in 1942, and became the distinctive hallmark of Airborne Forces.

ACKNOWLEDGEMENTS

I would like to thank everyone who has helped me to write this book, in particular the Commander of 5 Airborne Brigade, Brigadier Adrian Freer and his predecessor Brigadier Graeme Lamb for their support of the project; Major Matthew Lowe for his critical eye in checking detail; Jill Swift and Chris Fletcher at Media Ops and Mrs Belinda Brinton and her team at the Airborne Forces Museum; Irvin and GQ parachutes for their assistance; Julian Thompson for allowing me access to his own research material and Graham Bound who was in the Falklands at the time of the invasion. Thanks also go to Peter Darman and Iain Ballantyne; Major Chris Roper; Lieutenant-Colonel Simon Barry and Major Alan Flavell, who also provided constructive comments which helped to steer the direction of the book. In particular I would like to thank my wife Jessica, who spent hours at the computer checking my first and second drafts and was then forced to listen to me read the chapters to her.

PICTURE CREDITS

The Airborne Forces Museum; Teddy Nevill; The Defence Picture Library; MoD photographer Chris Fletcher; Simon Kelly; Guy Channing; Richard Spake; Carl Schulze; Bob Morrison; WO2 Peter Bristow; Graham Bound; Graham Slocombe; Jim Hunter (former Pathfinder); Peter MacDonald; Tom Hannon; Peter Holdgate; Captain Andy Reeds of 2 Para and award-winning photographer Andrew Chittock of DPL.

INDEX